Flag Burning

DATE DUE

	PRINTED IN U.S.A.

SOCIAL PROBLEMS AND SOCIAL ISSUES
An Aldine de Gruyter Series of Texts and Monographs

SERIES EDITOR
Joel Best, *University of Delaware*

Joel Best (ed.), **Images of Issues: Typifying Contemporary Social Problems** (Second Edition)

Joel Best (ed.), **Troubling Children: Studies of Children and Social Problems**

James J. Chriss (ed.), **Counseling and the Therapeutic State**

Donatella della Porta and Alberto Vanucci, **Corrupt Exchanges: Actors, Resources, and Mechanisms of Crime, Deviance, and Control**

Jeff Ferrell and Neil Websdale (eds.), **Making Trouble: Cultural Constructions of Crime**

Ann E. Figert, **Women and the Ownership of PMS: The Structuring of a Psychiatric Disorder**

Mark Fishman and Gray Cavender (eds.), **Entertaining Crime: Television Reality Programs**

James A. Holstein, **Court-Ordered Insanity: Interpretive Practice and Involuntary Commitment**

James A. Holstein and Gale Miller (eds.), **Reconsidering Social Constructionism: Debates in Social Problems Theory**

Philip Jenkins, **Intimate Enemies: Moral Panics in Contemporary Great Britain**

Philip Jenkins, **Using Murder: The Social Construction of Serial Homicide**

Valerie Jenness, **Making It Work: The Prostitutes' Rights Movement in Perspective**

Valerie Jenness and Kendal Broad, **Hate Crimes: New Social Movements and the Politics of Violence**

Stuart A. Kirk and Herb Kutchins, **The Selling of *DSM*: The Rhetoric of Science in Psychiatry**

John Lofland, **Social Movement Organizations: Guide to Research on Insurgent Realities**

Donileen R. Loseke, **Thinking About Social Problems: An Introduction to Constructionist Perspectives**

Leslie Margolin, **Goodness Personified: The Emergence of Gifted Children**

Donna Maurer and Jeffrey Sobal (eds.), **Eating Agendas: Food and Nutrition as Social Problems**

Gale Miller, **Becoming Miracle Workers: Language and Meaning in Brief Therapy**

Gale Miller and James A. Holstein (eds.), **Constructionist Controversies: Issues in Social Problems Theory**

Bernard Paillard, **Notes on the Plague Years: AIDS in Marseilles**

Dorothy Pawluch, **The New Pediatrics: A Profession in Transition**

Erdwin H. Pfuhl and Stuart Henry, **The Deviance Process** (Third Edition)

William B. Sanders, **Gangbangs and Drivebys: Grounded Culture and Juvenile Gang Violence**

Theodore Sasson, **Crime Talk: How Citizens Construct a Social Problem**

Wilbur J. Scott, **The Politics of Readjustment: Vietnam Veterans since the War**

Wilbur J. Scott and Sandra Carson Stanley (eds.), **Gays and Lesbians in the Military: Issues, Concerns, and Contrasts**

Jeffrey Sobal and Donna Maurer (eds.), **Weighty Issues: Fatness and Thinness as Social Problems**

Jeffrey Sobal and Donna Maurer (eds.), **Interpreting Weight: The Social Management of Fatness and Thinness**

Robert A. Stallings, **Promoting Health Risk: Constructing the Earthquake Threat**

Frank J. Weed, **Certainty of Justice: Reform in the Crime Victim Movement**

Michael Welch, **Flag Burning: Moral Panic and the Criminalization of Protest**

Carolyn L. Wiener, **The Elusive Quest: Accountability in Hospitals**

Rhys Williams (eds.), **Cultural Wars in American Politics: Critical Reviews of a Popular Myth**

Flag Burning

Moral Panic
and the
Criminalization of Protest

Michael Welch

ALDINE DE GRUYTER
New York

About the Author

Michael Welch is Associate Professor in the Administration of Justice Program, School of Social Work, Rutgers University, New Brunswick, New Jersey.

ALDINE DE GRUYTER
A division of Walter de Gruyter, Inc.
200 Saw Mill River Road
Hawthorne, New York 10532

This publication is printed on acid free paper ∞

Library of Congress Cataloging-in-Publication Data

Welch, Michael, Ph.D.
    Flag burning: moral panic and the criminalization of protest / Michael Welch.
        p. cm. — (Social problems and social issues)
        Includes bibliographic references and indexes.
        ISBN 0-202-30651-8 (cloth : alk. paper) — ISBN 0-202-30652-6 (pbk. : alk. paper)
        1. Flags—Desecration—United States. I. Title. II. Series.

    CR113.W44 2000
    929.9′2′0973—dc21   00-044196

Manufactured in the United States of America

10 9 8 7 6 5 4 3 2

To the memories of my
Irish-American grandmothers,

Katharene Walsh Householder
and
Mildred O'Brien Welch

CONTENTS

Acknowledgments   ix

I   THE EMERGENCE OF FLAG DESECRATION AND CIVIL RELIGION

1 Protest, Social Control, and the Semiotics of Flag Desecration   3

2 The Roots of Flag Desecration in American History   17

3 Civil Religion and the Flag as a Venerated Object   31

II   THE AUTHORITARIAN AESTHETIC AND ITS RESISTANCE

4 Questioning Authority in the Age of Protest   47

5 Flag Burning as Political Iconoclasm in the 1980s   61

6 Patriotism and Dissent in the Post-*Eichman* Era   79

III   MORAL PANIC OVER FLAG DESECRATION

7 Moral Panic and the Social Construction of Flag Desecration   101

8 Moral Entrepreneurs and the Criminalization of Protest   127

9 The Media and Its Contradictions in the Flag Panic   153

10 Resisting the Criminalization of Protest   177

References	189
Cases Cited	212
Name Index	214
Subject Index	216

Acknowledgments

This book is the culmination of years of work, and as a final product it embodies the assistance and cooperation of many people. At Rutgers University, many of my students in the Administration of Justice Program were instrumental in retrieving literature and assembling data: Jennifer Bryan, John Sassi, Allyson McDonough, Tom Ehrlich, Brian Homcy, Jennifer Mennel, Beth Raimondo, Kristin Mortellito, Laura Niedermayer, Kevin Tunney, Armando Patino, Leon Yin, Eric Price, Joseph Fredua-Agyman (a.k.a. Haas), Mike Spatola, Sheri McKay, and Cheryl Machleder.

Earlier in my career, Professors Henry Lesieur and Bill DiFazio at St. John's University (New York) significantly influenced my sociological understanding of the world, and at Rutgers University, several colleagues continue to support my scholarly journeys into controversial terrain, including Dean Mary E. Davidson, Lennox Hinds, Al Roberts, and Carol Fine at the New Brunswick campus, and Freda Adler and Gerhard O. W. Mueller at the Newark campus.

My editors at Aldine de Gruyter, Richard Koffler and Mai Shaikhanuar-Cota, were immensely helpful as I completed the manuscript. Likewise, series editor Joel Best along with Marilyn McShane and Trey Williams provided invaluable insight into the project. Also, the book benefits tremendously from the meticulous work of my copy editor, Peter Smith.

Finally, there are many political activists and artists who presented to me valuable opportunities to learn more about the ongoing struggle for free and critical expression; in particular, I am tremendously grateful to Shawn Eichman, Ron English, and Dread Scott.

I

The Emergence
of Flag Desecration
and Civil Religion

1

Protest, Social Control, and the Semiotics of Flag Desecration

"It is by the goodness of God that in our country we have those three unspeakable precious things: freedom of speech, freedom of conscience, and the prudence never to practice either of them."
—*Mark Twain*, Fenimore Cooper's Literary Offenses

SOCIAL CONTROL OF POLITICAL PROTEST

Throughout civilization, especially in societies steeped in hierarchy, elite rulers have gone to great lengths to legitimize and maintain their power over people. In doing so, authorities have targeted dissenters in a concerted effort to regulate political protest; indeed, even messages containing subtle nuances of an antiestablishment sentiment have been subject to repression. Consider, for instance, the 1968 Olympic Games in Mexico City. After finishing first and third in the 200-meter sprint, Americans Tommie Smith and John Carlos were awarded the gold and bronze medals, respectively, during the traditional Olympic ceremony. But while the American national anthem played, Smith and Carlos shocked the Olympic and U.S. establishment by raising their black-gloved fists in a gesture of Black Power. For their silent, though momentous, act of defiance, Smith and Carlos were suspended immediately from the U.S. Olympic team, evicted from the Olympic village, and forced to leave Mexico. Vice-presidential candidate Spiro Agnew and California Governor Ronald Reagan, among other establishment voices, branded Smith, Carlos, and other supporters of the Black Power movement "dangerous enemies of the state" (Lipsyte, 1993:8:11). The 1968 team arguably was one of the most accomplished in U.S. track and field history, but those athletes became the only group of Olympians never to be invited to the White House, a blunt reminder that public defiance, however subtle, would not be tolerated by the nation's top officials. If government leaders thought they would undermine the civil rights and Black Power movement by humiliating Smith and Carlos, they were sadly mistaken. A notable irony of social control is its tendency to produce contradictory results; the government's mistreatment of black activists would be no exception. By being vilified by the establishment, Smith and Carlos were elevated to the status of courageous dissenters; correspondingly, it empowered the civil rights movement for African-Americans, which gained considerable momentum at that time. Smith said his punch to the sky was a "silent gesture heard round the world." Bill Toomey, who earned a gold medal in the decathlon in the 1986 Olympics recalled: "It was a modest gesture that became one of the most dramatic—almost religious—symbols, saying we just want to remind you that all is not well." Fellow teammate Lee Evans, gold medalist in the 400 meters, insists that the gesture educated him: "1967 and 1968 were the best thing that ever happened to me. . . . The movement became my career. I'm still living it." (Lipsyte, 1993, Section 8:1, 11).[1]

Although officially snubbed by the U.S. government, what happened to American athletes Smith and Carlos in 1968 pales by comparison to the reprisals directed against Mexican protestors. In the months leading up to the Olympic Games in Mexico City, the government embarked on a repressive campaign, as police and federal troops attacked thousands of students demanding educational reforms and denouncing police brutality. During four months of unrest, federal troops occupied universities and repressed student activism; overall, more than one hundred people were killed, also hundreds of others were wounded and thousands arrested. So that political unrest would not disrupt the Olympics, Mexico's president agreed to some of the student demands, including willingness to uphold university autonomy. In the end, the Olympic Games in Mexico City were not sullied by protest, other than the Black Power salute by Smith and Carlos (Sobel, 1969).

The incidents in Mexico City offer lessons about the raw power of protest, including the extent to which political and cultural elites will go to stifle dissent. Moreover, brutal attempts to crush unwelcome criticism ironically escalate the degree of resistance, which in turn empowers opposition against the state (Marx, 1981).

Turning attention to social control of political protest in the United States, this book embarks on an in-depth examination of flag desecration and efforts to criminalize that particular form of dissent. Flag burning, like the Black Power salute of the 1960s, is a potent symbolic gesture conveying sharp criticism of the state. Still, the act of torching Old Glory differs qualitatively from other forms of defiance, especially because the flag is revered. With this distinction in mind, attempts to penalize and deter flag desecration transcend the utilitarian function of regulating public protest.

Because the essence of the flag is imbued with patriotic qualities of sacred proportion, campaigns to preserve its integrity invoke a higher moral obligation on the part of government and people. Indeed, flag desecration offends not only political elites but most American citizens as well. Given the deep emotional—virtually religious—attachment of most citizens to the nation's most cherished emblem, flag burning has been known to incite a full-fledged moral panic, a phenomenon marked by a turbulent and exaggerated reaction to a putative threat (Cohen, 1972; Goode and Ben-Yehuda, 1994). In 1989, flag hysteria reached unprecedented heights as moral entrepreneurs scrambled to criminalize such acts of political iconoclasm. Despite renewed interest in punishing flag burners, however, formal measures of social control—flag protection statutes—proved ironic insofar as they produced results contradictory to the crusade to save Old Glory. Although moral panic over flag desecration aroused considerable anxiety among citizens, the campaign to criminalize that expression of protest triggered resistance by First Amendment advocates committed to preserving the constitutional right to free speech.

Despite popular claims that American society is built on genuine consensus, the flag-burning controversy brings to light the contentious nature of U.S. democracy and its ambivalence toward free expression. The First Amendment of the U.S. Constitution often is viewed as one of the more unpopular additions to the Bill of Rights. According to constitutional commentator Nat Hentoff (1997), the First Amendment gives us the right to tell people what they don't want to hear. Similar reasoning has guided the U.S. Supreme Court for fifty years. In *Terminiello v. Chicago* (1949), the high court ruled that a fundamental function of free speech in a democracy is to invite dispute, and that speech should be protected unless it is likely to produce a clear and present danger. The Court, in *New York Times v. Sullivan* (1964), also determined that debate on public issues should be uninhibited and robust, and that it may well include unpleasantly sharp attacks on government. In a similar vein, the court emphasized that if the opinions of citizens are deemed offensive, they deserve constitutional protection (*FCC v. Pacifica* 1978; see Irons, 1997, 1993).

Exploring moral panic over flag desecration provides a unique opportunity to refine our understanding of adverse reactions to political dissent, especially toward protest considered so *offensive* that many people believe it ought to be treated as a *crime*. This work sets out to examine the sociological process facilitating the criminalization of protest by attending to moral enterprises, civil religion, authoritarian aesthetics, and the ironic nature of social control. Before embarking on some of the more conceptual features of this analysis, it is fitting that we review briefly flag desecration in American history.

AMERICA'S STRUGGLE WITH INCENDIARY DISSENT

Whereas many Americans are under the impression that flag desecration emerged initially during the Vietnam War era, the history of this caustic form of protest is traced to the period leading up to the Civil War. In promoting their respective causes, both the Union and the Confederacy resorted to symbolic warfare by relying heavily on flags; indeed, such symbolic crusades had substantive consequences. During the Union reoccupation of New Orleans in 1862, William B. Mumford was executed upon being convicted of treason in a military court for pulling down, dragging in the mud, and tearing to shreds an American flag.

Following the Civil War, flag protectionists targeted other forms of desecration, particularly abuses in the realm of commercialism. In 1907, the U.S. Supreme Court upheld *Halter v. Nebraska*, a case in which two businessmen were fined $50 for selling a bottle of "Stars and Stripes" brand beer—a violation of the Nebraska state flag desecration law. Soon the flag-protection movement would shift its focus from the commercial to the political arena in efforts to apprehend violators of flag desecration statutes. During the tense period leading up to U.S. involvement in World War I, the war itself, and the Red Scare of 1919–20, flag-protection enthusiasts set their sights on political dissidents, especially such leftists as pacifists, labor organizers, anarchists, and communists. Interestingly, though, even mainstream citizens who chose not to consecrate the flag were subject to draconian penalties. E. V. Starr was arrested under Montana law for refusing a mob's demand that he kiss the flag and for terming it "nothing but a piece of cotton" with "a little bit of paint." For this violation, Starr was sentenced to hard labor in the state penitentiary for 10 to 20 years, along with a $100 fine (*Ex Parte Starr*, 1920:146–47; see Goldstein, 1995; Welch, 1999a).

Enforcement of flag-desecration laws has ebbed and flowed throughout contemporary U.S. history; still, efforts to protect the flag are intensified during periods of war. At the height of the Second World War, more than 2,000 children of Jehovah's Witnesses were expelled from school for refusing to salute the flag while reciting the Pledge of Allegiance. For Jehovah's Witnesses, the act of saluting the flag is believed to be a form of idolatry, which is forbidden by their faith. For years, Jehovah's Witnesses were persecuted by vigilante mobs; eventually, though, the U.S. Supreme Court overturned its previous decision, and struck down compulsory flag salute and Pledge of Allegiance requirements (*West Virginia Board of Education v. Barnette*, 1943).

During the Vietnam War era, arrests for flag desecration in the form of burnings and especially alterations, such as superimposing a peace symbol on the flag, were commonplace. Once again, left-wing dissenters, particularly antiwar activists remained the chief enemy of the flag brigade. The lower courts handed down an array of inconsistent and contradictory rulings, adding to a sense that protestors were at the mercy of the state and its law enforcement apparatus. Robert Goldstein (1995) points out that the U.S. Supreme Court bears much of the responsibility for this legal quagmire since it refused to hear all but three cases involving flag desecration. Although the high court overturned convictions in *Street v. New York* (1969), *Smith v. Goguen* (1974), and *Spence v. Washington* (1974), it repeatedly sidestepped the fundamental issue: whether physical flag desecration used to express political speech was a form of symbolic speech protected by the First Amendment. It was not until *Texas v. Johnson* (1989) and again in *U.S. v. Eichman* (1990), that the Court ruled on the constitutionality of flag protection laws. In both decisions, Justice William Brennan certified that flag desecration, even flag burning, was symbolic speech protected by the First Amendment, insisting: "We do not consecrate the flag by punishing its desecration, for in doing so we dilute the freedom that this cherished emblem represents" (*Johnson*, 1989:397).

Rather than put the issue to rest, the court's ruling in *Johnson* triggered rage among politicians and their constituents. This collective burst of emotion contributed to the rise of moral panic over flag desecration, prompting legislative action to criminalize that particular gesture of dissent. Whereas the vast majority of lawmakers in the nation's capital supported measures to outlaw flag desecration, many did so to seek political cover since being labeled unpatriotic would virtually terminate their political careers. In addition to providing elected leaders political cover, the flag panic also served as political diversion, thus deflecting attention from substantive issues facing Americans, including economic strain, inaccessible health care, and inadequate education. Perhaps it was no coincidence that politicians instigated rather than assuaged public fear of flag burning at a time when large numbers of congressmen were implicated in two monumental scandals, the BCCI and the Savings and Loan debacle. Conveniently, hysteria over the flag provided corrupt lawmakers a safe sanctuary from public scrutiny (see Goldstein, 1996a; *New Republic*, 1990; Welch, 1999a). Sociologist Steven Dubin (1992: 17) elaborates the politics of diversion, saying that in the 1980s, "style took precedence over substance in politics." The emergence of mediated political messages in the form of "sound bites" and 30-second television spots contributes to the reduction of critical analysis of social problems by appealing to emotion through visual cues. In addition to the calculated use of the flag, Dubin reminds us that diversionary politics furnished government with another tactic to conceal its unwillingness or inability to remedy social ills. Consider the following state strategy:

A New York City program instituted in 1985 epitomizes this concern with maintaining a facade: abandoned buildings in the South Bronx and other ravaged parts of the city were outfitted with imitation windows, complete with paintings of curtains and potted plants. These facsimiles were literally window dressings, stand-ins for nonexistent programs to address the manifold problems of urban decay. (Dubin, 1992:17)

Still, moral panic over flag desecration in the late 1980s transcended the diversionary politics and the sanctuary of political cover for lawmakers. Riding the conservative wave of civil religion, special interest groups (e.g., Citizens Flag Alliance and the American Legion) lobbied on behalf of Old Glory, thus perpetuating flag legislation as a political agenda. Even though the Flag Protection Act of 1989 was struck down by the U.S. Supreme Court in *Eichman*, the moral campaign to protect the flag persists. In 1995, 1997, 1999, and 2000, a proposal for a constitutional amendment banning flag desecration passed overwhelming in the House of Representatives only to fail in the Senate by four votes (Alvarez 2000). In addition to this legislative activity, other measures of social control persist. By relying on antiquated criminal statutes such as inciting to riot and disturbing the peace, police, prosecutors, and judges have continued to punish protestors who exercise their right to desecrate the flag as symbolic speech. Between 1990, when the FPA was ruled unconstitutional (thus, invalidating all state flag-protection statutes), and 1999, dozens of incidents of flag desecration have been subject to formal actions by the criminal justice apparatus (see Chapter 6).

At a demonstration supporting the rights of Indians to spearfish from Round Lake, in Price County, Wisconsin, Indians Arthur Koser and Roger Stone were arrested and charged with using the U.S. flag improperly, a violation of a Wisconsin statute. The arrests occurred when Stone and Koser each displayed a U.S. flag on which a picture of a Plains Indian was superimposed. Both Stone and Koser were arrested, taken to the county jail, and released on $200 bail (*Koser v. County of Price*, 1993). The arresting officer was following orders from his superior who claimed that "the display of the flag would lead to a disturbance of the peace or even violence"— without any indication that violence was imminent (*Koser* 1993:307).

Tragically, even educators—who are expected to be a bit more enlightened than members of the criminal justice machinery—themselves have participated in the suppression of free speech. In 1991, administrators at Elk Grove High School (California) invited student organizations to decorate the walls of the school with murals representing their thoughts on civics. To depict American freedoms, students from the Model United Nations Junior Statesmen Club decided to paint a mural featuring a burning flag accompanied by statements explaining the importance of civil liberties. The principal refused to authorize the artwork because "the mural on school walls could easily be perceived as an endorsement of flag burning [and] many people in our community—and students as well—will find a mural depicting our flag in flames to be offensive" (Sanders, 1993a:A-1). Elk Grove students insisted, however, that their mural celebrated American freedoms and taught people about the U.S. Constitution. On their behalf, the American Civil Liberties Union (ACLU) filed suit, and the court found that the mural constituted "student speech and expression" protected under California Education Code. Elk Grove school officials appealed the decision but the ruling was upheld. In 1993, the mural was finally painted, but as if in riposte, Elk Grove school administrators passed a new policy banning all permanent murals. Demonstrating once again the irony of social control, the day after the policy was instituted, 100 Elk Grove High School students left class in protest and 48 students were suspended for three days when they refused to return to school (see Hoge, 1993a; *Markgraf v. Elk Grove Unified School District*, 1993).

In an act of defiance aimed squarely at the authoritarian aesthetic, managers at the Reid Municipal Golf Course in Appleton, Wisconsin, discovered their flag soiled with human feces. Old Glory was cleaned and returned to its post but once again was captured by some unknown persons who left a note reading: "The Anarchist Platoon has invaded Appleton, and as long as you [the rich golf club members] put flags up, were [sic] going to burn them" (Pommer, 1998:4-A). Eventually, police arrested 18-year-old Matthew Janssen, a punk rocker and anarchist who described his act of flag *defecation* as a form of government protest. A local prosecutor charged Janssen with theft and felony flag desecration under the Wisconsin flag protection law which includes penalties of up to two years in prison. Janssen argued that the Wisconsin flag statute was unconstitutional, and the county court judge concurred. Nevertheless, the prosecution pushed forward with its case against flag defecation and Janssen was convicted on two misdemeanor counts of theft and sentenced to nine months in the county jail (Pommer, 1998).

While considering the subjective imperatives of the authoritarian aesthetics and the enforcement of a particular version of beauty, it becomes clear that definitions dictating the proper presentation of images are fraught with contradictions (see Ferrell, 1996). Indeed, formal measures designed to protect Old Glory have yet to resolve semiotic and ontological questions over exactly what is a flag and precisely what is desecration. Given the central importance of these considerations to flag protection as a formal code of conduct, it is fitting that we explore further the semiotic and ontological dimensions of social control.

SEMIOTIC AND ONTOLOGICAL CONSIDERATIONS

Semiotics is the study of signs and the transmission of their meaning. While language appears to be the most conspicuous form of communication, semiotics directs attention to other types of signification in society and culture, assuming that *all* social actions are symbolic. From a semiotic point of view, a sign actually is not a *thing*; rather, it is a *representation* of something else. "By a sign is meant a three-termed relation formed when, for somebody, something (the signifier) stands in for something else (the signified) in some context (the ground)" (Mann, 1984:350; Eco, 1976; Gottdiener, 1995; C. S. Pierce, 1931; Saussure, 1966; Sperber, 1974). Culture serves as the context unifying the signifier with the signified, thus enabling the sign to be communicated clearly. More to the point for our analysis, it is through power relations in culture that meanings are constructed and manipulated (Barthes, 1967; Foucault, 1979). By the same cultural process, Barthes (1967) and Levi-Strauss (1963) demonstrate that myths, considered second-order systems of signification, also are shaped by the influence of power. The impact of semiotics on sociology is found in the work of Durkheim (1933 [1964]) who proposed that myths are compelling forces in social organization, particularly in the formation of collective representations of consciousness. Similarly, Marx (1867 [1967]) situated the role of myths in the construction of ideologies which are hierarchical symbolic systems propelled by political and economic imperatives, stratifying society into producers and consumers of culture (Gottdeiner, 1995; see Baudrillard, 1983; Derrida, 1976; Kevelson, 1990; Milovanovic, 1988).

At its most basic level of interpretation, the American flag signifies patriotism. Still, at a higher level of abstraction, Old Glory has been transformed from a secular object of nationalism into a sacred icon through an elaborate cultural process involving civil religion (see Bellah, 1988). As we shall explore further in Chapters 2 and 3, the Stars and Stripes is a cultural product of mythmaking and is embodied in such popular legends as Betsy Ross and General George Washington. Due to its sacred quality, the flag enjoys a degree of prestige not common in other national emblems, such as the bald eagle and the Statue of Liberty. It is precisely Old Glory's venerated status that makes its destruction such a potent form of protest and resistance; indeed, flag *desecration*—a religious term—often is likened to iconoclasm, the act of vandalizing holy symbols. According to Congressman Douglas Applegate:

> Yes, the flag is, in my estimation, an icon defined as an object of critical devotion. As such, it should not be destroyed for any reason by iconoclasts. . . .
> As a comparison, if one attempted to overthrow or destroy the Republic, we would be tried for treason and if found guilty, would be executed. While I do

not suggest this punishment for those convicted of burning or desecrating the flag. I do expect some restitution or punishment that fits the crime that I believe it is. (*CR*, July 20, 1989:E2593)

In expanding our appreciation for a semiotic approach to vexillogy—the study of flags the flag—let us also consider the ontological implications. As a branch of metaphysics, ontology explores the nature of being, or essence, and in what form things actually exist, if at all (Runes, 1968).[2] Ontologically, the flag's essence is significant because it is treated as much more than a mere symbol of American patriotism, liberty, and freedom. The crusade to protect the Old Glory has struggled to transform the symbol into a *thing*, a process called reification. Political commentator Sidney Blumenthal insightfully observed, "The Republicans, post-Reagan, adhere to a literalist faith in the power of elemental national symbols" (Blumenthal, 1990:13). Consider the thoughts by Representative Newt Gingerich (GOP, Georgia) who argued: "It's a very real issue because symbols matter" (quoted in Blumenthal, 1990:13). Grasping to comprehend the Republican party's ontology, Blumenthal concluded: "By this logic, an issue exists because a sign exists, making the issue a projection of a symbol, not the symbol the reflection of an issue" (Blumenthal, 1990:13; see Hitchens, 1997).

Reification manifests itself in the legislative process directed at criminalizing flag desecration, thus raising vexing questions about how the flag, which is really a symbol, can actually exist in material form. Editors at the *Nation* wondered aloud: "What exactly *is* a flag—and *when* is it? What if someone maliciously burns an old flag with forty-eight stars? Should that person go to jail? . . . Suppose someone burns a photograph of the flag? or makes a photocopy of the photograph and faxes it to a friend who burns it? Does the friend go to jail? or the sender?" (*Nation*, 1990:1). In addition to photographs, photocopies, and faxes, there are other technological developments confounding efforts to define the flag and its desecration. Nowadays, browsers on the World Wide Web can visit the Flag Burning Page where they can participate in a virtual flag burning.[3] Computer technology complicates further the semiotics of flag burning, especially from the standpoint of postmodernism and deconstructionism. Virtual flag burning underscores the critical observation that postmodern society is overrun by second-order signs that detach people from reality, producing a hyperreality. The notion of hyperreality draws attention to an endless play of signifiers, or infinite regress, in which signs are defined by other signs (Barthes, 1967; Baudrillard, 1983; Derrida, 1976; Gottdiener, 1995).

Ontological apprehensions have been confronted by many critics of the criminalization process, one of whom argues forcefully that the "American flag is an abstraction, and all material versions of it—even with 50 stars and 13 stripes—are mere representations, among which the law cannot clearly draw a line" (Judson, 1997:A-15; also see Trippett, 1989). In his commentary titled "Flagellation," Hendrick Hertzberg (1989:4–5) writes: "Amid the current hysteria an important ontological point has been: you can't burn the flag. It can't be done. A flag, yes. The flag, no. . . . A flag, any particular flag, is merely a copy. You can no more destroy the flag by burning a flag than you can destroy the Constitution by burning a copy of the Constitution."

Despite the merits of ontological questions concerning Old Glory, politicians have legislated to outlaw flag desecration on numerous occasions, dating back to the turn of the twentieth century. Interestingly, an object that resembles a flag but is not a flag was protected under the (former) Texas state law used to prosecute *Johnson*; in fact, the statute made it a crime to deface any representation of the U.S. flag publicly, regardless of how many stars and stripes it had. Furthermore, the so-called flag did not even have to be cloth. In his opposition to a flag-protection amendment, Congressman Gary Ackerman pointed out that Congress would then have the dubious task of determining exactly what a flag is and is not. Under the current proposal for a flag-protection amendment, everything from party napkins to boxer shorts could conceivably be targets of a federal antidesecration suit (Henderson, 1998). Ironically, many of the flag fashions and displays during the war in the Persian Gulf would have violated the flag protection statutes had they still been in effect; by contrast, "very similar clothing and displays had led to numerous prosecutions during the Vietnam War, when they were viewed as ridiculing the flag, instead of being patriotic" (Goldstein, 1996b:287–88).

Arguments favoring flag protection not only fail basic ontological scrutiny, they also defy the underlying principles of the U.S. Constitution, since such legislation would claim to uphold freedom of expression *except* in the case of flag desecration. Former solicitor general Charles Fried reminded members of the Senate judiciary committee that making exceptions to a principle contradicts the essence of what a principle represents. "The man who says you can make [such] an exemption [to the First Amendment] does not know what a principle is . . . just as the man who says, 'only this once let's make $2 + 2 = 5$' does not understand logic or mathematics" (*Congressional Record*, Senate Judiciary Committee, 1990:113).

In the event that a constitutional amendment banning flag desecration were to be passed, police would have the privilege of distinguishing between dignified and disrespectful treatments of the flag. With such discretionary powers, selective enforcement of flag legislation would be inevitable, and the arbitrary nature of law enforcement would likely discriminate not only against protestors but also other people pushed to the margins of American society. The policing of symbols has the eery potential to go well beyond protecting the American flag; indeed, social-control measures could be directed at citizens who bear the colors of their ancestors' heritage. In 1997, 15-year old Peter Riera was expelled from Boca Raton High School (Florida) for wearing a beaded Cuban flag necklace. School officials banned the ornament because the colors were "gang-related" and that the act of wearing the necklace was a "gang-related activity" as well. Like its American counterpart, the Cuban flag features red, white, and blue colors along with a star. On Riera's behalf, the ACLU filed suit against school administrators, arguing that "the young man's right to freedom of expression was being violated by the high school" and "students have the right to wear symbols of their heritage." Jim Green of the ACLU added, "Dress codes often contain an inherently racial or ethnic bias because they tend to focus on clothing associated with Cuban or African American groups while ignoring other groups such as Boy Scouts or cheerleaders" (ACLU, 1997:7–8). The suit against the school prevailed and Riera was then allowed to accessorize himself with the red, white, and blue. Still, social-control campaigns persist. In 1999, 15-year-old Ryan Green of Gulfport, Mississippi announced plans to file suit against Harrison Central High School, which had ordered him to remove a Star of David pin after the school board declared it a gang symbol (*New York Times*, August 19, 1999: A18).

STRUCTURE OF THE BOOK

This work rests firmly on the sociology of law and the sociology of knowledge; together these intellectual traditions contribute to a framework necessary to unveil the social construction of moral panic and the criminalization of protest. While providing a detailed narrative describing the nature of the flag-desecration controversy, this examination also delves into the conceptual and theoretical underpinnings of the phenomenon, thus offering an ongoing metanarrative. The chapters are presented in three major sections. The first traces the emergence of flag desecration along with a key social force, namely civil religion. As we shall see in Chapter 2, flag desecration as a means of political protest has its origins in the early civil liberties movements in England and America where radicals established the constitutional right to criticize government publicly. Nevertheless, some state leaders resisted such freedoms enjoyed by its citizens, occasionally passing sedition statutes as a mechanism to control political dissent. In its youth, the Republic struggled with a true sense of national and ethnic identity, a problem compounded by immigration. Soon a nativist movement emerged, adopting the flag to symbolize the prestige of citizens born in the United States to the exclusion of immigrants, who were perceived as cultural, political, and economic threats. Indeed, nativism reflected and exacerbated anxiety among Americans who felt that the nation was unraveling. This perception has persisted throughout U.S. history and it helps explain why political protest often frightens people into moral panic. Keeping a critical eye on the role of morality in shaping societal reactions, Chapter 3 explores how civil religion remains instrumental to the crusade to save Old Glory from desecration. Overall, the early chapters demonstrate that flag-related events become more significant during periods of war, including the Civil War and World Wars I and II; still other social forces, including nativism and civil religion, contributed tremendously to the distinct qualities of moral panic over flag desecration.

The second section of the book explores the authoritarian aesthetic attached to flag worship and its resistance. Beginning with Chapter 4 on the Age of Protest, flag desecration is contextualized within the civil rights movement and demonstrations against the Vietnam War. Beyond these well-defined social movements aimed specifically at government and its policies, the Age of Protest blossomed into a much larger and more general rejection of the establishment and its aesthetics. During the late 1960s and early 1970s, young people resisted conventional forms of art, fashion, and lifestyle, all of which contributed to alternative images of the flag. In addition to the rather concise political messages conveyed in flag burnings, there were other, more complicated, forms of antiestablishment expression common in avant-garde art and clothing accessories that featured other symbols superimposed over the Stars and Stripes. Ironically, during the Vietnam War, the authoritarian aesthetic governing the "proper" image of Old Glory was so reactionary and rigid that people were arrested for having sewn *peace* symbols onto the flag.

In the 1980s, the Reagan revolution and its conservative right-wingers steamrolled across America's political landscape; still, there were scattered bursts of resistance, though not on the scale of the Age of Protest. Unlike the massive antiwar rallies that characterized the 1960s and early 1970s, demonstrations protesting U.S. militarism in Central America and other hawkish campaigns by the Reagan administration were few in number; however, flag burnings by a small clique of radicals—the supporters of the Revolutionary Communist Party (RCP)—began to attract political and public attention. Whereas the 1984 flag burning outside the Republican National Convention in Dallas produced scant media coverage, the arrest and prosecution of Gregory L. Johnson, an RCP supporter, eventually escalated into a frenzy that sparked the 1989 flag panic (Chapter 5).

As we shall discuss in Chapter 6, the flag desecration controversy continues to spill over into other realms of society, including art and commerce, offering another glimpse of adverse societal reaction condemning acts construed as disrespectful toward the nation's most cherished emblem. The campaign to prosecute dissenters persists even after the U.S. Supreme Court in *Johnson* (1989) and *Eichman* (1990) ruled that flag desecration is a form of political speech protected by the First Amendment. Such prosecutions serve as tangible evidence of the state's interest in upholding the authoritarian aesthetic by punishing people who use the flag to criticize government.

In the final series of chapters, the theoretical and conceptual components of moral panic are presented in detail, especially as they manifested in the flag hysteria of 1989 (Chapter 7). While introducing the cast of characters in the drama of moral panic, particular attention is turned to moral entrepreneurs whose activities inside and outside of government propel the flag protection enterprise. Moral panic over flag desecration reached fever pitch and lawmakers scrambled to criminalize that form of protest by passing the Flag Protection Act of 1989. When the FPA was struck down by the High Court, moral entrepreneurs regrouped, embarking on another strategy to protect the flag, this time with a constitutional amendment, a crusade that persists today. By examining the *Public Papers of the Presidents* and the *Congressional Record*, we deconstruct political rhetoric characterized not only by moral panic but also other sentiments as well, most notably civil religion and nostalgia (Chapter 8).

Because they contribute significantly to moral panic over flag desecration, the media deserve a closer look, especially in light of their contradictory activities. Paradoxically, the media benefit by offering extensive coverage of flag desecration, but in doing so, they inflame flag panic to the extent that lawmakers organize to criminalize protest, thus placing restrictions on free speech. In Chapter 9, the media's contradictory role in promoting, then downplaying, moral panic over flag desecration is discussed.

The concluding chapter canvasses political and legal resistance to criminalizing protest embodied in flag protection laws and constitutional amendment proposals. Consistent with the notion of ironic social control, measures intended to ban flag desecration merely encourage acts of defiance, thereby illustrating the symbiotic relationship between and rule makers and rule breakers. As dissenters and their First Amendment defenders square off with flag protectionists bent on limiting free speech, we discover sharp contradictions in American society, whereby state hierarchies threaten to undermine democratic principles of free speech.

NOTES

1. During the 1960s and 1970s, Harry Edwards, sociology professor currently at the University of California at Berkeley and founder of the Olympic Project for Hu-

man Rights, became a key figure in promoting the raised-fist gesture of Black Power, continually reminding fellow activists of the compelling power of symbolism in protest.

2. According to Mann (1984) epistemology, a branch of philosophy concerned with the theory of knowledge, differs from ontology, the study of the nature of things; he concedes, however: "The relative primacy of ontology and epistemology is an ongoing debate in the history of philosophy, since the nature of things presumably determines our ability to know them, while on the other hand they can exist for us only through our knowledge of them" (p. 112).

3. The internet address of the virtual-flag-burning web site is: http://www.indirect.com/user/warren/flag.html

2

The Roots of Flag Desecration in American History

Patriotism is the last refuge of a scoundrel
—Samuel Johnson, April 7, 1775

Popular notions of American patriotism suggest that Old Glory has a deep and rich history dating from the birth of the nation. Upon closer examination, however, contemporary references linking the flag to the rise of the Republic are overstated, and perhaps in the end, little more than nostalgic myths. Historians discredit the enduring legend that "the Stars and Stripes leaped fully panoplied from the marble brow of the 'Father of His Country,' with Betsy Ross as midwife" (Mastai and Mastai, 1973:47). Rather than spring into full existence, the flag as we know it today evolved over time. The Continental Congress approved the flag's design in 1777; still, at that time—contrary to popular belief—the emblem lacked not only genuine enthusiasm, but strict standardization as well. There were many variations of stars and stripes, keeping the flag in metamorphosis until 1912, when an executive order specified its design and dimensions. The establishment of the flag was motivated not by a need for national identity but rather by practical concerns, such as locating U.S. ships at sea. Whereas American nostalgia through artistic renderings commonly depicts Old Glory at the center of momentous battles (e.g., paintings by Emmanuel Leutze, *Washington Crossing the Delaware* [1851–52] and Archibald M. Willard's *The Spirit of '76* [1875]), the U.S. Army fought under its own regimental unit flags, not the Stars and Stripes; in fact, the military did not carry the U.S. flag until the Mexican War in 1846. Further evidence that the flag generated little attention and interest resides in the observation that it rarely was deployed in symbolic political protest: until of course, the Civil War (Brinkley, 1990; Curti, 1968; Curtis, 1993a; Goldstein, 1995, 1996a, 1996b; Guenter 1990; Johnson, 1930; McPherson, 1989; O'Leary, 1999; Preble, 1917; Quaife, 1942; Smith, 1975; Zelinsky, 1988).

Whereas the flag desecration controversy in America is commonly associated with the Vietnam War era, surfacing once again in the late 1980s, scholars remind us that the struggle to protect the flag has ebbed and flowed since the Civil War period (Goldstein, 1995, 1996a, 1996b; McPherson 1989). During the Civil War, the Union flag emerged as a widely visible symbol of national unity, but after Reconstruction allegiance to it was relaxed. The flag was featured in fashion (e.g., dresses and scarves) and the advertisement of retail products (e.g., liquor, cigars, fruits, and even toilet paper) (Johnson, 1930; Mastai and Mastai, 1973; Preble, 1917). Soon politicians promoted themselves and their election campaigns with the flag; on the national stage, that form of promotion was first seen during the 1896 presidential campaign. In the tense period leading to the First World War, the focal point of the flag protection movement shifted from commerce and mainline politics to left-wing dissent: a development that would reemerge during the Second World War, the Vietnam War, and again in the late 1980s. This chapter explores early historical eras, illuminating the social, cultural, and political significance of flag desecration vis-à-vis flag protection. In doing so, we shall see that controversies surrounding the flag have not only symbolic repercussions but substantive consequences: especially in the form of arrests, prosecutions, and various punishments—including public humiliation, fines, and incarceration, as well as victimization by vigilante mobs.

THE ORIGIN OF FREE SPEECH AND EFFORTS
TO CRIMINALIZE DISSENT

Free speech in the United States is traced to seventeenth-century England where a group of Radical Whigs championed several key rights, including free speech and religious liberties. In addition to espousing limitations on the monarchy and Parliament, social reformers secured the right to criticize the state (Mayer, 1991). Although such monumental achievements in the realm of individual rights would become cornerstones of American constitutionalism, the right to criticize government would remain bitterly contested. Many early American government leaders favored restrictions on free speech, particularly as a strategy to stifle political dissent. Conversely, advocates of the Bill of Rights demanded that a set of additional constitutional safeguards was necessary to protect citizens against government and defend the minority, however small, against the majority, however large (Finkelman, 1992; Schwartz, 1971).

Throughout American history, government has challenged individual rights and liberties. Indeed, campaigns to restrict free expression occasionally have resorted to coercive mechanisms of social control, most notably criminalization. Among the first significant measures designed to limit free speech was the Sedition Act of 1789 under which certain forms of political dissent were criminalized. Sedition, an act of resistance or insurrection against government, was not only penalized but also politicized during the Presidency of John Adams. Whereas Congress set out to guard federal officials from false, scandalous, and malicious criticism, the scope of protection was astonishingly uneven; the Sedition Act prohibited criticism of President Adams but not of Vice-President Thomas Jefferson. Since Jefferson was poised to face Adams in the presidential election of 1800, the Sedition Act was used as an instrument of power enjoyed by the incumbent. Beginning with the Sedition Act trials and continuing throughout U.S. history, prosecutors argued that criticism of government undermined the legitimacy of the president, and as a result, threatened national security. During the Jefferson presidency, however, the Sedition Act expired. Ironically, prohibiting criticism of government had come to be viewed by citizens as a tyrannical act, which in turn diminished rather than affirmed the legitimacy of the state (Curtis, 1993a; Gibson, 1986). As we shall see later, efforts to suppress and criminalize political protest would persist with various degrees of intensity throughout American history.

NATIVISM AND THE FLAG IN ANTEBELLUM AMERICA

Whereas the roots of flag adoration *and* desecration in American history are found principally in the Civil War era, key developments in the antebellum period mark the emerging role of nativism in shaping of popular images patriotism and nationalism. As the United States expanded geographically—from sea to shining sea—during the 1840s so did a popular belief in manifest destiny: a cultural ideology resonating a sense of superiority among White Anglo-Saxon Protestants (WASPs) who believed they were an elite people chosen by God to cultivate and civilize the nation. As discussed in Chapter 3, civil religion has had a tremendous impact on the transmission of American culture and patriotism. In a parallel vein, civil religion has contributed to a pernicious version of nativism that not only discriminated against foreign-born people and their children but also led to violence against them. The nativist movement targeted immigrants who were characterized as cultural, political, and economic threats to WASP-Americans; at that point, the ethnic and religious groups in the direct line of fire were German-Americans and Irish-Americans, many of whom were Catholics. In addition to the Native American Party, the American Republican Party had emerged as a premier nativist organization: later that group was nicknamed "the Know-Nothings" because its members guarded the party's secrets by pretending to know nothing. In proclaiming their patri-

otism, the American Republican Party adopted the flag along with the eagle and an etching of George Washington as symbols of their ethnic—and
patriotic—purity (Baker, 1977; Guenter, 1990).

In Philadelphia, nativist sentiment reached a flash point in 1844 when
Native American Party supporters and Irish-American Catholics clashed,
sparking three days of violence known as the Kensington Riots, in which
the homes, schools, and churches of Irish immigrants were burned and
razed. Not to be lost in this wave of ethnic violence was the Stars and
Stripes. Whereas nine people perished in the fighting, the death of nativist
George Shiffler became symbolically relevant since he died while trying to
protect the flag from desecration. In fact, Shiffler's supporters iconized that
very flag by parading it through the streets and then displaying it with a
placard inscribed in large letters: "This is the Flag that was trampled on by
Irish Papists" (Guenter, 1990: 56). Nativists immediately canonized Shiffler
as a martyr and vowed to rid "their" country of foreigners who came to
steal America from the descendants of the Revolution. "For the Native
Americans, who already felt their public schools threatened by Roman
Catholic efforts to discontinue readings from the King James version of the
Bible, the death of Shiffler and the simultaneous desecration of the flag demanded revenge" (Guenter, 1990:55–56). Nativist rioters announced that
they would burn the dwellings of Irish Catholics; in response, residents of
all ethnic backgrounds in Kensington adorned their homes with makeshift
U.S. flags in an effort to defend themselves against arsonists.

The Kensington Riots became a defining moment in the construction of
history and nationalism for nativists, especially with regard to the flag. On
the next Independence Day in Philadelphia, nativists commemorated their
fallen as over three thousand participants marched, many of whom carried
Old Glory. Due to that nativist (and exclusionary) pageantry, immigrants
would continue the struggle to be viewed as "real" Americans. In years to
come, other nativist organizations would embrace the flag as an emblem
of a racially and ethnically pure Protestant America, including the Ku Klux
Klan and the post-Holocaust American Nazi Party (Baker, 1977; Guenter,
1990). In 1915, the Klan was reborn in Atlanta through the efforts of Colonel
William J. Simmons, who remained fervently devoted to "pure Americanism" in the tradition of the Know-Nothings. The Klan adopted the Flag
Code and instructed the adolescent member of its Junior Order in flag etiquette; requirements for membership in the Klan included an oath of allegiance to the flag and the Constitution. Later photographs would show
hooded Klansmen standing in front of a fiery cross and clutching the Bible
while holding the flag. In 1925, more than forty thousand hooded Klansmen carrying flags marched down Pennsylvania Avenue in Washington,
D.C. "Such an image could, with good reason, disturb a modern-day patriot; it does, however, demonstrate how nativist groups often incorporate

the national banner into their symbology, interpreting it as an affirmation of their particular ideological beliefs" (Guenter, 1990:179; see Chalmers, 1981; Johnson, 1923; O'Leary, 1999; Rice, 1972).

THE CIVIL WAR ERA AND THE EMERGING SIGNIFICANCE OF THE FLAG

Not to diminish the importance of the Kensington Riots, the Civil War era marks the beginning of what has become identified as the flag desecration phenomenon; until that time, the American flag generated little popular interest and was used rarely for political protest. During the Civil War era, however, the flag was increasingly politicized and as a result of civil religion, granted sacred meaning by government and its supporters. This development is significant sociologically because the newly enshrined status of the flag would cue protestors that the symbolic power of the flag could be easily reversed by flag desecration, an act of iconoclasm that punctuated criticism of government. In Northern states, abolitionists flew flags upside down and draped them in black to protest the Fugitive Slave Act of 1850, under which runaway slaves were extradited to their owners (McPherson, 1989; Paludan, 1975). As secession spread in the South, the Confederacy denounced the Union, leading to a war that combined military force with political symbolism. While the Union draped its flag over military installations, government buildings, and schools, the Confederacy retaliated with its own brand of semiotics. In addition to encouraging secessionists to destroy and burn the Union flag, Southern political and military leaders decorated their campaign against the North with its own flag. The Confederate, or rebel, flag quickly became a formidable rival to the U.S. flag, setting off a controversy that would linger into the twenty-first century. While firing shots at Fort Sumter (South Carolina), Confederate soldiers aimed deliberately at the Stars and Stripes. The incident became legendary, mythologized in battle cries in the North where Union military efforts received popular support. Civic leaders spoke at ceremonial flag raisings, and for the first time in American history, citizens began flying the flag from their homes (Preble, 1917).

Shortly after the flag became a consecrated emblem of the Union, government and military elites developed tactics to defend it. In 1861, Treasury Secretary John Dix instructed a clerk in New Orleans to shoot on the spot anyone who attempted to confiscate the flag. As the Civil War erupted, Old Glory was publicly desecrated in many Southern cities, and in what is believed to be the first political protest of its kind, a flag was burned in Liberty, Mississippi. Official measures of social control in the form of using military personnel to punish flag desecrators in regions controlled by the Union were complemented by informal efforts. In the North, vigilantes coerced citizens and businesses to drape the flag in support of the Union. Due to those formal and informal activities, the nation had become much more flag conscious; similarly, as the Civil War deepened, stories spread of dying soldiers reaching out to the flag for solace, love, and even invigorating strength (Eggenberger, 1964; Goldstein, 1995; Guenter, 1990; O'Leary, 1999; Preble, 1917; Smith, 1903).

Another significant event during the Civil War era involved William B. Mumford, who was convicted of treason for desecrating the U.S. flag in New Orleans during Union reoccupation of the city. In 1862, Union general Benjamin Butler, nicknamed the Beast of New Orleans, ordered Mumford to be executed by hanging. Mumford would have been spared the death penalty on the condition he swear allegiance to the Union, but he spurned the ultimatum. Deposed Louisiana governor Thomas Moore memorialized Mumford's resistance against Northern forces: "Scorning to stain his soul with such foul dishonor, he met his fate courageously, and has transmitted to his countrymen a fresh example of what one will do and dare under the inspiration of fervid patriotism" (Parton, 1864: 353).

PARTISAN POLITICS AND FLAG DESECRATION

Whereas the Civil War era marked an important period in the development of the flag's consecrated status, by the 1890s, Old Glory was being used to promote political parties and their candidates. Nearly a century before George Bush and the Republicans embraced the flag as a patriotic challenge to Democrat Michael Dukakis, GOP candidate William McKinley, in 1896, relied on a similar tactic against Democratic-Populist candidate William Jennings Bryan. Although the flag had been used in partisan politics as early as the 1840s, when it was common for candidates to have their names and slogans superimposed on the flag, McKinley was the first to place the flag at the center of his campaign. McKinley's supporters not only produced massive flag displays to amplify their candidate's reverence for the flag, but, much like the Bush campaign in 1988, the strategy was designed to raise questions concerning Bryan's patriotism. McKinley waxed nostalgic by reminiscing about the virtues and triumphs of the Civil War, and the campaign reached a crescendo when it founded the first annual national Flag Day in honor of McKinley. Republicans invested heavily in the McKinley campaign, both financially and symbolically. The Bryan campaign, however, took exception to the insinuation that their candidate lacked sufficient loyalty to become president. Supporters of Bryan attacked posters and flags bearing McKinley's name; during the 1896 election there were about twenty incidents in which the flag was defaced, torn, and burned (Goldstein, 1995; Goodwyn, 1978; Guenter, 1990; Jones, 1984). The flag-protection movement drew heavily on its objections to the flag's mistreatment in partisan politics; still, such misuse of the flag was not the sole target of the flag crusade. By the end of the nineteenth century, efforts to ban flag desecration with criminal statutes also were motivated by adverse reactions to commerce and advertising.

PROHIBITING FLAG COMMERCIALISM

The flag protection movement gained considerable momentum in the decades following the Civil War. Beginning in the 1890s, several veteran and patriotic organizations (e.g., the Loyal Legion, the Grand Army of the Republic, and the Sons [and Daughters] of the American Revolution) joined forces with the American Flag Association. Together, these groups campaigned to protect the flag from desecration, particularly from businessmen who misused the flag in the course of commerce (Mastai and Mastai, 1973; O'Leary, 1999). In a series of legal victories, the flag-protection movement sponsored legislation that was adopted in every state between 1897 and 1932 (Goldstein, 1995). As a result of this legislative activity, the flag, for the first time in U.S. history, was officially designated a venerated object whose desecration was criminalized.

Soon the constitutionality of flag-protection laws was challenged in court, as judges began invalidating bans on desecration. Manufacturers who used images of the flag to hawk their wares argued that flag-protection statutes infringed on their private property rights. In *Ruhstrat v. People* (1900), the first of only a few landmark decisions on flag desecration, the Illinois Supreme Court determined that the Illinois flag-desecration statute impinged on personal liberty rights; hence, using the flag for business advertising was ruled a legitimate occupational pursuit. A key decision in *Halter v. Nebraska* (1907), however, pumped new life into the then-wavering flag-protection movement. In *Halter,* two businessmen appealed their convictions and fines of $50 for selling a bottle of "Stars and Stripes" brand beer decorated with an image of the flag. Attorneys for the businessmen argued that the state of Nebraska had unlawfully interfered with their property rights in pursuit of a legitimate business venture. The Nebraska and U.S. supreme courts rejected the arguments of the defendants and upheld their convictions and penalties (*Halter,* 1907).

As the flag crusade targeted businessmen for the improper use of the nation's emblem, their efforts ironically contributed to the commodification of patriotism. Historian Cecilia O'Leary examined the role of the Grand Army of the Republic (GAR) in the emerging paradox of American patriotism, noting that the business community found a kindred soul in the GAR, "not only because patriotism boosted consumerism but also because the GAR's emphasis on an orderly, hierarchical society . . . resonated with capital's attempts to impose social stability" (1999:41). The contradiction between the GAR's commitment to preserving the dignity of America's memories embodied in the flag and other emblems (i.e., military uniforms from the Civil War) and its willingness to become a cultural and business monolith was not easily resolved. "Although the commercialization of nineteenth-century culture often exploited national symbols and messages in ways that the GAR would later condemn as sacrilegious, technological changes in manufacture and the expansion of markets made patriotic symbolism a ubiquitous commodity" (O'Leary, 1999:43). Soon mass production of flags and images of Old Glory would demonstrate the intimate connection between American culture and commerce. Still, the GAR and other groups involved in the flag lobby were left uneasy about the commodification of patriotism since there would forever exist a fine line between promoting heartfelt nationalism and crass commercialism.

The campaign to protect the flag by lobbying the government to pass legislation during the turn of the century is particularly significant for several reasons. First, early state statutes banning flag desecration would endure until 1989, when the U.S. Supreme Court in *Johnson* would invalidate them on constitutional grounds; but for nearly a century, thousands of American citizens would be arrested and funnelled into the criminal justice system for violating antidesecration laws. Second, the commercial rationale for laws against flag desecration would be replaced with a different legislative focus. Flag protectionists soon would become concerned more with political protest and less with the commercial misuse of the flag. Finally, the sociological significance of early flag-protection statutes is evident insofar as a government decree officially elevated the flag to a venerated status. Indeed, that final aspect of the flag-desecration phenomenon has strong implications for civil religion, whereby secular objects are granted sacred meaning (Bellah, 1988, 1978, 1975, 1970).

FLAG CONTROVERSIES DURING THE WORLD WARS

Due to massive immigration, urbanization, and industrialization, America underwent rapid social change during the first two decades of the twentieth century. Relatedly, key shifts in the economy prompted labor unrest and various strains of political radicalism. Whereas the intent of the flag-protection movement at the turn of the century was to ban profane uses of the flag in such mainstream pursuits as commerce and advertising, the flag desecration issue was transformed significantly some 20 years later. By 1920, the political milieu had been altered by several key events:

the tense period leading up to America's entry into World War I, the war itself, and the postwar "Red Scare" of 1919–20 (Jaffe, 1972; Murphy, 1972). Together, these events reshaped flag-protection efforts by focusing on political dissenters who challenged the traditional political order: pacifists, militant trade unionists, and domestic Communists inspired by the 1917 Russian Revolution (Chafee, 1919; Lewis, 1991; Peterson and Fite, 1957). As Prosser (1969: 161) notes, those dissidents often were victims of political oppression in the United States; however, "they occasionally provoked this response by using the American flag to demonstrate dissent." Since then, flag enthusiasts have directed more energy to protecting the flag from political dissenters than from mainstream businessmen. Of the 55 flag-desecration incidents uncovered between 1907 and 1964, 45 involved perceived political dissent (Goldstein, 1995).

Wartime remains a significant social context for flag desecration prosecutions; after all, public dissent often intensifies during periods of war, thus prompting the concern of government. Of the 45 prosecutions for flag desecration (as political protest) between 1907 and 1964, 35 occurred in wartime (Goldstein, 1995, 1978; Jaffe, 1972; Murphy, 1972; Walker, 1990). In the years leading up to U.S. involvement in the First World War, perceived threats to the American way of life compelled lawmakers to formulate legislation designed to protect the nation's security. A key tactic in such campaigns was the enforcement of loyalty. Efforts to shield the flag quickly extended beyond promoting national pride to protecting domestic tranquility against sedition, treason, and anarchy. In 1918, J. M. C. Smith, Representative from Michigan, spoke at a congressional hearing: "This is a time [during World War I] above all when I think that sedition should be suppressed" (House Judiciary Committee Subcommittee No. 1, *To Preserve the Purity of the Flag*, 62nd Congress, 2nd session, 1918:1). Smith's remarks about sedition prefaced his support for a federal flag-protection statute. Two types of flag desecration were labeled federal offenses: mutilation and contempt. Mutilation referred to physically injuring the flag, while contempt encompassed verbal insults. During the proceedings, Smith was asked if he believed that "a man who would wipe his hands on the flag is an enemy of this country." (Ibid.) Smith answered affirmatively and concurred with fellow congressmen who proposed that flag desecrators "should either be shot or locked up." (Ibid.) During that period, there were several well-organized campaigns to pass a federal flag-protection law, but each failed. Still, similar legislative efforts persisted. In 1918, Congress passed the Sedition Act, which included flag-protection provisions along with a ban on criticism of the U.S. government and its armed forces. Whereas sedition is generally defined as advocating a violent overthrow of the government, the Sedition Act of 1918 was written so broadly that it applied sweepingly to many activities deemed unpatriotic, including flag mutilation and contempt. Under the act, statements (spoken or written) or actions deemed disloyal to the United States were punishable by a fine of not more than $10,000 or imprisonment for not more than twenty years, or both (U.S. Code, 40 *Statutes* 555).

The Sedition Act of 1918, along with state flag-protection laws, served more than mere symbolic objectives. During the First World War, those statutes were enforced for the purpose of suppressing political opposition to U.S. involvement in the war; as a result, thousands of antiwar activists were arrested, prosecuted, convicted, and imprisoned (Rabban, 1997; see Goldstein, 1978; Walker, 1990). Although defendants appealed their cases on grounds that their right to criticize the government—the *sine qua non* of free speech—had been violated, the courts often upheld their convictions. Typically, such cases involved defendants who had been charged with obstructing the war effort and attempting to interfere with the military draft; those violations were widely enforced and applied to delivering speeches as well as distributing leaflets denouncing American militarism.

In disputes over free speech, the U.S. Supreme Court routinely sided with the government and reminded citizens that First Amendment protections diminish during wartime, even to the point of restricting antiwar activities that promote peaceful political change (Curtis, 1993a). As a case in point, socialist leader Eugene Debs was convicted of draft obstruction for giving a speech in Canton, Ohio, in which he commended imprisoned draft resisters for defying the state (*Debs v. United States*, 1919; see also *Schenck v. United States*, 1919). From behind prison bars, Debs campaigned for president, drawing nearly a million votes. Anarchist Emma Goldman similarly spent several years in a federal penitentiary for issuing antiwar speeches and publishing remarks critical of the government in her journal *Mother Earth*. Goldman and fellow radical Alexander Berkman loathed compulsory patriotism, insisting that flag glorification diverted public attention from capitalist exploitation and militarism. In his anarchist publication *The Blast*, Berkman referred to the flag as a sacred rag. "The very fact that men are sent to prison for 'desecrating' a rag proves that there is no freedom of conscience under that flag. No decent man or woman can respect the symbol of such tyranny" (Berkman, 1916:5). *Mother Earth*, *The Blast*, and other subversive political works were censored by the Postmaster General, who exercised the authority to suppress journalism critical of the war effort.[1]

On a parallel plane, the Red Scare produced the Palmer Raids of 1920, whereby private homes and offices of antiwar activists and other libertarian radicals were ransacked in 33 cities. Under the Sedition Act, U.S. Attorney General Alexander M. Palmer, who had strong presidential ambitions, authorized government agents to seize papers and literature regarded as disloyal and seditious. More than 4,000 persons (U.S. citizens and aliens alike) were arrested and many were jailed for more than a week without charge. Indeed, the criminalization of dissent during the First World War extended well beyond measures to suppress free speech and enforce compulsory patriotism; deportation campaigns became emblematic of the government's renewed interest in nativism by removing radical immigrants. Overall, more than 3,000 aliens described as "politically dangerous" by the government were arrested, detained, and subjected to deportation hearings: approximately 800 people were deported, many of whom were communists, anarchists, and members of the Industrial Workers of the World (Wobblies). Emma Goldman and Alexander Berkman were among those banished from the United States. The deportation delirium, as it became known, was fraught with violations of due process but none of these cases was reviewed by the Supreme Court (Goldstein, 1978; Donner, 1990; Rabban, 1997; Rehnquist, 1998; Robins, 1992; Sifakis, 1992; Walker, 1990).

During World War I, state flag-protection statutes (and the federal Sedition Act of 1918) were used not only to suppress radical activism but were enforced in ways that penalized even nonradicals for violating orthodox patriotism. According to Guenter (1990: 167): "Fear of treachery by enemy supporters at home drove many Americans to demonstrate their patriotism by reporting supposed traitors." Against this wave of compulsory patriotism, mainstream citizens who chose not to consecrate the flag were subject to draconian penalties. In 1918, Tony Deidtman, a naturalized U.S. citizen born in Germany, was convicted of sedition in Montana for making a comment sympathetic to German civilians who were suffering during the war; he was sentenced to not less than ten years at hard labor. In compliance with Section Three of the Uniform State Flag Law, subversive elements could be arrested not only for supporting the enemy, but also casting contempt upon the flag by word or deed (Guenter, 1990). In a case that demonstrates the unforgiving nature of compulsory patriotism during that period, E. V. Starr was arrested under the Montana sedition law for refusing a mob's demand that he kiss the flag and for denouncing it as "nothing but a piece of cotton" with "a little bit of paint." For that transgression, Starr was sentenced to hard labor in the state penitentiary for 10 to 20 years, along with a $100 fine (*Ex Parte Starr* 1920; refer to Chapter 3). Incidentally, the Montana sedition law (replete with provisions for flag protection) served as a model for the federal Sedition Act. During the First World War, several states increased penalties for flag desecration: in Louisiana and Texas violations were punishable by five and twenty-five years in prison, respectively.

Although American history is scattered with cases of flag defilement by nonradicals, bona fide political dissidents typically bear the brunt of such prosecutions. Consider the cases of clergyman pacifist Bouck White, who presided over the "Church of the Social Revolution." White was arrested, charged, and convicted of insulting the flag in 1916 and again in 1917 for flag desecration. In the first case, White circulated an antiwar cartoon depicting the flag on the ground near a bag of money with a serpent entwining them and the word "WAR" printed across the top. Despite the clear attempt to express political dissent, government authorities prosecuted White for violating penal law banning use of the U.S. flag for advertising purposes. On the eve of his first trial, White and members of his congregation held a meeting at which Old Glory and several emblems of other nations (e.g., a British flag) were burned in a large kettle dubbed "the melting pot" symbolizing international brotherhood (*New York Times* June 2, 1916:53). The incident became especially significant because it was the only prosecution for flag *burning* to be recorded until the Vietnam War era. During White's first trial, Judge McInerney echoed the sentiments of outraged Americans petitioning the government to strip White (who was U.S.-born) of his citizenship by asking rhetorically: "Why don't you go off and live in some other country? Why don't you find a country that likes to have its flag desecrated?" (*New York Times* June 3, 1916:10). White was convicted and sentenced to 30 days in jail and fined $100 for insulting the flag.

In 1917, White and two of his followers, Edward Ames and August Henkel, were found guilty of burning the flag. Judge McIntyre proclaimed to the jury "your verdict goes out to the world and shows to the people the American flag must be revered and respected." Thinking aloud about punishing White, Assistant District Attorney Alexander Rorke drew references to justified homicide: "If an American in his indignation had shot White dead on the night of the flag burning, I doubt if you could find a juryman who would vote to convict him" (*New York Times* March 15, 1917:1). White and his two codefendants were sentenced to 30 days in jail and fined $100 for torching the flag, but the judge regretted not having the power to extend the sentence to several years. Judge McIntyre's "America, Love it or Leave It" message was geared similarly toward immigrants, proclaiming that the verdict "is a warning to the aliens in this country that American institutions must be accorded proper respect, especially in these momentous days in the nation's history" (*New York Times,* March 16, 1917:12). Referring to the perceived threat of radical immigrants, the judge noted "in recent years there has been coming into our country certain elements . . . [who] have dared to suggest destruction to our institutions. To these and all others this court sends a warning that hereafter it must be 'hats off to the flag'" (Ibid.). While in jail, White, Ames, and Henkel were assigned daily flag duty. During his first flag raising behind bars, White remarked: "It looks good to me but I wish my flag was there too." When asked about his flag of choice, White proclaimed, its "the red banner of internationalism" (*New York Times,* March 16, 1917:12). Soon red (and some black) flags, which were increasingly being condemned by patriotic Americans, also would be outlawed by many states.

Whereas the World War I era prompted government officials to become increasingly vigilant in efforts to shield Old Glory, it was during the Red Scare of 1919–20 that red flags and other subversive emblems were formally suppressed. Stemming from Russia's Bolshevik Revolution in 1917, the red flag emerged as an international symbol of socialism. At the height of the anticommunist hysteria, 32 states and several cities outlawed displays of red flags and similar opposition symbols. Penalties for violating red flag laws were generally harsher than those of the flag desecration statutes; typically, such offenses were punishable by fines of up to $500 and sentences of as much as six months in jail (Chafee, 1941; Goldstein, 1978; Jaffe, 1972; Million, 1940–41; Murray 1955). The constitutionality of red flag laws eventually was confronted by the U.S. Supreme Court in 1931 when Yetta Stromberg, a 19-year-old member of the Young Communists League, appealed her conviction that she had unlawfully engaged in a red flag ritual. The incident occurred at a camp where she served as counselor, and her activities with the children included teachings of history and economics, including class consciousness and the solidarity of the workers. In its landmark decision, *Stromberg v. California* (1931), the court ruled that such laws blatantly violated First Amendment freedoms, especially when red flags were displayed to express peaceful and orderly opposition to the state.

Between the First World War and the Vietnam War era, there were very few prosecutions for flag desecration, even during World War II. Ironically, it was at the height of U.S. involvement in the Second World War that incidents involving Jehovah's Witnesses generated enormous public outrage, culminating in vigilante violence. In what has been characterized as compulsory patriotism during World War II, many school districts required students to salute the flag while reciting the Pledge of Allegiance as part of the daily ritual to inculcate loyalty to the country. The act of saluting a flag, however, conflicts with the religious beliefs of the Jehovah's Witnesses, who regard such gestures as idolatry. Adhering to their religious convictions, Jehovah's Witnesses instructed their children not to salute the flag, even though it was required by school-district policy. Staunchly enforcing the flag-saluting requirement, educators began expelling from school the children of Jehovah's Witnesses; more than 200 were suspended in twenty states. Labeled as unpatriotic, Jehovah's Witnesses faced fierce hatred and discrimination in their communities, where vigilante mobs persecuted and attacked them (Manwaring, 1962). Eventually, the controversy reached the courts. In 1940, the U.S. Supreme Court in *Minersville School District v. Gobitis* upheld the legality of school policies that enforced flag saluting, but three years later reversed its decision in *West Virginia Board of*

Education v. Barnette, which struck down the compulsory ritual and prohibited school officials from punishing students who did not salute the flag. In light of the enormous relevance of flag-saluting requirements to civil religion, this example of moral panic over flag desecration will be explored fully in the next chapter.

CONCLUSION

Because flag desecration accompanies related phenomena, it ought to be understood as an epiphenomenon. Indeed, protests featuring the Stars and Stripes do not occur in a vacuum, rather they transpire in the context of several social forces, including nationalism, nativism, militarism, politics, and economics. As shown in this chapter, American history is replete with political struggles between the state and its citizens; moreover, political dissent often is shaped by the very institutions it opposes. As the state confronts defiant citizens, conflict between authorities and dissidents often is escalated rather than suppressed.

Whereas the flag crusade has its roots in civic activities aimed at promoting patriotism, over time that enterprise has been coopted by the state, using flag protection as a means of regulating political protest. Nevertheless, citizens overwhelmingly support legislative measures criminalizing flag desecration, a development with troubling implications to democracy. In framing the Bill of Rights, several advocates of free speech anticipated a tyranny of the people; consequently, they amended the Constitution in ways that guarantee protections for the minority, however small, from the majority, however large. Despite freedom of expression and the right to criticize government, the struggle between compulsory patriotism and political dissent persists.

NOTE

1. Other notable arrests for flag desecration include that of Bill Haywood of the International Workers of the World (the Wobblies), who used Old Glory as a protest poster in demonstrations supporting the rights of striking miners between 1901 and 1903 (Green, 1988).

3

Civil Religion and the Flag as a Venerated Object

The constant invocation of the notion of "desecration" suggested that a secular symbol was being endowed with religious majesty, which dictates spiritual reverence. And the supporters of the flag demonstrated a remarkable literalness in their beliefs, directly equating a piece of cloth with what it represents.
—*Steven Dubin*

Never corrupt patriotism by mixing it with religion.
—*William Safire, "Fourth of July Oration"* New York Times

In American culture, reverence for the U.S. flag is emblematic of nationalism and patriotism; at a higher level of abstraction, however, it also embodies civil religion. As a public theology or religion of the nation, civil religion denotes a nonsectarian faith in which secular objects are transformed into sacred icons (Bellah, 1967). Indeed, elements of civil religion are clearly evident in flag-protection crusades, most notably expressed in legislation intended to guard the flag, a *venerated* object, from *desecration*. A nationwide Gallup poll in 1992 indicated that 77 percent of Americans surveyed believe that the physical act of burning the flag is not protected as freedom of speech by the First Amendment. Similarly, 82 percent of citizens polled believe that the American people should have the right to determine by vote whether or not the U.S. flag should be protected and, when asked if it were put to a vote today, 81 percent said they would vote for a constitutional amendment (Gallup, 1992). Currently, the crusade for a constitutional amendment to shield the flag continues to marshal considerable support in Congress, and because civil religion shapes significantly the course of American culture, efforts to criminalize flag desecration are likely to persist.

As a social movement propelled by civil religion, the flag-protection campaign has captured the attention of intellectuals from various academic disciplines, including historians (Guenter, 1990; Mastai and Mastai, 1973; O'Leary, 1999; Preble, 1917; Quaife, 1942; Smith, 1975; Zelinsky, 1988), political scientists (Goldstein, 1995, 1996a, 1996b; Rotnem and Folsom, 1942), legal scholars (Curtis, 1993a; Nahmod, 1991; Prosser 1969), and journalists (Hentoff, 1995; and Hess, 1989). Conspicuously absent from the discourse on flag desecration, however, are sociologists (see Welch, 1999a). In light of its relevance to civil religion, the dearth of sociological analysis on flag desecration is especially disconcerting. While attending to key conceptual, historical, and cultural considerations, this chapter explores the sociological significance of the flag-protection enterprise. Keeping civil religion at the center of our analysis, this chapter examines the emergence of formal flag codification, informal control, and patriotic socialization by the state.

FLAG DESECRATION AND CIVIL RELIGION

Moralism is a trait found typically in both religion and patriotism, contributing to a profound sense of righteousness, which prompts people to defend the eternal good (see Katz, 1988). From an anthropological standpoint, rallying around the flag is a ritual infused with patriotic fervor, and in a more primal state resembles nondescript religion. Although the separation of church and state in the United States is formally established by its constitution, in the sphere of American culture, religion and civics are deeply interwoven, commonly expressed in the benediction, God Bless America. Numerous civic exercises are imbued with religion; for example, the bible is used in courtroom protocol to *swear* in witnesses and induct public officials into government office. Similarly, U.S. currency also features explicit references to the deity, including the phrase "In God We Trust" printed on bills and embossed on coins. Although the Constitution proclaims a separation of church and state, these two institutions frequently operate in concert to promote religion and patriotism, together becoming a potent unifying force in American culture (Gibbs, 1991; Greenhouse, 1998; Welch and Bryan, 1997; Wills, 1990).

Conceptual Considerations

Whereas Rousseau initially used the term civil religion in *Social Contract* to capture the transcendental quality of political states, sociologist Robert Bellah (1988, 1978, 1975, 1970, 1967) redirected the concept to formal and informal links between religion and state. Specifically, Bellah viewed civil religion as a public theology whereby secular objects are transformed into sacred icons. Other sociologists have elaborated on the notion of civil religion: pointing out that it signifies "the collection of beliefs and symbols connected to the polity" (Williams and Demerath, 1991:417). Described further as America's "politicomoral" ideology, civil religion "has combined moral absolutism, competitive individualism, and a messianic conception of the United States into a consistent worldview" (Anthony and Robbins, 1982: 215; see Demerath and Williams, 1985; Hammond, 1976; Hughey, 1983; Mathisen, 1989; Nahmod, 1991; Sperber, 1974; Wimberley, 1980; Zelinsky, 1988).

Returning to Bellah's approach to civil religion, he insists that the religious dimension of social life permeates all other social spheres, suggesting that even the most secular aspects of social life are shaped by religious experience. Bellah's work derives heavily from Durkheim (1912 [1954]) who proposed that society in its cohesiveness possesses a *sacred* character, thereby evoking awe and devotion among its people. Durkheim concluded that even in secularized societies, religion—albeit in a noninstitutional form—manifests itself in symbolic and metaphorical expressions of society in its ideal image. In that sense, the function of religion serves to unify society with common values, commitments, and sanctity of the normative boundaries (Durkheim, 1912 [1954]; see Alpert, 1939). In modern society, civil religion provides an additional source of social solidarity, and in the realm of American patriotism, the flag stands as a consecrated symbol of nationalism and unity. Flag protection, as a patriotic duty, represents a moral obligation in which activities in the sphere of the profane (i.e., citizenship) permeate the sphere of the sacred or transcendental (i.e., religion). Civil religious rituals and affirmations promote communal devotion to the nation's symbols. Furthermore, in a Durkheimian sense, celebrating nationalism is a projection of societal power that citizens share, transmit, and reproduce. Patriotism transcends individual existence; accordingly, citizens assign sacred significance to the flag as a medium, in order to visualize the power of nationalism. In the end, that sanctity, though largely unconscious, provides aura and meaning for Americans.

The civil-religious dimensions of flag adoration extend beyond its rituals and affirmations; by virtue of legislation, the flag's status as a *venerated* object had been officially designated. The flag's sanctity in American culture has been maintained by legal language specifically referring to the flag as a venerated object (along with monetary currency, draft cards, and the presidential seal). Moreover, violating a flag-protection statute constitutes an act of *desecration*. Legal terms such as *venerated* objects and *desecration* verify how deeply religious forces penetrate the civic arena. The iconization of the flag, by which civil-religious status was afforded formal protections, is traced to specific activities and events occurring in the 1890s. During that era, intense lobbying by influential figures in the flag-protection movement led to the flag's transformation into a venerated object (see

O'Leary, 1999). As a result of that process, the flag was anointed as a sacred icon, but characteristic of civil religion, it has also retains its secular qualities insofar as it represents nationalism and patriotism. The veneration of the flag has enjoyed lasting success, culminating in a form of civil religion that has endured for more than a century.

Historical and Cultural Considerations

The religious aura surrounding the adoration of the flag—as a venerated object and consecrated national symbol—illuminates the importance of civil religion in American culture (Welch and Bryan, 1997). National history, along with legends and "harmless" myths, are driving forces behind the reproduction of civil religion. The transformation of the flag from a secular object into a sacred icon occurred during the antebellum period and was shaped significantly by a nativist social movement. From that time on, Old Glory—a nickname immersed in civil religion—has been revered by rituals which honor, worship, and adore the flag's *sanctity*. These patriotic rituals inculcate in citizens the flag's significance in the nation's history, heritage, and culture (Andrews, 1890; Colgrove, 1896–97; Guenter, 1990; Wilson, 1899).

Inspired by nostalgic visions of the American Revolution and the Civil War, a social movement dedicated to promoting patriotism by protecting the flag was forged during the 1890s. That network of flag enthusiasts consisted of several veterans and hereditary patriotic groups, including the Grand Army of the Republic (mostly Union Civil War survivors), the Sons of the American Revolution, and the Daughters of the American Revolution (O'Leary, 1999). As noted previously, early efforts to protect the flag were aimed at commercial and partisan political misuses of the flag, and later attempts to guard the flag were redirected to suppress political opposition. With those developments in mind, it is important to explore the historical and sociological processes by which the flag has been transformed from a highly respected—albeit secular—object into a civil-religious icon whose reverence and etiquette would be enforced by legal mandate. From its inception, flag-protection legislation was rooted in civil religion. In what was the first legislation of its kind, the House of Representatives in 1890 passed a bill to prevent flag desecration. Without hearings or floor debate, the bill targeted commercial misuse of the flag in advertising and relied heavily on civil-religious reasoning. The flag "should be held a thing sacred, and to deface, disfigure, or prostitute it to the purposes of advertising should be held to be a crime against the nation and be punished as such" (CR, 1890:10697). Although the federal bill did not become law, its penalties were later adopted by state statutes: a fine of $50, or imprisonment for less than thirty days, or both.

It has been suggested that early flag lobbyists, who were middle class and upper-middle class, moved to protect the flag for reasons of nostalgia in the face of the perceived threat that *their* traditional America would become overrun by a new class of businessmen (Goldstein, 1995; Guenter, 1990; O'Leary, 1999). As is often the case with perceptions of social threat, sources of anxiety are complex and incorporate several aspects of rapid social change. During the 1890s, urbanization, industrialization, and immigration contributed to political, socioeconomic, and cultural shifts away from the status quo. Sociologically, flag protection represented resistance to imminent social change insofar as Old Glory would become a perpetual symbol of *their* America; indeed, from the beginning, the flag-protection movement was founded on rigid notions of nativism and cultural elitism. Reactions by flag enthusiasts against commercialism and the misuse of the flag by rising businessmen were drawn along lines of old money and new money, which generated profit by the use of gaudy advertising. At that time, the advertising world was highly stratified socioeconomically and aesthetically; thus, the advertising profession was respectable, provided it relied on dignified imagery and upscale messages. The elitist reaction to the misuse of the flag marks the emergence of an authoritarian aesthetic; interestingly, the flag-protection movement was spearheaded by Charles Kingsbury Miller, a wealthy retired newspaper advertising executive. Miller offered his advertising acumen to the flag-protection enterprise; he designed and distributed pamphlets that instructed citizens and politicians in the proper way to display the flag. Along with Union army veteran Captain Philip Reade, Miller and the flag brigade promoted an aesthetic based on civil religion whereby the flag was to be treated with dignity.

In a 1898 address, Miller pleaded for flag protection by resorting to themes of civil religion: "Those three sacred jewels, the Bible, the Cross, and the Flag, command our national reverence." Moreover, Miller's speech also exuded elitist paternalism when insisting that flag desecration by partisan politics and commercialism "sets a bad example to the lower classes, who degrade the flag to its nadir; and has deadened the sentiment that the emblem of our republic should be kept as inviolate as was the Holy of Holies in King Solomon's temple" (1898:1). Miller's sense of nativism also surfaced in his address when he referred to "uneducated foreigners who land upon our friendly shores [who] are ignorant of everything pertaining to American institution, even after many years' residence" (1898:1). Similarly, Miller took aim at political radicals, whom he called "the world's worst enemies, the anarchists, [who] flock to this country to find a safe and free asylum" (1898:1). Blending flag protection with civil religion, nativism, and elitism, Miller exhibited moral panic, fearing that the nation was perilously close to unraveling into mayhem. In one of his many pamphlets, Miller (1901:1) wrote: "The red flag of danger flies in America. Anarchy is rampant. . . . [I]ncreasing pauper immigration is deteriorating our citizenship." Whereas the rhetoric of flag protectionists, such as Frances Saunders Kempster of the Daughters of the American Revolution and Col. Ralph Prime of the Sons of the American Revolution and President of the American Flag Association, was not as inflammatory as Miller's pamphlets, there remained a persistent reliance on civil religion, often comparing the flag to the Christian cross (see Daughters of the American Revolution Flag Committee, 1899; Goldstein, 1996b; O'Leary, 1999; Zelinsky, 1988).

Generally, sociologists and historians have overlooked an important element of civil religion that seems to violate the principle of the separation of church and state. For nearly 150 years, many churches have displayed the flag along with their various religious symbols and statues. It has been reported that the incident at Fort Sumter during the Civil War prompted ministers to show support for the Union by draping the flag inside and outside their churches. It is believed that houses of worship embraced the flag to ensure that their religion was viewed as favorably as *American*. Given the degree of animosity harbored by nativists toward Roman Catholics in the nineteenth century, Old Glory became instrumental in keeping Catholicism free of suspicion. More recently, the Nicheren Shoshu of America, a sect of Buddhists, have begun to incorporate not only massive flag displays but also baton twirlers and cowboys into their patriotic and religious extravaganzas (Guenter, 1990).

Formal Flag Codification and Civil Religion

The flag crusade in the late nineteenth century was more than a political lobby aimed at persuading legislators to pass antidesecration statutes; given the degree of commitment to civil religion, early flag enthusiasts participated in a form of fanaticism typical of a cult. The flag cult developed elaborate customs, codes, and rituals that would later be adopted by other patriotic groups and clubs (e.g., the Boy Scouts of America and the Girl Scouts of America). Codification of the flag emerged initially at the turn of the twentieth century when several states passed flag-protection laws; in 1923, codification was established further when the Second National Flag Conference finalized a formal code of flag etiquette. The following year, 28 states adopted the code for school instruction. The Flag Code consisted of specific instructions dictating the manner of displaying the flag: in all, 15 items pertaining to the flag ritual were detailed meticulously in the code along with 15 cautions. The flag should be flown only in good weather, and if displayed at night it should be illuminated; the flag ought not to touch the ground; the flag is required to be folded according to a precise angular pattern; when the flag is flown at half-staff—to honor the death of significant countrymen—it is raised initially to the top of the pole then lowered to its midpoint, following the same procedure in removing the flag from the pole. Perhaps ironically, the proper and respectful way to dispose of an old and worn flag is to burn it in a solemn ceremony, marking its formal retirement. The Flag Code concluded its list of instructions for proper flag display with a notation on criminalization by supporting penalties (i.e., fine and imprisonment) for public mutilation, abuse, or desecration of the flag (see Guenter, 1990).

Rituals and rules of etiquette resemble primal forms of religious fanaticism. Such superstition was reinforced by a flag cult that viewed Old Glory as having magically powerful qualities that are necessary to hold the nation together, especially in times of crisis. During the First World War, the flag cult reached its zenith in mystical ceremonies invoking the holy power of the flag; the Freemasons and their auxiliary organization Eastern Star paid formal homage to the flag in their assemblies. Indeed, some Masons went to great lengths to claim mystical connections among their group, the birth of the Republic, and the emergence of the flag. John W. Barry constructed an elaborate symbology in which the colors and the design of Old Glory had their origin in the Masonic version of manifest destiny. Barry's interpretation of history (or legend) suggested that George Washington, himself a Mason, engineered the flag and commissioned Betsy Ross to sew a design that would reflect the traditions of the brotherhood of Masons (Barry, 1924). Likewise, Eastern Star, a secret society for Protestant women, professed a mythical history of the nation that integrated Aryan racial pride, the bible, numerology, and the flag. In *Mystic Americanism,* Eastern Star member Grace Kincaid Morey reads into Old Testament accounts symbolic references and predictions associated with the nation and its flag (Morey, 1924).

Another profound manifestation of civil religion as a cult was expressed by William Norman Guthrie who published a tract titled *The Religion of Old Glory* in 1918. Guthrie advocated nondemoninational public religious ceremonies worshipping the Stars and Stripes akin to mystical rituals; his "Ceremony of Worship Unto Old Glory" combined pagan forms of idolatry with Christian prayers and genuflections. At a higher level of devotion, Guthrie's flag fanaticism projected into the afterlife, as shown by his belief that the U.S. flag was the flag of God, and service to it continues after death (Guthrie, 1918). Admittedly, Guthrie's ceremonies were extreme forms of civil religion; however, formal links between nationalism and religion continue to merge. Recently, federal legislators sponsored an elaborate assembly billed the Congressional Flag Day prayer concert, which was staged in Washington, D.C. in 1997 (Clines, 1997). Over the course of American history, however, reverence for the flag has persisted among mainstream citizens due not to fanaticism but rather to subtle but powerful influences of civil religion. "Almost all Americans admittedly in varying degrees, have been culturally conditioned to respond to the symbol of the flag as a representation of a spiritual reality we all share. Many would agree that the flag is the most significant symbol of our civil religion; it certainly is the most ubiquitous" (Guenter, 1990:22; Welch and Bryan, 1997).

Civil Religion as Informal Control

Despite mainline respect for the flag, U.S. history also includes incidents of fanaticism and fetishism, culminating in informal social control and vigilante justice (Welch, 1992). Punishment for flag desecration, from a Durkheimian perspective, represents a communal reaction to violations of the sanctity of nationalism, a defense mechanism situated at the moral center of American society. Whereas the formal penalties for violating flag protection laws are based on legal constructs borrowed from the religious sphere (i.e., desecration of a venerated object), informal punishments also reflect religious ideation in enforcing patriotism and condemning outcasts. Throughout the history of the flag-protection crusade, especially during World War I, vigilante mobs forced persons of questionable patriotism to kiss the flag (Peterson and Fite, 1957; also see Watkins, 1993). Kissing the flag is a symbolic expression of respect firmly rooted in formal religious rituals, resembling the kissing of the holy cross, holy relics, rosaries, and finger rings of bishops, Cardinals, and the pontiff.

Perhaps the most draconian punishment for (oral) flag desecration was imposed on E. V. Starr in Montana during the First World War (see Chapter 1). The sentence was upheld on appeal, as federal judges concurred with the *Halter* precedent. Interestingly, though, District Court Judge George M. Bourquin admonished the sentence as "horrifying," but was himself powerless to overturn it. "In the matter of his offense and sentence, obviously petitioner was more sinned against than sinning. It is clear that he was in the hands of one of those too common mobs, bent upon vindicating its peculiar standard of patriotism and its odd concept for respect for the flag by compelling him to kiss the latter" (*Starr*, 1920, 146). Referring to the unruly mob's "unlawful and disorderly conduct . . . they, not he, should have been punished" (*Starr*, 146). Clearly, the *Starr* controversy blurs the line between formal and informal measures of social control. Indeed, government and law enforcement officials often turned a blind eye to vigilante violence and in some cases participated in the victimization of flag desecrators and those unwilling to defer to the Stars and Stripes (see Peterson and Fite, 1957).

In a similar incident of victimization, a Wyoming mob attacked a man who praised the German Kaiser in 1917; he was nearly hanged to death but was revived by a city marshal, then forced to *kneel* and *kiss* the flag. During that era, similar incidents of coerced flag kissing imposed by vigilante mobs were reported in Chicago, Iowa, Ohio, Boston, and New Haven (Peterson and Fite, 1957; also see Watkins, 1993). Elements of civil religion permeate the flag-protection movement by underscoring a sense of moralism and righteousness; moreover, such victimization was reminiscent of the persecution of heretics, a common manifestation of moral panic. From a Durkhemian perspective, punishing flag desecrators serves the moral order by defining moral boundaries and upholding the sanctity of national symbols, namely Old Glory.

As mentioned previously, perhaps one of the most ironic twists in the flag-protection movement was the controversy over the compulsory flag salute involving the Jehovah's Witnesses in the late 1930s and 1940s (Barber, 1947; Gilkey, 1957; Lewis, 1991; Manwaring, 1962; Murphy, 1972; Walker, 1990). Indeed, those events illuminate how civil religion and institutional—albeit nonmainstream Christian—religion are occasionally at odds. During that period, many states had laws that required teachers and students to salute the flag while reciting the Pledge of Allegiance during the daily ritual of affirming their patriotism. Resisting the state and its rules of conduct, hundreds of students refused to salute the flag, a transgression constituting insubordination punishable by expulsion. Many of those students were children of Jehovah's Witnesses who refused to salute the flag because the act violated their religious beliefs against idolatry. According to *Exodus,* Chapter 20, verses 4 and 5: "Thou shalt not make unto thee any graven image . . . ; thou shalt not bow down thyself to them nor serve them." Adhering to a literal interpretation of scripture, Jehovah's Witnesses considered the flag an image within that command and refused to salute it; consequently, as many as 200 children in about twenty states were expelled from their schools by 1940 (*West Virginia Board of Education v. Barnette,* 1943; Manwaring, 1962). Compounding their victimization, Jehovah's Witnesses came under attack by citizens who questioned the religious sect's patriotism, especially at a time when Americans were distressed over U.S. involvement in World War II (Jaffe, 1972; Murphy, 1972).

Eventually the courts were drawn into the fracas. In 1940, the U.S. Supreme Court upheld a school district's right to expel children from school on the grounds that they refused to salute the flag (*Minersville School District v. Gobitis,* 1940). In justifying its decision, the high court referred to national unity and national security, thus inflaming moral panic. As many as 2,000 Jehovah's Witnesses children were expelled from school for refusing to salute the flag; similarly, their parents were harassed and beaten by townspeople. The ACLU reported that almost 1,500 Witnesses were victims of vigilante mobs in 355 communities in 44 states between May and October 1940 (*Gobitis,* 1940; Manwaring, 1962; Walker, 1990).

Amid the flag mayhem in 1943, the U.S. Supreme Court reversed itself,

striking down compulsory flag salute and Pledge of Allegiance requirements (*Barnette*). In his landmark opinion, Justice Robert Jackson articulated that "we apply the limitations of the Constitution with no fear that
freedom to be intellectually and spiritually diverse will disintegrate the social organization . . . no official, high or petty, can prescribe what shall be
orthodox in politics, nationalism, religion or other matters of opinion"
(*Barnette*, 1943:415). *Barnette* remains enormously significant. By ruling
against compulsory patriotism, the court issued a powerful declaration of
individual constitutional rights against the will of the people, reiterating
that the purpose of the Bill of Rights was to withdraw certain subjects from
the vicissitudes of political controversy and place them beyond the reach
of the majorities and government officials (also see Andersen, 1940–41;
Danzig, 1993a, 1993b; Fennell, 1941; Grinnell, 1939; Rotnem and Folsom,
1942).

Oddly, though, in the early 1970s, the courts again were entangled in a
flag-saluting case in Henrietta, New York. High school art teacher Susan
Russo stood silently at attention during daily classroom recitation of the
pledge of allegiance. School regulations required her to participate by
saluting the flag and when Russo was hired in 1969, she was required to
sign a loyalty oath affirming her support of the constitutions of the United
States and of New York state. Consequently, her refusal to salute the flag
violated a condition of her employment and she was discharged by school
officials. Russo resorted to a civil rights action by insisting that her em-
ployer violated her First Amendment rights (*Russo v. Central School District
No. 1*, 1972). In 1984, Susan Shapiro, a high school senior in Randolph, Massachusetts, caused a stir by not standing for the playing of "The Star Span-
gled Banner," saying that: "The flag don't mean nothing. It's important to
some people, but not to me." Shapiro said that she was humiliated and harassed by teachers and students; she also received hate mail reading: "It
can't happen here! Think about it Jew!" (Margolick, 1984: 35).

In a recent event somewhat reminiscent of the persecution of the Jehovah's Witnesses, professional basketball player Mahmoud Abdul-Rauf
was suspended without pay in 1996 by the National Basketball Association (NBA) for refusing to stand during the national anthem, a violation of
league policy. Abdul-Rauf, a devout Muslim, proclaimed that he "doesn't
believe in standing for any nationalistic ideology" and referred to the U.S.
flag as "a symbol of oppression, of tyranny" (*New York Post*, 1996:56). Abdul-Rauf's disobedience brought harsh criticism from fans, sportswriters,
and veterans' organizations. Ed Wearing of the American Legion suggested that Abdul-Rauf should renounce his citizenship, insisting that "refusing to stand up and recognize the unity of this nation as embodied
under the flag is tantamount to treason" (*New York Post*, 1996: 56). Returning fire, Nat Hentoff editorialized: "You would have thought that J. Edgar

Hoover had never died. While some sportswriters supported Abdul-Rauf, most did not. [The star sports columnist of the *Daily News* [NY]], Mike Lupica, kept alive the traditions of the Know-Nothing Party of the 1850s. He said, 'If this young man finds living in this country, abiding by the rules of his sport, so offensive, then he should leave'" (1996:10).

The Abdul-Rauf incident was not the only time a basketball player had been criticized by self-described patriots. During the Persian Gulf war, Marco Lokar, an Italian citizen playing for Seton Hall University (N.J.), refused to wear a U.S. flag patch on his basketball uniform. Fans and veterans groups chided Lokar, even though he eloquently cited moral and religious principles in denouncing the war (Harvin, 1991; *New York Newsday*, February 12, 1991; Vecsey, 1991). Incidentally, the tradition of playing the "Star-Spangled Banner" at sporting events is traced to the 1890s when millionaire sporting goods manufacturer Albert Goodwill Spalding aligned nationalism with baseball. It was during the Spanish-American War that musicians first performed the national anthem on opening day at New York City's Polo Grounds (Guenter, 1990).

In another recent case of compulsory flag veneration, Deiter Troster, a corrections officer for the State Correctional Institution at Greensburg, Pennsylvania, refused to wear a U.S. flag patch on his uniform. Troster's insubordination violated a new uniform regulation mandating the display of the flag patch on the right sleeve of the uniform shirt. Troster, a retired Army major, argued that "state-compelled display desecrates the flag and debases it [because] . . . the American flag symbolizes freedom from state-coerced political or patriotic speech" (*Troster v. Pennsylvania State Department of Corrections et al.*, 1995:1088). For refusing to wear the flag patch, Troster was suspended and faced dismissal from his job.

Patriotic Socialization by the State

As civil religion shaped American culture in the mid-nineteenth century, the responsibility of teaching patriotism was transferred from the home to schools, marking a key shift in socialization. Guenter reminds us of the important "historical relationship between the school and the forces of American civil religion, forces that would raise the flag to the pinnacle of holiness" (1990:43; O'Leary, 1999). While educating children about civics, American schools deliberately cultivate patriotism by transmitting history, and equally important, legends and myths. Such pedagogies exemplify what Neitzche described as society's impulse to create myths that become indispensable elements of culture. "Even the state knows no more powerful unwritten laws than the mythical foundation that guarantees its connection with religion and its growth from mythical notions" (Neitzche, 1967:75; see Nahmod, 1991). More to the point, many patriotic legends are taught as history. Consider the popular tale of Betsy Ross, the Philadelphia seamstress credited with making the first American flag at the request of General George Washington. Without verifiable evidence, the story has been uncritically accepted by Americans beginning in the 1870s, remaining a staple in American education. Although nowadays the Betsy Ross story is considered a harmless fabrication, it continues to glorify the flag in ways that allow educators "to introduce an active female character into the pantheon of political heroes" (Guenter, 1990:101; O'Leary, 1999; Smith, 1975). Unlike such feminist heroes as Joan of Arc and Susan B. Anthony, however, Betsy Ross' contribution to history reinforces traditional sex roles for females, becoming famous for carrying out a domestic chore at the request of a powerful military man.

Whereas the role of nativism was instrumental in the flag-protection movement, its influence also is found in the state's campaign to Americanize children in public schools. Initially, patriotic socialization for America's youth was underwritten by veterans' organizations and hereditary societies, but later the efforts of George T. Balch proved particularly significant. Balch introduced patriotic rites for the classroom consisting of flag glorification and the recitation of the Pledge of Allegiance. While employed as a New York City auditor in 1886, Balch was alarmed by various "tenement-house problems" associated with the living conditions of recent immigrants whom he referred to as "human scum, cast on our shores by the tidal wave of a vast immigration" (Balch, 1898: ix). Balch professed that patriotic ceremonies in public schools would *regenerate* the immigrant population by immersing them in American culture. For students, Balch developed lockstep training to instil good citizenship that was so dogmatic that it was commonly referred to as a catechism, a term laden with civil religion. During the Spanish-American war and into the twentieth century, flag protocols for schools spread quickly across the nation. State laws were instituted, requiring pupils and teachers to observe the flag ritual at the beginning of each school day (Manwaring, 1962).

Nativism and its animosity toward recent immigrants remained underlying themes of the patriotic movement. While saluting the flag, students were instructed to chant the phrases: "We offer our Heads and our Hearts to our God and Country! One Country! One Language! One Flag!" (Balch, 1898:16). "It is no coincidence that Balch's plan encouraged the use of the flag in spreading not only love of country but also a code of moral behavior. He spoke candidly about the use of the flag as a tool in the Americanization of the foreign element" (Guenter, 1990:116). The intensity of Americanism in socializing children fluctuated over the next several decades, becoming more pronounced during wartime. Prior to U.S. involvement in World War I, teaching children patriotism regained interest as Old Glory was placed center stage in daily school rituals. In 1915,

Theodore Roosevelt recommended that citizenship training be appended to a renewed cultural movement involving nativism (Sica, 1990). In a speech to the Knights of Columbus, Roosevelt proclaimed that "duties of patriotism required giving up all other loyalties—to old country, ethnic group, and class" (Kazin, 1989:19). Although civil religion in American culture is believed to promote solidarity and facilitate assimilation, it is fraught with contradictions, producing divisiveness and exclusion (Demerath and Williams, 1985). Moreover, civil religion in the realm of flag adoration lends itself to strict political orthodoxy. As we shall explore further, protestors commonly are marginalized and ridiculed by mainline citizens.

CONCLUSION

Historically, political symbols have been used by authorities to establish a particular culture conducive to state power (Hayes, 1960; Lerner, 1937; Nahmod, 1991). The American experience is no exception; over time, the flag has become a sacralized object steeped in legends, myths, and mysticism, all of which add to an aura of American culture. As a civil-religious icon, Old Glory has been employed by the state for purposes of reproducing its power over citizens. From a critical standpoint, civil libertarians oppose the government's reliance on images to manufacture consent among citizens (Herman and Chomsky, 1988; Welch and Bryan, 1997, 1998, 1999; also see Greenberg, et al., 1995). Nevertheless, defenders of the state argue that the Stars and Stripes warrants unique status due to the "almost mystical reverence with which it is regarded by Americans" (Rehnquist dissenting in *Johnson*, 1989:2533, 2552). Supreme Court Justice Rehnquist reminds us that the flag inspires poetry and song which are quintessential vessels for cultural myths and beliefs about the birth of the nation; moreover, he insists that sacralizing the flag is necessary for purposes of empowering the state. Sheldon Nahmod respectfully disagrees with Rehnquist: "We have come too far as a nation, with our tradition of tolerance for controversial and unsettling ideas, and should, by this time, be too mature as a political community to punish heretics by establishing a blasphemy exception to the first amendment" (1991:511).

Moral fervor contained in civil religion continues to permeate the contemporary flag protection movement; in fact, proponents of flag-protection legislation cite moral justifications for defending the flag from desecration. During the flag flap of the late 1980s, Representative James Sensenbrenner reacted to the flag-burning controversy by pleading: "Is it too much to ask those who consider themselves Americans to be required to have respect for our flag? In this day and age, when it seems that perversion is accepted and morality is a taboo perhaps this small mandate is not asking too much" (Waldman, 1989:15). Similarly, at the 1997 Flag Day prayer concert in Washington, D.C., Congressman Bob Barr instructed his constituents to "simply stand up and say our flag needs protection" (Clines, 1997:A-22).

Against the prevailing tide of Americanism, however, critics denounce the flag crusade for endorsing compulsory patriotism and promoting a national religion. Ira Glasser, Executive Director of the ACLU, compared flag protection to religious fanaticism, and likened the effort to eliminate the "offensive" display of burning flags to the Muslim condemnation of author Salman Rushdie for his so-called blasphemous book *The Satanic Rituals*. "Blasphemy might be a crime in Iran but it ought not be a crime in America. Yet, in attempting to convert the flag from a political symbol into a religious icon, that is precisely what George Bush has proposed" (Glasser, 1989:A-23).

II

The Authoritarian Aesthetic and Its Resistance

4

Questioning Authority
in the Age of Protest

Flag protection marks a rediscovery of the core American values, like respect for authority, and a rejection of the counterculture values of the 1960s and the anti-authoritarian attitude and anti-Americanism.
—*Senator Chuck Grassley*, Congressional Record

The period between the mid-1960s and the mid-1970s was so rife with dissent that it has become popularly known as the Age of Protest (Kittrie and Wedlock, 1986). Whereas the Vietnam War fueled much of the opposition against the state, other forms of dissent also mounted, especially the civil rights campaign and the counterculture. Given our focus on First Amendment freedoms it is fitting that we acknowledge one of the early events shaping the Age of Protest, the 1964 Free Speech Movement at the University of California at Berkeley. Upon his return from civil rights work in Mississippi, Mario Savio defied the university's policy restricting leafletting, a popular vehicle among students for communicating ideas on social issues. At the heart of the conflict between students, particularly those committed to the civil rights movement, and university administrators was freedom of speech. Soon Savio and other student leaders organized sit-ins and other public protests, forcing the administration to repeal its prohibitions on leafletting (Miller and Gilmore, 1965; Savio, 1965; see Kittrie and Wedlock, 1986). Among the valuable lessons learned from the Free Speech Movement at Berkeley was the realization that civilian dissent can—and should—redirect government policy, and in the end, alter the course of history.

With peace, civil rights, and militarism at stake, questioning authority would become the *zeitgeist*'s prevailing theme. At the center of the turbulence were fundamental First Amendment liberties, most notably rights to assembly and free speech. Events in that period are significant to this discussion, given that public political dissent often was stifled by government, and occasionally criminalized. Among the most heavily regulated forms of protest was flag desecration. During the 1960s and 1970s, flag desecration became a complex social phenomenon taking on many different manifestations, ranging from flag burning as part of public protest against the Vietnam War to wearing flag patches on clothing to signify popular culture.

Flag desecration is a particularly significant act because it represents a type of dissent that spawns unique forms of social control. Whereas semiotics, civil religion, moral panic, and authoritarian aesthetics contribute to the social construction of flag desecration, the importance of social movements ought not be neglected. Although the notion of social movements can be applied to political protests during previous moments in American history (e.g., World War I), the term takes on greater meaning during the Vietnam War era due the vast scale and intensity of dissent. In this chapter, we explore flag desecration in the Age of Protest, attending to societal conditions and political events that not only triggered dissent but also shaped an emerging counterculture.[1]

SOCIAL MOVEMENTS IN THE AGE OF PROTEST

Adding to the turbulence in the Age of Protest were various forms of collective behavior that appeared to drift without any particular goal other than rejecting a culture reproduced by the establishment. In sharp contrast to the amorphous character of this counterculture, however, several social movements emerged as highly organized campaigns with crystallized objectives. Protest of that nature relied on well-defined strategies that steered their opposition against the status quo. Whether the movements were devoted to establishing civil rights or ending the war in Vietnam, they channeled their outrage into public acts of defiance. Because the Age of Protest was becoming such a defining historical period, American sociologists concluded that social movements were not mere collective behavior but rather a distinct phenomenon deserving a closer look. Herbert Blumer was among those sociologists turning attention to social movements and their impact on social change. According to Blumer, "social movements can be viewed as collective enterprises seeking to establish a new order of life" (1974:4). As antecedents, social problems and significant events (e.g., the repression of civil rights and war) create conditions of unrest that spark social movements; before such movements take form, however, they exist loosely as primitive rebellion lacking organization, continuity, and leadership.

The Age of Protest provided a timely opportunity for sociologists to realize that there were several *different* types of social movements. A typology of social movements not only permits us to appreciate the nuances of protest but similarly identify various contours of flag desecration. Blumer (1974) distinguishes among general, specific, and expressive social movements in an attempt to reveal their unique characteristics. General social movements tend to mirror cultural drift, whereby the ideas, beliefs, and values of people begin to stray from convention. In the 1960s, the counterculture exemplified a *general* social movement, representing cultural drift from the establishment but in ways that were broad and relatively unorganized. The counterculture was an influential force insofar as it contributed to various social movements, encouraging young people to reject authority. Manifesting as *specific* social movements during that era, the civil rights and antiwar campaigns conformed to principles of organization that enabled them to influence social change.

Drawing considerably from the counterculture, another form of collective behavior emerged as expressive social movements. Unlike the well-orchestrated activity of specific movements, expressive social movements of that era did not necessarily set out to alter the institutions of the social order; rather, they exerted energy toward aspects of popular culture such as art and fashion. Those expressive social movements reinforced the prevailing attitude of antiauthoritarianism, and through the prism of avant-garde art and fashion, they gave the *zeitgeist* a distinctive look and posture (Welch, 2000).

THE AUTHORITARIAN AESTHETIC AND FLAG DESECRATION

As discussed in previous chapters, the symbolic value of Old Glory commonly transcends earnest patriotism, reflecting deeper components of state power. In an authoritarian manner, political and economic elites go to great lengths to defend their aesthetics, producing an array of social-control measures commonly found in the flag crusade. A key form of social control intended to preserve the flag's sacred status has been criminalization. The word *offense* enjoys two basic definitions; it can mean either a criminal act or an insult. In the realm of flag desecration, the term offense combines both meanings since the state—in an effort to promote its authoritarian aesthetic—legislated that it would be a crime to insult the Stars and Stripes. Empowering the campaign to enforce rigidly defined notions of flag beauty and respect, the criminalization process was further set into motion as the state authorized agents of the criminal justice apparatus to arrest those who violate the establishment's aesthetic. Simply put, flag desecration had been deemed imagery so *offensive* that authorities banned such expression. Flag desecration is remarkable because it targets not only the state but also the authoritarian aesthetic by attacking its symbols. In doing so, flag desecrators invert an established state symbol, producing a contrary political message. Because flag desecration takes place in public space, it shocks the consciousness of authorities, prompting greater social control for political symbols and the regulation of public space.

During the Age of Protest more Americans were prosecuted for desecrating the flag than at any previous time. It is difficult to determine exactly how many people were arrested and prosecuted for flag desecration since many cases never reached the appellate courts; as a result, they were never catalogued into standard legal documents. An unsourced report of approximately 1000 cases by the *Christian Science Monitor* (May 15, 1973) is considered an underestimate by the ACLU; in fact, Burt Neuborne of the ACLU mentioned to a journalist in 1972 that he had personally handled more than 300 flag desecration cases (ACLU, 1970, 1971; see Goldstein, 1996b, 1995; Hopkins 1991; Murphy 1972). In his comprehensive survey of flag desecration, political scientist Robert Goldstein (1995: 140) found 60 cases that were definitely adjudicated between 1966 and 1976, and 60 percent of those cases ended in acquittals. As general support for the Vietnam War declined during the late 1960s, acquittals were more common. Despite being exonerated, however, the process of being arrested (or merely hassled) by law enforcement officers is a humiliating and degrading experience.

Based on his examination of flag desecration cases during the Vietnam War era (60 cases), Goldstein (1995:140–41) presents four basic categories: flag burnings (9 cases), wearing the flag (16 cases), superimposing symbols (15 cases), and miscellaneous charges (20 cases). Whereas each category of flag desecration is distinct, they share a unifying theme of challenging the authoritarian aesthetic. Certainly, flag burnings represent the boldest form of iconoclasm and criticism of the state; still, other violations of the authoritarian aesthetic, such as those featured in art and fashion, remained culturally significant. As we proceed through each of the four types of flag desecration prevalent during the Age of Protest, it is fitting that we acknowledge the varieties of resistance. Despite their apparent individuality, each of these forms of resistance occurred within a distinct cultural and political *zeitgeist* (see Ewick and Silbey, 1992; Scott, 1985).

Burning the Flag

The authoritarian aesthetic imbued in Old Glory hinges on a subjective sense of respect, given that not all acts of flag burning are universally interpreted as desecration. As noted previously, the *proper* way to dispose of old and worn flags is to burn them, a ritual and ceremony observed each year by the American Legion. During the Vietnam War era, authorities were quick to determine whether flag-burning incidents occurred in the context of social protest; if so, such antiestablishment gestures were deemed so disrespectful that the state treated them as a crime. Unlike people who were arrested for wearing the flag (or cited for various miscellaneous acts of flag desecration), flag burners often were prosecuted to the full extent of the law. Of the nine cases of flag burning between 1966 and 1976 discovered by Goldstein (1995) only three were acquitted and two of these acquittals were based on highly technical rather than First Amendment grounds. In *Alford v. Sacramento Judicial District* (1972:68), a California appeals court rejected the state flag desecration law on the grounds that it was so broad that it could apply to "a martini toothpick mounted with a Flag designed to spear an olive."

The media play a unique role in moral panic over flag burning. Whereas only a scattering of flag desecrations were reported by local media in 1966, the following year was a watershed for national news coverage of flag violations. The most heavily publicized flag burning occurred during a massive antiwar demonstration with more than 200,000 protesters gathered in New York City's Central Park on April 15, 1967. Weeks later, the House Judiciary Committee began four days of hearings on flag-desecration legislation, leading to the first federal statute banning such acts.

An integral feature of social movements is a shift in collective perceptions whereby a certain social problem no longer is viewed as a mere misfortune, but is reframed as an *injustice*, provoking outrage and a demand for social change (Turner, 1974). With that in mind, many flag burnings in the Age of Protest were expressions of outrage directed at a particular injustice, especially the Vietnam war and the repression of civil rights. A case in point was the first reported flag burning of the 1960s. On April 12, 1966, a flag was ignited during a theater presentation of an antiwar skit entitled "LBJ" in New York City. Municipal officials considered revoking the theater's license but later terminated their investigation of the incident. Elsa Tambellini, the theater's producer, conceded that the piece was a "very strong protest" against the Vietnam War; still, the flag burning was directed at a "symbol of the extraordinary brutality that America has become" (*New York Times*, April 12, 1966:1). Furthermore, Tambellini viewed the licensing investigation as a repressive measure designed to stifle political dissent.

Similarly, Sidney Street, a black 47-year-old Brooklyn bus driver, who had been awarded a Bronze Star for his heroism during the Second World War was arrested for violating New York's statute prohibiting flag desecration. On June 6, 1966, Street received news of the shooting of James Meredith, a civil rights leader in Mississippi and "took from his drawer a neatly folded 48-star American flag [and went to a nearby intersection where he] lit the flag with a match" (*Street v. New York*, 1969:576). A police officer later testified at the trial that he asked Street whether he had burned the flag. "Yes, that is my flag" Street responded, "I burned it. If they let that happen to Meredith we don't need an American flag" (*Street*: 576). Street's conviction was upheld by two New York State appeals courts. However, the U.S. Supreme Court reversed the decision on technical grounds that the record did not preclude the possibility that Street had been convicted solely for his words rather than for his act of burning the flag. In its ruling, the Supreme Court refused to address the constitutionality of flag-dese-cration laws, thereby contributing to years of contradictory and inconsis-tent rulings (see *Crosson v. Silver*, 1970).

Generally, violations of flag-protection laws were classified as misde-meanors; even when jail terms were imposed, desecrators rarely spent more than a few weeks or months behind bars. A notable exception, how-ever, was the Texas state law banning flag desecration, a code established decades earlier but still enforced during the Vietnam War era. The Texas statute, the toughest in the nation, treated flag desecration as a felony, pun-ishable by sentences of up to 25 years in prison. In 1970, 19-year old Gary Deeds was arrested for burning a piece of flag bunting in protest of the Vietnam War. In what is considered the harshest penalty for flag desecra-tion, Deeds was sentenced to four years in prison for *insulting* the flag. It was reported that on the first jury vote, some of the jurors proposed that Deeds be punished by 20 years in prison, but a couple of moderate jurors were able to persuade their colleagues to reduce the sentence to four years. Deeds appealed his conviction and contended that four years' confinement constituted cruel and unusual punishment, but the court "found no merit in this contention" (*Deeds v. State*, 1971: 718; see *State v. Farrell*, 1974; and *Sutherland v. DeWulf*, 1971).

Wearing the Flag

During the Vietnam War era, wearing the flag was interpreted by au-thorities as another assault on the establishment's aesthetic. Paradoxically though, the authoritarian aesthetic rested heavily on a double standard, distinguishing between people who supported the status quo and those who opposed it, even mildly. As part of an expressive social movement, many young people threatened the authoritarian aesthetic by sporting ca-sual attire, along with beads, beards, and long hair. The long arm of the law had difficulty controlling those who rejected conventional notions of ap-pearance; nevertheless, flag desecration laws furnished agents of social control with the means to penalize people who wore the flag in defiance of the authoritarian aesthetic. As a category of desecration, wearing the flag was all-encompassing; enforcement campaigns included prosecutions of those who wore flag shirts, flag capes, flag vests, and flag patches on jackets and pants.

One of the more colorful cases of flag desecration during the Vietnam War era involved Abbie Hoffman, the counterculture icon and leader of the Youth International Party ("Yippies"). As a political activist and self-proclaimed "cultural revolutionary," Hoffman not only understood the importance of publicity through the mass media for purposes of amplifying protest, but also the power of unconventional clothes as symbols of rebellion. It was said of Hoffman that "his was a radicalism of deed, not word" (Raskin, 1996: xiv). With these considerations in mind, Hoffman formulated a tactic for his appearance at the congressional hearings of the House Committee on Un-American Activities. "Abbie did not want to let the HUAC steal the media spotlight. He wanted what *he* was about to be on the evening news, and not what *they* were about. Abbie had the idea of wearing a flag shirt and saying 'I'm more American than you' (Lefcourt quoted in Raskin, 1996:178). Hoffman realized that he would be arrested for violating the federal flag desecration law, and the incident would get more publicity than the committee hearings. Hoffman also anticipated the cops tearing the shirt from his back and then *they* would be guilty of flag desecration. Preparing for a confrontation with police that would result in having his shirt confiscated, Hoffman had an image of the Viet Cong flag painted on his back. According to plan, while walking in front of the Canon Office Building, law enforcement officers approached him, forcibly removed the flag shirt, and charged him with flag desecration. But without a shirt covering Hoffman's back, the Viet Cong emblem represented another attack on the authoritarian aesthetic. Hoffman was the first person to be convicted under the 1968 Federal Flag Desecration Law and sentenced to a 30-day jail term and $100 fine. At his sentencing, Hoffman exclaimed sarcastically to the court: "I regret that I have only one shirt to give to my country!" (Lefcourt, 1989; Raskin, 1996).

In *Hoffman v. U.S.* (1971), the District of Columbia Court of Appeals struck down Hoffman's conviction, citing that the shirt was store-bought apparel. The court noted further that Hoffman purchased the shirt but did not engage in physically desecrating it; moreover, the item was a shirt and *not* a flag. Hoffman aptly pointed out that the federal flag desecration law was so vague that would criminalize the attire of drum majorettes and anyone wearing an Uncle Sam suit. Consistent with the equivocal nature of the authoritarian aesthetic, the enforcement of flag laws is highly selective. In the 1960s and 1970s, celebrities Roy Rogers and Dale Evans routinely wore flag shirts while advertising dog food on television. Hoffman had written about his experience being arrested for flag desecration in an essay entitled "Fuck the Flag" concluding that the government's motto is "We can put anybody in jail we don't like no matter what the Constitution says" (1989:130; also see Raskin, 1996; Sloman, 1998).

In a related incident involving the authoritarian aesthetic, Hoffman, appearing on the Merv Griffin television show, held Mao Tse-tung's *Little Red Book* in one hand and a marijuana cigarette in the other. During the interview, Hoffman removed his jacket, thereby exposing his flag shirt. CBS executives must have thought that the flag shirt was more controversial than a communist book or a joint since they edited the footage in a way that obscured Hoffman wearing the Stars and Stripes, a tactic that Hoffman called electronic fascism. Still, CBS aired commercials featuring the flag, and that hypocrisy was not overlooked by critics who said "the flag could be used to sell products, but not to make a political statement" (Raskin, 1996:189).

To elaborate further on the authoritarian aesthetic, similar cases involving flag capes are revealing. Several convictions of flag desecration were upheld by the courts by relying on *Halter*: in particular, the contention that insults to the flag can lead to a breach of peace (e.g., *Deeds, Farrell, Sutherland*). In many cases, however, prosecutors failed to present any evidence of actual or threatened disorder—as in *State v. Waterman* (1971), in which the defendant was convicted for wearing the flag as a cape (also see *State v. Saionz,* 1969). Conversely, a California appellate court upheld the state's conviction in a flag vest case (*People v. Cowgill,* 1969) because even though there had been no breach of peace at that particular moment, the court maintained that a disturbance might occur in future instances. In another flag-vest case, the Virginia Supreme Court overruled a conviction because there was no evidence of defilement (*Franz v. Commonwealth,* 1972). At the trial, Edward Franz forcefully rejected the political radicalism of the time, describing himself as someone who was responding to popular fashion by saying he found the flag vest and wore it because he thought it was "cool." To persuade the court that he was not affiliated with the counterculture, Franz introduced character witnesses who portrayed him as "a former Cub Scout, a former Boy Scout, active in his church, a loyal American citizen, and as one who worked well with colors, forms, and objects" (*Franz,* 1972:71). In overturning the conviction, the court concluded that Franz did not intend to disrupt the authoritarian aesthetic and that he possessed qualities consistent with the traditional values of the establishment.

As further evidence that the flag symbolizes the authoritarian aesthetic, it is worth noting that many civilians were arrested for having flag patches stitched to their clothing; ironically, such arrests were carried out by police who themselves had flag patches sewn on their uniforms. Although prosecutors were unwilling to acknowledge the apparent contradictions in cases where defendants were charged with flag desecration for wearing flag patches, eventually the courts confronted those inconsistencies. In a New Hampshire case involving a flag patch worn on a jacket, a federal appeals court invalidated the state's flag-desecration law since it was deemed unconstitutionally vague (*Royal v. Superior Court of New Hampshire*, 1976; see also *Parker v. Morgan*, 1971).

The campaign to ban flag patches on civilian clothing also extended to pants. More to the point of authoritarian aesthetics, flag patches located on the seat of trousers especially infuriated law enforcement officers and some of the courts. In *Delorme v. State* (1973) the Texas Court of Criminal Appeals upheld a conviction, concluding that wearing a flag on the seat of one's pants cast contempt on Old Glory (see also *State v. Van Camp*, 1971). In a similar case, an Ohio appeals court upheld a lower court conviction of a man who wore a flag patch on the back pocket of his pants. The prosecution claimed the flag patch was located "over the anus, . . . a part of the human body universally considered unclean . . . [and thus] was a clear act of defilement" (*State v. Kasnett*, 1971:636, 637, 639). The Ohio Supreme Court, however, overturned the conviction by noting that no physical damage was done to the flag; in fact, the court noted, the patch was placed over the back pocket and not the anus. The court went on to challenge the vagueness of the law and arbitrariness of its enforcement. "Is a flag worn by a policeman over his heart, or on his sleeve, or on his helmet permissible, and the same flag worn by a student impermissible depending upon which part of his anatomy it is upon or near?" (*State v. Kansett*, 1973:537, 538).

Flag patches sewn on the crotch of pants similarly made the authorities bristle. In *State v. Mitchell* (1972), an Ohio appellate court upheld a conviction by ruling that a flag patch attached to the crotch seam of a pair of jeans defiles the flag. The court also offered references to law-enforcement uniforms but rather than question the arbitrary nature of flag-protection statutes, the justices invoked the authoritarian aesthetic. According to the court, flag patches "were a far cry from the use made by a patrolman who wears [a flag patch] on the sleeve of his blouse or attached to a shirt covering his breast" (p. 220). Still, inconsistencies plagued court rulings on other flag-patch cases, and in Washington a state appeals court rejected such a conviction (*State v. Claxton*, 1972; also see *People v. Vaughan*, 1973; *Goguen v. Smith*, 1972).

Superimposing Symbols on the Flag

During the Age of Protest, the enforcement of the authoritarian aesthetic was manifested in arrests for superimposing symbols onto the flag. In support of the antiwar campaign, it was common for students to place a peace sign over the Stars and Stripes, a modification that some agents of social control viewed as desecration. The irony of a *peace* symbol producing an adverse—or even violent—reaction by supporters of the status quo makes sense only in a culture that conforms to rigid notions of nationalism. Several courts relied on the legal premise of preventing breaches of the peace in convicting defendants who had altered the flag with a peace symbol. In some of those cases, however, higher courts contested the state's argument of disturbing the peace. In one such peace-symbol case, the Iowa Supreme Court overturned a conviction by rejecting the state's claim that hanging a replica of the flag upside down behind a peace symbol in the front window of his home, the defendant might have provoked public disorder (*State v. Kool*, 1973). In a similar case, a college student in Texas was sentenced to 10 years' probation for flying a peace-symbol flag. The appeals court, however, overruled the conviction on grounds of prosecutorial misconduct because prosecutors repeatedly referred to the defendant as a "hippie," "anti-Christ," and "communist" (*Renn v. State*, 1973:932). Likewise, another college student was arrested and charged with unlawfully and willfully exposing a "contemptuous representation of the American flag on the rear window of his automobile" (*State v. Liska*, 1971:598). In that case, the "contemptuous" figure was a decal composed of red and white stripes with a peace symbol. At trial, Liska described himself as a conscientious objector to the Vietnam War, and as a pacifist, he displayed the decal to make a political statement of peace. On appeal, Liska's conviction was overturned on the grounds that he was expressing his aspiration for peace" and the decal was not contemptuous (see also *Herrick v. Commonwealth*, 1972; *Long Island Vietnam Moratorium Committee v. Cahn*, 1970; *Miami v. Wolfenberger*, 1972; *State v. Nicola*, 1971; *State v. Zimmelman*, 1973).

Protesting the U.S. invasion of Cambodia and the killing of four students by the National Guard during an antiwar rally at Kent State University, Harold Spence displayed from his apartment window a flag to which he had attached black tape in the form of a peace symbol. The 23-year-old Spence was convicted by a Seattle court for violating the state ban on flag desecration: in his defense, Spence said he intended to associate the flag with peace instead of war and violence. Following conflicting appellate rulings, the U.S. Supreme Court intervened. In one of only three flag cases heard by the High Court (i.e., *Goguen, Street*), the justices struck down the conviction in *Spence v. Washington* (1974). Unfortunately for the sake of clarity, the U.S. Supreme Court once again failed to deliver a ruling that could have mapped out the limits of freedom of expression.

During the Age of Protest, rejections of the authoritarian aesthetic and the culture it symbolizes also included imagery that attacked the political economy in addition to the Vietnam War. In 1966, an antiwar demonstrator was arrested for displaying a flag that featured dollar signs in lieu of stars. A Hawaii circuit court sided with the defendant who claimed that he was making a statement about what the flag has come to represent; thus, his action was not a form of flag desecration but a criticism of commercialism in American culture (*State v. Kent*, 1966). The varieties of resistance expressed in superimposing symbols on the flag went beyond peace symbols and dollar signs, both of which seem to have drawn sympathy from the appellate courts. The courts were less sympathetic to other forms of imagery that established a different tenor of criticism. In 1971, a Ohio man was convicted in a municipal court for driving a truck that featured a painting of an American flag with the face of Mickey Mouse superimposed over the field of stars. The court was not amused by the defendant's attempt to mock the government and ruled it was in the state's interest to preserve loyalty and patriotism represented by the flag (*State v. Saulino*, 1971).

Miscellaneous Charges of Flag Desecration

Clashes between the campaign to uphold the traditional aesthetic of the flag and the antiwar movement surfaced in numerous other cases, including alternative flag displays, published photography, and various political messages contained in art. Elizabeth Hubner, a mother of two, was arrested, fingerprinted, and detained on $500 bail by Mineola (N.Y.) police for displaying the flag upside down. Though Hubner was eventually acquitted, the humiliating experience served as a memorable punishment for violating the authoritarian aesthetic. The hypocrisy of the authoritarian aesthetic was not overlooked when a nearby American Legion post displayed the Stars and Stripes upside down to protest the North Korean capture of a U.S. naval ship; not surprisingly, nobody was arrested for that gesture (Frisbie, 1971; also see *Commonwealth v. Lorenc*, 1971; *State v. Hodsdon*, 1972).

Official efforts to defend the integrity of the flag ventured into another realm of imagery and expression, most notably photography. In *Korn v. Elkins* (1970) and *People v. Keough* (1972), the defendants were convicted for releasing publications featuring a flag burning and a flag accompanied by a nude subject, respectively. Appeals courts, however, overruled both convictions on the grounds that such imagery posed no realistic threat to public peace (also see *State v. Hershey*, 1972).

Other artistic expressions critical of government, however, were not given the benefit of the doubt, and the Stephen Radich affair is a classic illustration of how authorities can staunchly enforce the establishment's aesthetic. Radich, owner of a New York City art gallery, was arrested in 1966 for displaying an exhibit by artist Marc Morrel that included sixteen sculptures and paintings. Morrell, an ex-marine, developed a stark antiwar motif in his work. One piece featured a flag shaped into an image of a cadaver hanging from a noose; another sculpture was formed into a erect phallic symbol covered with a flag and attached to the base of a cross wrapped in a religious garment entitled "The United States Flag as a Crucified Phallus." Overall, the exhibit intended to denounce those who engaged in aggressive acts and support war in the name of organized religion; as one critic observed, Morrel's work was a type of "protest art" and the phallic flag equates "social military violence" and "sexual violence" (Kramer, 1967; 1970). For reasons never made public, Radich—not Morrell—was the target of the prosecution under the state flag desecration statute. In their defense of Radich, the ACLU characterized the incident as a case of cultural suppression: numerous artists and art dealers offered their support, realizing that if Radich were convicted, police involvement in the arts would be inevitable and tragic. At the trial, the assistant district attorney argued that the art display would generate public outrage to the point that a riot could ensue, and therefore the gallery was not entitled to First Amendment protection ("A Test for Old Glory," 1967; Adams, 1976 Baldwin, 1974; Crow, 1996; Graham, 1971).

In a 1967 ruling that cited *Halter* and clung to the premise that the state should preserve the public peace (per the New York state flag statute), Radich was convicted and sentenced to a $500 fine or a 60-day jail term: though appealed, the conviction was upheld repeatedly at the state and federal levels. Along the way, several judges dissented, including Court of Appeals Chief Justice Stanley Fuld, who accused the prosecution of political censorship. Art critic Hilton Kramer, who testified at the Radich trial, charged that the court's opinion was "full of strange and frightening details," which threatened "the display of art that protests the political policies of the government" (*U.S. v. Radich*, 1970:856). Moreover, Kramer thought that if the court was correct that the Morrel constructions posed a threat to peace, "then our society is already far more fragile than even its severest critics have yet supposed" (*New York Times*, March 1, 1970:A1). After eight years of litigation, in 1974 Radich was acquitted in federal court, thereby overturning the original 1967 conviction in federal appeals court on constitutional grounds (see also *People v. Lindsay*, 1972; see Dubin, 1992; Goldstein, 1995; Hendricks and Toche, 1978; Lippard, 1972).

CONCLUSION

At the outset of this chapter, social movements were introduced as a means of contextualizing political activities among those who reside outside the immediate orbit of state power. The Age of Protest will be remembered for its varied social movements, including a general movement in the form of the counterculture, along with specific movements such as the civil rights campaign and demonstrations against the Vietnam War. Adding to the *zeitgeist*, which encouraged America's youth to question authority, were several nondescript, expressive social movements found in avant-garde art and unconventional fashion.

Despite the enormity of dissent in the Vietnam War era, a regressive social movement was manifested in several campaigns denouncing social protest. On July 4, 1970, more than 250,000 conservatives congregated at an "Honor America Day" assembly in Washington, D.C. where evangelist Billy Graham condemned "extremist elements" who had "desecrated our flag, disrupted our educational system, laughed at our religious heritage and threatened to burn down our cities" (*National Observer*, June 1, 1970:1). Similarly, the hard-hat demonstrations of 1970 served as an outlet for the status quo. Amid the rage resonating from the U.S. invasion of Cambodia and the National Guard shootings of students at Kent State University, New York City Mayor John Lindsay, at the urging of antiwar protestors, sympathetically lowered the flag at City Hall to half-staff. In sharp reaction, thousands of construction workers stormed City Hall demanding that the flag be raised to full-staff, along the way, they harassed and assaulted peace activists. For nearly a month, hard hats wearing flag decals on their helmets paraded with flags through Manhattan's financial district (Guenter, 1989; Pullen, 1971). As a regressive social movement, the hard hats symbolized iron-fisted support for the state and its military, posting signs calling Mayor Lindsay a "rat, a Commy rat, a faggot, a leftist, a neurotic, an anarchist, and a 'traitor'" (Bogart, May 16, 1970:A1). In an interview with a journalist, one "hard hat" said that he would kill his own son if he defiled the flag, since flag desecration was "the worst thing" antiwar demonstrators had ever done (Goldstein, 1995:160).

In the Age of Protest, regressive social movements contributed enormously to the crossfire between advocates of social progress and those defending the status quo. Whereas the debate over the Vietnam War and civil rights remained prominent features of social conflict, important cultural shifts also were evident, particularly the rejection of the establishment, its authority, and its aesthetics. In many ways, the panic over flag desecration serves as a reminder of those profound changes in American society.

NOTE

1. Given the direction and scope of this chapter, several constitutional issues were deliberately omitted from the discussion on flag desecration. It should be noted that some of the landmark First Amendment cases that figured prominently in the constitutional debate over flag desecration were *U.S. v. O'Brien* (1968), *Tinker v. Des Moines* (1969), and *Cohen v. California* (1971). Those cases contribute to a critical understanding of the political symbolism and the authoritarian aesthetic, especially since they involve draft-card burning (*O'Brien*), wearing black armbands (*Tinker*), and a jacket bearing the slogan "Fuck the Draft" (*Cohen*).

5

Flag Burning as Political Iconoclasm in the 1980s

This is a sick and dying empire that is desperately clutching at its symbols
—*Joey (Gregory L.) Johnson,* Revolutionary Worker

After the Vietnam War, flag desecration and subsequent media coverage subsided, virtually falling off the nation's collective conscience. Still, efforts to preserve the authoritarian aesthetic by protecting the Stars and Stripes surfaced in a few incidents in which demonstrators were prosecuted for setting the flag ablaze. Unexpectedly, however, those isolated cases would gain momentum and eventually become highly significant in the realm of civil liberties. Indeed, by the end of the 1980s, the controversy over flag desecration would become reinvented in ways that would consume politics, ultimately compelling the U.S. Supreme Court to rule on the constitutionality of criminalizing that particular form of dissent.

As a social phenomenon, flag desecration during the Age of Protest was manifested typically in individualized acts of resistance rather than group activism; from a sociological viewpoint, such dissent stemmed from a *general* rather than a *specific* social movement. Conversely, flag desecration in the late 1970s and the 1980s was qualitatively different from previous protests insofar as it was part of a specific social movement mobilized by the Revolutionary Communist Party (RCP). During that period, the RCP, a small but boisterous radical clique, staged several flag burnings, and in doing so they dared authorities to unleash the repressive tendencies of the state. Rather than ignore the RCP, the government participated in one of the great *ironies* of social control. By prosecuting supporters of the RCP in flag-desecration cases, the state inflamed an issue that probably would have remained dormant. Paradoxically, while the obscure RCP made headline news, the government wound up in court faced with the task of defending its campaign against political protest. Along the way, other specific social movements, comprising mostly civil libertarians, quickly joined forces in time to participate in a landmark battle over First Amendment freedoms. This chapter explores extreme-leftist resistance aimed at the Reagan and Bush administrations. In addition to examining the role of the RCP in the reification of the flag panic, we take into account societal reaction and state response to three major sociolegal developments: *Texas v. Johnson,* the Flag Protection Act of 1989, and *U.S. v. Eichman.* So that these political events remain situated in their proper social context, we begin with an overview of the prevailing *zeitgeist* of the 1980s in which the Reagan and Bush presidencies figured prominently.

THE REAGAN REVOLUTION AND THE RENEWED
PATRIOTISM OF BUSH

Marking the beginning of a new era, 1980 has become a political benchmark in large part due to the social and cultural significance of the "Reagan Revolution." To his supporters, President Ronald Reagan represented a vision of conservatism that appealed widely to both young and old. Reagan's background in movies served him well since he not only mastered the art of media politics but also comforted his constituents with a unique brand of nostalgia commonly found in old-fashioned cinema. Whereas the Age of Protest reminded citizens of the complex nature of politics, Reagan borrowed pages from American history, particularly the 1950s and the Cold War. Reagan adopted traditional enemies abroad such as communism and the Soviet Union—which he dubbed the Evil Empire. With regard to domestic policy, Reagan scoffed at progressive liberalism; he gutted social programs, generously increased military spending, and deregulated key financial institutions. Altogether, these developments produced what conservatives hailed as the Reagan Revolution. To his detractors, Reagan's sense of nostalgia offered mainstream Americans a false sense of security; even more to the point, deregulation set the stage for the savings & loan scandal and other financial woes (Calavita, Pontell, and Tillman, 1997; Friedrichs, 1996; Nelson, 1990a, 1990b). Consistent with the conservative philosophy, Reagan's economic policy catered to the wealthy and turned its back on the impoverished (Phillips, 1990). The Reagan Revolution was criticized for creating socialism for the rich and leaving free enterprise for the poor (Harrington, 1989; see Aronowitz and DiFazio, 1994; Welch, 1998; 1996b).

The anticommunist motif of the Reagan Revolution is an important consideration for this discussion. Reagan not only "talked the talk," but he occasionally "walked the walk," especially when the United States invaded Grenada, a tiny Caribbean island that military advisors claimed was a haven for Marxist guerrillas. More to the point, Reagan justified military support to the *contras* in Central America in the name of fighting communism: a policy that spiraled out of control, culminating in the Iran-Contra affair. Concerned over the threat of communism, it is not entirely surprising that authorities (i.e., Federal Bureau of Investigation) monitored domestic groups suspected of subversive activities, in particular, the Committee in Solidarity with the People of El Salvador (CISPES) (Bonner, 1984; Dickey 1985; Dillon, 1991; Kahn, 1996: *Nation*, 1998). Skeptics of Reagan's foreign policy, however, took notice. Even overseas, Reagan faced criticism over U.S. militarism in Central America. While touring Ireland in 1984, Reagan was confronted by protestors who burned Old Glory. Joining the more than five thousand demonstrators, Julie O'Donoghue asked rhetorically: "Do the American people realize that we're not falling in love with his [Reagan's] love of the leprechaun nonsense? We are a Catholic country. What the Americans are doing in El Salvador and Nicaragua is just another form of tyranny?" (Kilborn, 1984:12). In another demonstration denouncing U.S. policy in Central America, William C. Cary of Minneapolis torched the Stars and Stripes. Cary was arrested and convicted of violating the federal flag-desecration statute; moreover, a federal appeals court upheld the conviction in 1989 (*Cary v. U.S.*, 1990; *New York Times*, October 16, 1990).

Similarly, Carlos Mendoza-Lugo was arrested for violating the U.S. federal flag antidesecration statute when he burned an American flag in front of a post office in Puerto Rico in 1987. Menodoza-Lugo, a Puerto Rican nationalist, pleaded guilty to flag desecration and was sentenced to a one-year prison term at the federal penitentiary at Atlanta. In his defense, Mendoza-Lugo said: "It wasn't an act of vandalism: I was protesting. . . . It's unconstitutional for me to be in jail when I was making use of my freedom of speech" (*Washington Post*, July 2, 1989:A3). His sentenced was later reduced to seven months in prison. Interestingly, officials at the federal Bureau of Prisons say that they do not maintain records on the number of prisoners serving sentences for flag desecration. As we shall address later with the Revolutionary Communist Party, it is in this political climate of suppressing dissent that even relatively unknown fringe groups were met with the strong arm tactics of the state, including surveillance, infiltration, intimidation, and even prosecution for desecrating the flag.

Leaping forward to the Bush administration, certain remnants of the Reagan Revolution persisted, but over time emerged as unique qualities of a new presidency. Many of the defining characteristics of George Bush were established while running against Democratic rival Michael Dukakis. Like his predecessor and mentor Reagan, Bush played the military and nostalgia cards; however, his version of "the good ole' days" struck political paydirt with his campaign for patriotism. Pundits agreed that symbolism was a powerful force in the election of Bush. Reminiscent of the

McKinley campaign at the turn of the century, Bush publicly questioned the patriotism of Dukakis. With a steady stream of political jabs, Bush reminded voters that Governor Dukakis had vetoed a law requiring the recitation of the Pledge of Allegiance in Massachusetts schools. In Chapter 6, we revisit the political implications of patriotism in the Bush presidency, especially in the context of the Persian Gulf War.

RESISTANCE AND SOCIAL MOVEMENTS: THE EMERGENCE OF THE RCP

In deciphering the complex structure of specific social movements, sociologists look to the distinct role of key participants as well as their activities. Lofland, Colwell, and Johnson (1990) constructed a typology of activists consisting of six different roles: Transcenders, educators, intellectuals, and prophets are involved *indirectly* in bringing about social change while parliamentarians and protestors participate *directly*. Still, parliamentarians work inside the system in an effort to reform society, whereas protestors operate outside the system, typically engaging in public demonstrations. Although each type of activist contributes to social change, for the purpose of this analysis we focus on protestors—in particular, flag burners who resort to a provocative form of resistance commonly known as agitation (see Welch, 2000).

As noted in the previous chapter, national newspaper coverage catapulted flag burning onto the political landscape in 1967 when Old Glory was torched during a massive antiwar demonstration in New York City's Central Park. Likewise, the media played a similar role in the next flag-burning controversy when worldwide television news broadcasted stunning images of Iranian citizens burning the U.S. flag during the hostage crisis in 1979. While mainline Americans were deeply *offended* by these acts of iconoclasm, many radicals realized that flag burning still had enormous protest potential. Soon, supporters of the RCP captured the flag, and in a manner of speaking held its symbolism hostage while voicing the movement's demands for social change. Before we examine those particular incidents of flag burning, it is important to place the RCP and its unique form of resistance within the context of a social movement.

Although there exist strict ideological differences between the Communist Party of the United States and the Revolutionary Communist Party (see Klehr, 1988), there are similarities with respect to the issue of membership, particularly the actual number of people who belong to these organizations. During the McCarthy communist witchhunt in the 1950s (reminiscent of the Red Scare of 1918), the government operated on the belief that communism in the United States posed a viable threat to national security, in large part due to the perception that Communist-Party membership was vast and quickly growing. Experts insisted, however, that the threat of communism in America was symbolic rather than substantive; indeed, McCarthyism was a product of moral panic (Goode and Ben-Yehuda, 1994). First-Amendment commentator Anthony Lewis insisted on that view by noting that membership in the Communist Party of the United States during the 1950s was minuscule; still, that did not dissuade the FBI from infiltrating the party. Lewis delivered a standard joke of that era, saying facetiously: "There were only 702 members of the Communist Party and 680 of them were FBI agents" (*History of the ACLU*, 1998; also see Lewis, 1991; Walker, 1990).

On a parallel plane, the actual membership of the RCP also is considered to be relatively small—estimates hover around 500 nationwide (which includes its student group, the Youth Brigade, and its other faction, the Vietnam Veterans Against the War—Anti-Imperialist) (Klehr, 1988). Nowadays, the size of the membership is not known publicly. A supporter of the RCP, asked how many people belonged to the party, replied, "Those who know, do not say, and those who say, do not know." To reiterate, the RCP, much like the Communist Party of the United States, does not appear to pose a serious threat to national security, but given its radical, anticapitalist ideology represents a symbolic threat, or folk devil. Perceptions of that threat contribute to moral panic, especially in the context of reactionary conservatism. The RCP's public display of resistance through flag burnings symbolizes not only an attack on the state, but at a higher level of iconoclasm, it represents an assault on state symbolism.

Unlike the larger, free-floating social movements discussed in the previous chapter, specific movements constitute a highly structured form of social activity; they are complex, formal organizations resting on hierarchical authority figures who lead their supporters according to ideologies and rules of conduct unique to that group. As crystalized campaigns, specific social movements operate with a distinct sense of purpose aimed at sharply defined objectives (Blumer, 1974). Typically, specific social movements involve several similar social-movement organizations; in fact, the RCP is just one of many communist groups in the nation. The RCP grew out of the radical 1960s in Berkeley, where one of its founders, Bob Avakian, resigned from the Students for a Democratic Society in its final days of existence. Avakian joined forces with other like-minded revolutionaries in that region and eventually laid the groundwork that would spawn the Maoist RCP. Much of their activism occurred on a small scale; nevertheless, in 1976, the RCP staged its most successful project called "Get the Rich Off Our Backs," a counterbicentennial march that attracted 3,000 participants in Philadelphia. Soon, internal upheaval and political disputes with rival Maoist groups altered the ideological infrastructure of the RCP, culminating in a split between competing factions in 1977.

A prominent characteristic of a specific social movement vis-à-vis a general social movement is its reliance on *instrumental* protest rather than solely on *expressive* dissent. Whereas expressive protest commonly manifests itself as angry and emotional outbursts (e.g., *Street, 1969*), instrumental protest is more calculating, rational, and designed to achieve a particular goal (e.g., *U.S. v. Eichman*, 1990, 1991). Instrumental protest is a common tactic of agitation. Indeed, the RCP has become known outside radical circles for its ability to agitate the government, engaging in shocking demonstrations that generated publicity, a strategy used by anarchists in the early twentieth century. Burning flags has become an RCP trademark, and by doing so, the group conveys its theory of social change based on the notion of a single spark. "The Party's strategy is to seize any spark of struggle, try to fan it and spread it" (Klehr, 1988: 95; see also newspapers *Revolutionary Worker* and *Revolution*, published by the RCP).

The role of agitation is vital to group activity within a specific social movement. As a form of resistance, agitation serves two basic functions: it shocks the public conscience with a political message, and it attracts new recruits. According to Blumer (1974: 8), agitation "is essentially a means of exciting people and of awakening within them new impulses and ideas which make them restless and dissatisfied. Consequently, it acts to loosen the hold on them of their previous attachments, and to break down their previous ways of thinking and acting." Jarring demonstrations, especially flag burnings, facilitate the basic functions of agitation, thereby contributing to shifts in consciousness necessary for a specific social movement.

Given that fire evokes primal human emotions, flag burnings should be viewed as a unique form of resistance, blending revolutionary iconoclasm with the power, danger, and aura of fire. Anthropologically, flag burnings by the RCP represent ceremonial behavior contributing to an in-group esprit de corps. Alluding to the mystical quality of fire and the magnetism of rebellion manifesting in collective behavior, RCP activist Shawn Eichman intuitively proclaimed: "To the oppressed, burning the flag is a celebration" (Affidavit by Shawn Eichman in *U.S. v. Eichman*, 1990:1; see Welch, 1992). Adding to the intensity of agitation is the societal reaction flag burnings evoke. While horrifying onlookers, flag burnings hurl police into action, culminating in the arrest and formal degradation ceremony of the demonstrators. Paradoxically, though, arrests rarely discourage dissent; indeed, being processed into the criminal justice system strengthens the morale and solidarity of the protest group. From the perspective of the RCP, being arrested by the enemy's social control apparatus reinforces the party's belief that its members are unjustly punished by a repressive state bent on stifling political dissent. Several RCP supporters arrested for flag burning insist that they wear their arrests as badges of honor. In their eyes—and in the eyes of their comrades—being arrested for flag desecration engenders a sense of martyrdom. Flag burning is an intriguing type of dissent due to the ironic responses it produces. Agitation in the form of flag burning baits police into arresting demonstrators; consequently, relatively minor incidents are escalated into media events, furnishing publicity for protestors while making the state's agents of social control appear repressive.

The first of a string of flag-burning cases involving RCP supporters was noticed during the 1979 hostage crisis, when Americans were held in the U.S. Embassy in Iran. Global television coverage regularly broadcast footage of Iranian protestors burning the Stars and Stripes, thereby prompting the RCP to imitate these political demonstrations designed to shock the public conscience. Initially those scattered flag burnings by RCP supporters generated little media attention; however, over time they would became increasingly significant as their cases penetrated the judiciary. Having flag-burning cases adjudicated—and appealed—is another tactic of activism that keeps the RCP committed to fighting the system. Those events reinforce a symbiotic relationship between rule enforcers and rule breakers, thus escalating rather than deterring public protest.

In 1980, RCP supporters Teresa Kime and Donald Bonwell participated in a political protest in front of the Federal Building in Greensboro, North Carolina. To draw attention to a May Day rally organized by the RCP, Kime and Bonwell torched Old Glory. As expected, local police sprang into action, arresting Kime and Bonwell on charges of violating the federal flag protection law; likewise, U.S. attorneys prosecuted them to the full extent of the law. Kime and Bonwell were convicted and sentenced to eight months in jail, and on appeal, their convictions were upheld (*U.S. v. Kime*, 1982). Kime and her codefendant petitioned the U.S. Supreme Court, but their appeal was denied, ending that particular judicial journey for the RCP. The high court had previously intervened in only one flag-burning case (*Street*). Still, Justice Brennan's dissent in *Kime* would later weigh prominently in striking down the federal flag desecration act. Citing a litany of landmark First Amendment decisions (*Stromberg, Barnette, Street, Spence*, and *O'Brien*), Brennan argued that the state was suppressing free expression (Dissent by Justice Brennan from refusal of the U.S. Supreme Court to grant certiorari in the 1982 case of *U.S. v. Kime*, 459 *United States Reports* 949).

Also in 1980, Diane Monroe, another supporter of the RCP, was convicted for misuse of the national flag under Georgia state law. The case stemmed from a 1979 incident in Atlanta where the RCP staged a flag burning as part of a demonstration condemning American foreign policy. Monroe was sentenced to 12 months' imprisonment, a ruling upheld on appeal by the Georgia Supreme Court (*Monroe v. State,* 1982). In 1984, however, a three-judge federal appeals court overturned Monroe's conviction on the grounds that the Georgia statute was unconstitutional as applied; interestingly, the panel relied heavily on Brennan's ardent remarks in *Kime,* marking the first time that a federal appellate court invalidated a flag-burning conviction on the basis of the First Amendment (*Monroe v. State Court of Fulton County,* 1984). Progress in the courts became a source of inspiration for the RCP's struggle against the state; moreover, the willingness of law enforcement to arrest flag burners, coupled with the perception that the federal judiciary would rule in favor of the RCP, led to several other demonstrations in which the flag was burned.

TEXAS v. JOHNSON

In 1984, President Ronald Reagan was renominated by his party at the Republican National Convention in Dallas. If reelected, Reagan promised to continue his conservative mandate, including a foreign policy aimed at thwarting communism, a political motif reminiscent of the 1950s Cold War. Interestingly, the GOP meeting in Dallas would become pivotal to the freedom-of-expression movement due to events occurring *outside* the convention hall. In a showdown that could have been scripted by Hollywood screenwriters, a little-known communist and supporter of the RCP would antagonize the Reaganites in a protest entitled the "Republican War Chest Tour." Activists enthusiastically joined in several anti-American, anticapitalist, and anti-imperialist chants, including: "Fuck America" and "Red, white, and blue, we spit on you. You stand for plunder, you will go under" (*Texas v. Johnson,* 1989:53). The rising intensity of the demonstration peaked as Old Glory burst into flames. When the smoke cleared, Gregory L. Johnson, a member of the Revolutionary Communist Youth Brigade (a youth group of the RCP), was arrested for disorderly conduct. That charge was later replaced with desecration of a venerated object under the Texas Law of the Parties.

Few Americans had heard of Johnson or the RCP in 1984, but over the next five years, citizens and politicians would harbor a deep resentment of Johnson and his band of communist agitators. Johnson, a self-described "army brat" who delivered the military newspaper *Stars and Stripes* while living with his stepfather on a military base in Germany, saw himself and his comrades as being pushed to the bottom of society: "I have nothing to lose. I am not an American, I'm a proletarian internationalist, a Maoist. . . . We are preparing the ground for revolution." Johnson viewed the flag as representing a "racist and oppressive society. . . . Liberty and justice for all is a lie" (Meier, 1989:5). Taking full advantage of a federal judiciary that appeared primed to test the constitutionality of flag desecration, Johnson and his supporters prepared for their day in court. In short order, government leaders, the media, and flag lobbyists as well as citizens would be consumed by moral panic over flag burning.

During the trial, the prosecution refuted claims that Johnson himself did not burn the flag, and even if he had not torched Old Glory, prosecutors insisted that he be convicted because the Texas Law of Parties extends to persons who encourage, direct, or aid others in desecrating a venerated object. With such a sweeping law at the state's disposal, Johnson was convicted on December 13, 1984, and sentenced to the maximum penalty: one year in jail and a fine of $2,000. Johnson did not testify during the initial phase of the trial in which guilt or innocence is determined; still, he conducted his activism in the halls of the courthouse, distributing news releases and holding press conferences. During the sentencing stage, however, Johnson took the stand to answer questions put forth by Assistant District Attorney Michael Gillett. Sanctimoniously, Gillet continued to expose Johnson's political worldview, a courtroom strategy that the defendant relished. Gillett taunted Johnson, asking "Do you think the American flag represents anything good at all?" Johnson, sporting a T-shirt with RCP's logo featuring a silhouette of a man holding a rifle, responded "no" and elaborated: "I think it is an honor to be compared to the Iranian people . . . in 1953, the United States put a bloody dictator in power, then people [Americans] want to know why the Iranian people use the American flag to carry trash in" (*Texas v. Johnson*, 1984:764).

Drawing attention to the prosecution's hypocrisy of upholding the Law of Parties and promoting compulsory patriotism while circumventing the First Amendment, Johnson volunteered: "It's revealing as to the compulsion that you feel to enforce patriotism, it's a desperation that you feel, the weakness that you feel, and the need to enforce patriotism to demand it from everyone." Gillett defensively berated Johnson, projecting a sense of patriotic purity found commonly in nativism: "If you don't like the country and you don't like the way it's run, why don't you just leave? . . . [I]f you dislike it so much, why don't you just move to Russia?" Again, Johnson welcomed the opportunity to share his worldview: "Well, . . . I don't consider it [Russia] to be any sort of society that people in the world who are striving for a future without oppression should look to for—for guidance. . . . If anything, I think that there are more similarities between the United States and the Soviet Union. They mutually possess over 50,000 nuclear weapons." Commenting on what he believed to be the subtext of the trial, Johnson referred to the power of labeling and social control, adding that the underlying message of the prosecution was to tell "anyone who has unpatriotic beliefs to keep them to yourself" or risk being officially branded as "thought criminal" by the state. Gillette urged the jury to punish Johnson with the maximum penalty on the grounds that he had "offended the nation" and was "creating a lot of danger for a lot of people by what he does and the way he thinks" (*Texas v. Johnson*, 1984: 781).

In 1986, the Court of Appeals for the Fifth Judicial District of Texas affirmed the judgement of the trial court. In its ruling, the appellate court concluded, "While the State has no legitimate interest in compelling respect for the flag [citing *Barnette*], we disagree with the Eleventh Circuit in *Monroe* and hold the State does have a legitimate and substantial interest in protecting the flag as a symbol of national unity (*Johnson v. State*, 1986). Johnson's luck, however, began to change when he appealed his case to the Texas Court of Criminal Appeals, where in 1988 his conviction was overturned. That court found *Texas v. Johnson* lacking in key areas of prosecution, including a condition of the state law that required a breach of the peace (*Johnson v. State*, 1988:97, 755 *South Western Reporter*, 2d series, 92). Dallas District Attorneys set out to reinstate Johnson's conviction and petitioned the U.S. Supreme Court to review its appeal in 1988. There, Dallas prosecutors insisted that Johnson's conviction was justified on two state interests: preserving the peace and protecting the flag as a symbol of national unity. Moreover, the state of Texas maintained that "an act of flag burning does not constitute 'speech' entitled to First Amendment protection because the conduct involved is essential neither to the exposition of any idea or to the peaceful expression of an opinion" (*Brief for Petitioner*, in the case of *Texas v. Johnson*, in the U.S. Supreme Court, October, 1988).

In its brief for the respondent, Johnson's lawyers maintained that the Texas flag-desecration law was unconstitutional both on its face and as applied to symbolic speech for which he was convicted. Citing *Barnette*, the brief reminded the court that the dual principles of freedom of expression and government by the people restricts the state from "mandating respect for its icons by imprisoning those who express disrespect" (Brief for Respondent, in the case of *Texas v. Johnson*, in the U.S. Supreme Court, October, 1988). During oral arguments before the U.S. Supreme Court on March 21, 1989, Dallas County Assistant District Attorney Kathi Drew reiterated the state's interests in protecting the flag; however, she was interrupted repeatedly by questions from Justices Scalia and Kennedy. While explaining the rationale of Texas law to protect the flag as a symbol of nationhood, Scalia asked abruptly: "Now, why does the . . . defendant's actions here destroy the symbol? His actions would have been useless unless the flag was a very good symbol for what he intended to show contempt for. His action does not make it any less a symbol." Kennedy inquired: "Could Texas prohibit the burning of copies of the Constitution?" "Not to my knowledge, Your Honor," answered Drew. Kennedy continued: "Well, how do you pick out what to protect? . . . [I]f I had to pick between the Constitution and the flag, I might go with the Constitution" (Oral arguments before the U.S. Supreme Court, March 21, 1989, in the case of *Texas v. Johnson*).

By contrast, the court generally was more hospitable to veteran civil liberties lawyer William Kunstler, who revisited the profoundly important precedent in *Barnette*. Quoting Justice Jackson in *Barnette*, Kunstler said: "Those who begin coercive elimination of dissent soon find themselves eliminating dissenters. Compulsory unification of opinion achieves only the unanimity of the graveyard. The First Amendment was designed to avoid these ends by avoiding these beginnings" (Oral arguments before the U.S. Supreme Court, March 21, 1989, in the case of *Texas v. Johnson*). Maintaining a strict commitment to freedom of speech, however offensive and shocking, Kunstler reminded the court that the function of the First Amendment is to protect the right for people to express ideas that others do not like.

Amid the flag panic that had been mounting for much of 1989, the U.S. Supreme Court delivered its decision on *Texas v. Johnson* on June 21. In its ruling, the court upheld the decision by the Texas Court of Criminal Appeals that had overturned Johnson's conviction. In a 5–4 vote (with Justices Brennan, Blackmun, Marshall, Scalia, and Kennedy in the majority) the high court ruled that desecrating the flag constitutes a form of political protest that is protected by the First Amendment of the U.S. Constitution. That final word on *Johnson* marked a critical moment in the history of the First Amendment; moreover, the decision immediately invalidated the federal flag-desecration law as well as similar statutes in 48 states. In his majority ruling opinion, Justice Brennan explained the court's rationale in reaching its painstaking decision. Combining sincere patriotism with sound legal reasoning Brennan proclaimed: "We do not consecrate the flag by punishing its desecration, for in doing so we dilute the freedom that this cherished emblem represents" (*Johnson*, 1989:420; see Bloom, 1990; Collins, 1991; Curtis, 1993b; Goldstein, 1996a: 1996b, 1990; Greenawalt, 1990; Loewy, 1989; Massey, 1990; Michelman, 1990; Mullins, 1989; Tushnet, 1990).

Chief Justice William H. Rehnquist dissented vehemently in an opinion that honored the nation and its cultural traditions. Departing from standard legal prose, Rehnquist's statements took the form of a stylized essay blending the nostalgic imagery of Americana and the virtues of militarism with the serenity of poetry. References to civil religion were evident in his plea to shield the flag, as he quoted verses from Emerson's "Concord Hymn." Legal scholars were quick to point out, however, that as chief justice, Rehnquist offered surprisingly little legal analysis in his opinion (Curtis, 1993b; Goldstein, 1996b). Senator Robert Kerrey told his colleagues that he was dismayed by Rehnquist's dissent, whose "argument appears to stand not on 200 years of case law which has supported greater and greater freedom of speech for Americans, but on a sentimental nationalism which seems to impose a functional litmus test of loyalty before expression is permitted" (*CR*, July 18, 1989:s8102-3). Rehnquist also resorted to hyperbole by insinuating that flag burning was a serious criminal offense. In what could be interpreted as moral panic, Rehnquist wrote: "Surely one of the high purposes of a democratic society is to legislate against conduct that is regarded as evil and profoundly offensive to the majority of the people— whether it be murder, embezzlement, pollution or flag burning" (*Johnson*, 1989:435).

THE FLAG PROTECTION ACT OF 1989

In the wake of *Johnson*, public outcry erupted as citizens, war veterans' organizations, and politicians denounced the U.S. Supreme Court. Congressman Dan Burton rancorously addressed his colleagues in the House: "Mr. Speaker, the Judiciary in this country has gone too far. Shame on these judges" (*CR*, June 22, 1989:H3002-04). The bitter societal reaction to *Johnson* was significant sociologically, considering that public and political rage laid the crucial groundwork for an impending criminalization campaign to ban flag desecration. That feverish response to flag burning, compounded by the ruling in *Johnson*, featured all the qualities of a classic moral panic. Congressman David Applegate clamored: "Mr. Speaker, I am mad as heck. We have witnessed the greatest travesty in the annals of jurisprudence when the U.S. Supreme Court allowed the destruction of our greatest American symbols. What in God's name is going on? . . . Are there any limitations? Are they going to allow fornication in Times Square at high noon?" (*CR*, June 22, 1989:H3002-04).

In words reeking with nativism, Senator Bob Dole pontificated in bold print: "PEOPLE [WHO] HATE THE FLAG . . . OUGHT TO LEAVE THE COUNTRY. . . . IF THEY DON'T LIKE OUR FLAG, GO FIND ONE YOU DO LIKE" (*CR*, July, 18, 1989:S8103). Citizens were equally infuriated by the Supreme Court's decision to extend First Amendment freedoms to flag burners. In a national poll conducted shortly after the *Johnson* ruling, 65 percent of Americans disagreed with the ruling, and 71 percent supported a constitutional amendment to protect the flag as a tactic to circumvent the Court's decision (*Newsweek*, July 3, 1989).

To put the prevailing societal reaction to flag desecration in context, it is important to consider the cultural and political *zeitgeist*. Patriotism had once again become popular in the late 1980s, as politicians across the country relied on the nationalistic imagery and rhetoric to promote election campaigns. Most notably, George Bush spun patriotic themes into his bid for the presidency, including a visit to Flag City, U.S.A., and several tours of flag factories. At his June 30, 1989, speech at the Iwo Jima Memorial, Bush continued his strategy of keeping the flag at the forefront of his presidency. Taking a cue from civil religion, Bush emphasized "what the flag embodies is too sacred to be abused. . . . God bless this flag. And God bless the United States of America" (*Weekly Compilation of Presidential Documents*, 25, no. 26, July 3, 1989: 1006–8). Running counter to the wave of criticism in *Johnson*, Senator Robert Kerrey insightfully captured the essence of moral panic. In a statement to Congress, Kerrey blamed the president for inflaming the hysteria over flag desecration: "President Bush did not stand before the angry and distressed mob to stop us in our tracks before we had done something we would regret. He did not offer words that calmed us and gave us the assurance that the Nation was not endangered. Instead of leading us, President Bush joined us" (*CR*, July 18, 1989:S8102–3).

Against this political and cultural backdrop, the flag-protection movement was revived dramatically as droves of congressmen rushed to overturn *Johnson*. In the days leading up to the Fourth of July (1989), 172 representatives and 43 senators sponsored 39 separate resolutions: each of them recommending a constitutional amendment. However, as elected officials debated the issue, Democrats began to reconsider the wisdom of a congressional amendment to protect the flag. As Republicans remained committed to amending the constitution, Democrats were cautious not to be depicted as unpatriotic, thus they opted to defend Old Glory with federal legislation. Democrats believed that they could draft a statute that would protect the flag *and* pass constitutional muster in the courts; consequently, they could promote themselves as devoted patriots without meddling with the constitution. On October 19, 1989, a constitutional amendment failed to achieve a two-thirds majority in the Senate, but the movement to protect the flag remained alive as both houses of Congress endorsed a flag-protection statute. On October 28, Congress passed the Flag Protection Act of 1989 (FPA). Subsection (a) of section 700 of title 18, U.S. Code reads: "Whoever knowingly mutilates, defaces, burns, or tramples upon the flag of the United States shall be fined under this title or imprisoned for not more than one year, or both" (see Faigman, 1990; Van Alstyne, 1991).

U.S. v. EICHMAN

The day the Flag Protection Act of 1989 officially took effect, several demonstrations protesting the new statute were staged around the nation, some of which involved flag burnings. Two incidents, in Seattle and Washington, D.C., were particularly noteworthy because dissenters who torched flags were arrested and charged under the revised federal statute.

In Seattle, RCP supporters Mark Haggerty, Jennifer Campbell, Darius Strong, and Carlos Garza were apprehended for burning the Stars and Stripes outside a U.S. post office shortly after midnight on October 28, moments after the law took effect. Later that day in Washington, D.C., four supporters of the Revolutionary Communist Youth Brigade (RCYB) were arrested for burning three flags outside the Capitol building. That assembly, known as the D.C. 4, included David Blalock, a member of the Vietnam Veterans Against the War (Anti-Imperialist); Shawn Eichman, a New York City revolutionary artist and member of the Coalition Opposed to Censorship in the Arts; and Dread Scott, also a revolutionary artist who earlier had gained notoriety by constructing a controversial art display at the School of Art Institute of Chicago. The fourth demonstrator arrested in Washington, D.C., that day was Gregory L. Johnson. Oddly, Johnson was not indicted, but joined the defendants as an unindicted co-conspirator.

In each case, federal district judges in Seattle and Washington, D.C. dismissed charges brought against the demonstrators. U.S. attorneys appealed both decisions directly to the U.S. Supreme Court for expedited review; as a result, the two cases (*U.S. v. Eichman*, 1989 and *U.S. v. Haggerty*, 1989) were consolidated into *U.S. v. Eichman* (1990), which would serve as a test case for the revised federal flag-protection statute. As part of the materials filed on their behalf, defendants Blalock, Eichman, Johnson, and Scott included a statement first issued when they were arrested for burning a flag on the steps of the U.S. Capitol. In challenging the FPA, this RCYB collective unleashed caustic attacks on the government for its tireless effort to stifle political protest. Punctuating their criticism of the state, the "D.C. 4" addressed an array of social problems along with the danger of civil religion:

> [E]specially in a political climate marked by increasing racism, assaults on women's rights, calls for an enforced oppressive moral code, censorship, intervention in other countries and overall escalating attacks on the people, all [flag burners] deeply felt the need to defy a law that would make the flag a religious icon and its worship mandatory. . . . FIGHT THE FASCIST FLAG AMENDMENT, NO FLAG AMENDMENT, NO MANDATORY PATRIOTISM. (Statement issued by D. Blalock, S. Eichman, J. Johnson, and D. Scott on October 30, 1989; Affidavits by David Blalock and Shawn Eichman in *U.S. v. Eichman*, 1990.)

During oral arguments on May 4, 1990, Solicitor General Kenneth Starr of the U.S. Justice Department reiterated the state's interest in preserving the national symbol as embodied in the FPA insisting the revised statute was constitutional. Conversely, William Kunstler, representing the respondents, argued that the FPA was unconstitutional and cited *Johnson* as the controlling precedent, emphasizing that there was no basis to accept the government's invitation to overturn last year's ruling (Oral arguments before the U.S. Supreme Court, May 4, 1990, in the consolidated case of *U.S. v. Eichman and U.S. v. Haggerty*, Nos. 89-1433 and 89-1334).

The U.S. Supreme Court promptly delivered a 5–4 decision in *Eichman* on June 11, 1990. In what essentially turned out to be a repeat of the *Johnson* ruling, the Court held that the prosecution of the defendants under the revised federal statute violated the First Amendment. In his majority opinion, Justice Brennan squarely applied *Johnson* to *Eichman* in affirming the judgements of the district courts. "Government may create national symbols, promote them, and encourage their respectful treatment. But the Flag Protection Act of 1989 goes well beyond this by criminally proscribing expressive conduct because of its likely communicative impact" (*U.S. v. Eichman*, 1990:310). The FPA's failure in the courts, however, did not derail the flag crusade; in fact, the campaign to pass a constitutional amendment gained considerable momentum in 1990 as a direct result of the *Eichman* ruling (Collins, 1991; Kmiec, 1990a; Nahmod, 1991).

MORAL PANIC OVER FLAG ART

Moral panic over flag desecration in the late 1980s spread to other spheres of American culture, most notably modern art. Deeply offended by avant-garde expression, Senator Jesse Helms launched a moral crusade to sanitize art. First Amendment advocates, however, ardently supported the art community, denouncing proposals for censorship. Some critics compared Helms' crusade to Hitler's Degenerate Art Show, a propaganda campaign designed to marginalize artists, intellectuals, and political dissenters (Abrams, 1991; *Degenerate Art*, 1993; Dubin, 1992; Kimmelman, 1991; New York Public Library, 1993; Wallach, 1991).

Dramatizing their defense of modern art, Ron English and Shawn Eichman, along with the Coalition Opposed to Censorship in the Arts, curated the Helms' Degenerate Art Show. In their curatorial statement, the organizers explained that the show "presents a parallel between Hitler's suppression of art and Helms's fascistic attempt to silence provocative art" (English and Eichman, 1989). The Helms' Degenerate Art Show toured each of the five boroughs of New York City in 1989 and 1990. The exhibit comprised numerous works attacking the authoritarian aesthetic and the state's preoccupation with compulsory patriotism, including a piece by Liana Tomchesson in which miniature flags serving as candles were set ablaze on top of a birthday cake. Supporting a similar leitmotif, English unveiled his "Piggy Bank": a freshly slaughtered pig, wrapped in the American flag, and stuffed with scores of one- and five-dollar bills. Eichman introduced "Alchemy Cabinet," a china cabinet containing numerous items including a coat hanger placed next to a vial containing fetal tissue—from an abortion that she underwent. The purpose of the Helms exhibit, according to Eichman, was "to show that the government and the churches don't have any right to censor art" (Johnson, 1989:6).

Contributing to moral panic over flag desecration in 1989, artist Dread Scott, a supporter of the RCP, exhibited his controversial work "What Is The Proper Way to Display the U.S. Flag?" at the School of the Art Institute of Chicago (SAIC). In that piece, a flag was deliberately placed on the floor of the gallery near a podium furnished with a ledger book. Given the flag's location on the floor, visitors could either walk on Old Glory or step around it while entering into the ledger book their thoughts about the proper way to display the flag. Although Scott's piece had already been on display at Near NorthWest Arts Council Gallery in Chicago months earlier without incident, public and political interest in it mounted on February 23 when a news crew aired footage showing the flag on the floor of the gallery (Hochfield, 1989). Reacting to the news report, veterans embarked on a militaristic mission to rescue the flag. Failing to capture it, the veterans engaged in a repetitive ritual in which they removed the flag from the floor and ceremoniously folded it and respectfully placed it on the shelf with the ledger book. Gallery attendants then returned Old Glory to its original location on the floor, thereby prompting the flag protectionists to repeat their rite (Hess, 1989:20).

Moral panic over the flag inside the gallery spilled into the streets, where thousands of demonstrators held a vigil, blaring patriotic hymns and pep-rally-type chants: "One, two, three, four, get the flag up off the floor." On March 5, an estimated 2,500 flag enthusiasts decked out in military garb and red, white, and blue hats gathered in front of the Art Institute to denounce Scott. A week later, the size of the crowd nearly tripled as approximately 7,000 protestors jammed Michigan Avenue to picket the exhibit. Amidst hundreds of flags waving in the stiff breeze stood picket signs connoting the perception of cultural threat: "Stop Commie Art." One participant supporting the nationalistic assembly wondered ontologically, "Without symbols, how will we know who we are?" (Finley, 1989:1). The circus-like atmosphere swirling around the exhibit attracted politicians, who used the event to stump their patriotism. President Bush reaffirmed his commitment to Old Glory by condemning Scott and his display. Locally, Chicago elected leaders fueled the frenzy in an effort to enhance their political careers. Alderman Ed Vrodolyak, who was running for Mayor, desperately tried to energize his lagging campaign by pressuring his opponent Richard M. Daley, then the state's attorney general, to arrest someone for desecrating the flag (Royko, 1989:Sec. 1, 3).

Initially, Chicago veterans filed an injunction to keep the flag off the floor of the gallery; however, the judge ruled that the exhibit did not violate state or federal flag-desecration laws. Nevertheless, the Chicago City Council passed a resolution denouncing the exhibit and criticized—and marginalized—the SAIC administrators for not ending the controversy: "They're dreamers. They're probably all artists." The measure's sponsor echoed the growing moral panic, shouting "There has never been a more dastardly act in the City of Chicago" (Recktenwald and Strong, 1989: Sec. 2: 9). The city council also urged schools "to teach respect for the flag as a national symbol" (Fulton and Seaman, 1989: 31). At the conclusion of the exhibit, both the city council and the state legislature passed revised flag-protection laws that included a ban on displaying the flag on the floor. Suggesting a contagion effect, similar prohibitions were passed in Indiana and were included in the revised Federal Protection Act of 1989.

Due to its interactive quality, Scott's flag art illuminates many sociological forces, including nostalgia and social control aimed at promoting cultural conformity and the authoritarian aesthetic. The context of the moral panic enveloping the flag flap of the late 1980s includes other controversies: according to Dubin (1992: 118) "this conflict dipped into the same reservoir of communal anxiety that fed controversies dealing with race, religion, and sex."

CONCLUSION

As a political shift to the conservative right, the Reagan Revolution recreated a sense of nostalgia, marking a return to yesterday's villains, including communists. Fittingly, the RCP baited political reactionaries into a skirmish over the flag. Whereas Bush insisted that the popularity of Old Glory reflected consensus and national unity, Bob Avakian, Chairman of the RCP, spun an alternative interpretation. "The flag was painted on Fat Boy, the atomic bomb dropped on Hiroshima; it flew over American slavery; it rode with the calvary in the wars of genocide against the American Indians and the theft of Mexican land; the flag graced the sides of the planes that dropped napalm on the Vietnamese people; and is sewn on the uniforms of the [U.S.] 'advisors' of the 'Contras' in Central America" (Avakian, quoted by the Emergency Committee to Stop the Flag Amendment and Laws, 1989).

In one of the most unpopular decisions handed down by the high court, the majority ruled that the state could no longer criminalize flag desecration since it constituted symbolic speech shielded by the First Amendment (*Johnson*, 1989). Refusing to accept *Johnson* and *Eichman* as the final word on flag desecration, the flag crusade pushed forward, reviving interest in a constitutional amendment. Exhibiting a sense of urgency, Congressman James Sensenbrenner desperately asked his constituents: "Is it too much to

ask those who consider themselves Americans to be required to have respect for our flag? In this day and age, when it seems that perversion is accepted and morality is a taboo perhaps this small mandate is not asking
too much" (Waldman, 1989:15).

Becoming a major social force in the late 1980s, moral panic over flag
desecration entered the sphere of modern art where moral entrepreneurs
portrayed unconventional imagery as dangerous. Denouncing Scott's flag
art, Illinois State Senator Walter Dudyez argued: "Clearly the flag was being desecrated. It was on the floor and it was filthy. There is an accountability here that they haven't been fulfilling, and the Legislature is
responding. What if an artist was to put a loaded gun on a pedestal and
ask, 'What is the proper way to use a gun?' There has to be some sort of
policy" (Wilkerson, 1989: Section 4, 4). Many of those who toured Scott's
installation expressed similar outrage at modern art and its nontraditional
use of the flag. The following entries in Scott's ledger book were commonplace: "Dread Scott is a commie pig and should be strung up by his
balls and fed to leeches. Artsy-fartsy people suck." "You commie bastard.
Someone should throw you down and trample you." Offering a disturbing view of democracy, another visitor wrote: "I believe in your right as a
citizen to express your view. Be aware, however, that 'majority rules' in our
democracy. If the majority believe your choice is wrong—it will follow you
the rest of your life.—NAME, 3rd grade teacher and proud to pledge each
morning!" Clearly, Scott's flag art, along with other political and cultural
events of the late 1980s, fueled perceptions of social threat, resulting in repressive campaigns aimed at criminalizing unpopular ideas and imagery.

6

Patriotism and Dissent in the Post-*Eichman* Era

Those protestors were exercising free speech right up until they burned the flag, then they were expressing violent conduct. This kind of conduct should not be tolerated in a free and democratic society.
—*Major General Patrick Brady, Chairman of the Citizens Flag Alliance (CFA, 1998b).*

The [U.S. Supreme] Court routinely overrules the actions of local police boards, boards of education, and state laws under which they act. The beneficiaries of the Court's protections are members of various minorities, including criminals, atheists, homosexuals, flag burners, illegal aliens including terrorists, convicts, and pornographers.
—*Patrick Buchanan, 1996*

Although moral panic is among the most significant social forces shaping the flag-desecration controversy, it is also important to consider the clash between competing social movements. Compounding social conflict and moral panic is the reactionary claim that public protest aimed at the establishment represents an outward sign that society is becoming unglued and overrun by radicals. That perception was evident in 1989 and again in 1990 after the U.S. Supreme Court handed down its *Johnson* and *Eichman* decisions. Due to those rulings, the high court established a unique era of political expression; for the first time in U.S. history, flag desecration was constitutionally protected. Still, the Supreme Court did not resolve the battle over flag protection; rather, the unpopularity of *Johnson* and *Eichman* merely inflamed moral panic, and the crusade to protect Old Glory raged into the 1990s. As the debate over flag protection was taking place in the mannerly decorum of Congress, efforts to repress political dissent in the streets took on a brutish quality as police continued arresting protesters for desecrating Old Glory.

The social and political *zeitgeist* surrounding those events figured prominently in the enforcement of antiquated laws banning flag desecration. As mentioned in the previous chapter, the Reagan and Bush presidencies marked a distinct return to nostalgic visions of American life, replete with flag waving and military actions against "evil" dictators. The prevailing regressive social movement, however, had formidable opponents in American society, especially the campaign opposing the Persian Gulf War. While President Bush spoke proudly of a New World Order, critics denounced his worldview as imperialistic and mocked his foreign policy, calling it the New World *Odor*. Our discussion begins with an overview of the political landscape of the late 1980s, continuing into the 1990s. Attending to key social and political developments, repressive actions by the state aimed at promoting compulsory patriotism and regulating political protest are examined. Despite the constitutionality of flag desecration as political protest, formal and informal measures of social control persist in the post-*Eichman* era.

DESERT STORM AND THE NEW WORLD ODOR

As an extension of the Reagan Revolution, the Bush administration spawned a patriotic movement charged with protecting the flag from desecration. Moreover, a renewed sense of nationalism empowered U.S. foreign policy and militarism. In 1989, American military forces invaded Panama, an action the Department of Defense argued was necessary in fighting the war on drugs, despite its clear violations of international diplomacy. The following year, Bush's critics realized that the military maneuver in Panama had served as a mere tuneup for the high-tech attack in the Persian Gulf (Craig, 1996; Johns, 1991, 1996; Welch, Bryan and Wolff, 1999; Welch, Wolff, and Bryan, 1998). Proclaiming a New World Order, Bush and Desert Storm enjoyed massive popular support. In January 1991, backing for the war reached nearly 80 percent from an increasingly patriotic public, many of whom went to great lengths to express their renewed faith in U.S. military policy (*Time* 1991).

Despite its general popularity, however, the war in the Persian Gulf drew sharp criticism. Detractors interpreted Bush's political and military show of force as a transparent attempt to shed himself of the wimp label. In calling for an end to the "Vietnam Syndrome", Bush celebrated once again the nostalgic virtues of militarism. Curiously, mainline Americans who felt ambivalent about their government's bombing of Iraq were assuaged by the realization that they could support the troops but not the war. Incorporating commerce and consumption with fashion and culture, American patriotism during the Persian Gulf War manifested in tacky tee-shirts, some bearing the intrepid slogan "Red, White, and Blue: These Colors Don't Run" (Broad, 1998; Swank, 1993).

Desert Storm enthusiasts also accessorized their clothing with yellow ribbons, prompting adverse reactions by employers committed to strict dress codes. In 1990, a court officer in Worcester, Massachusetts, earned the right to wear a yellow ribbon below the badge on his uniform. A gate attendant at Miami's Opa-Locka Airport was told to remove her yellow ribbon from her uniform but she refused saying: "If they want my ribbon and my flag, they'll have to take my shirt with it" (*Time*, 1991:55). Due to overwhelming pressure from its employees, Disney World management departed from its strict uniform policy by allowing its workers to wear yellow ribbons on the job during the Gulf War (*Time*, 1991).

Despite resounding civilian support for Desert Storm, there was notable antiwar resistance. Peace activists staged rallies across the nation, a movement that caught the ire of self-described patriots. In Maplewood, Missouri, Timothy Dunn found his antiwar sign torched in his front yard. In another Missouri town, prowar demonstrators attacked a car draped with a peace sign and shoved flagpoles through the windows and shouted "Commie Faggots!" at the two passengers. At Fort Ord in California, a car belonging to a decorated Vietnam War veteran was impounded after he refused to remove PEACE IS PATRIOTIC and SAY NO TO WAR signs from the vehicle's window (*Time*, 1991:55). As another example of repression, JMB Realty blocked the New Jersey Coalition Against the War from distributing antiwar leaflets in its suburban New Jersey malls. The coalition sued on the grounds that JMB Realty violated its First Amendment right to political expression, and in a significant legal victory for anti-war activists, the New Jersey Supreme Court concurred (*Rutgers Focus*, 1996). In an intriguing case, police arrested 18 anti–Persian Gulf War demonstrators protesting the Operation Welcome Home parade in New York City in 1991. The incident began when prowar enthusiasts harassed and assaulted several of the outspoken pacifists; police quickly intervened but arrested only the protestors, not their attackers (*Revolutionary Worker*, December 21, 1991; January 26, 1992; Defense Campaign for the War Parade 18, No Date).

FLAG INCIDENTS IN THE POST-*EICHMAN* ERA

As mentioned, the U.S. Supreme Court in *Johnson* and *Eichman* established a distinct period in American history in which flag desecration is explicitly protected as free speech. Despite its constitutionality, however, flag desecration continues to be met with considerable resistance from the criminal justice apparatus.

Although it is difficult to determine the precise number of flag incidents in the post-*Eichman* era, between 1990 and 1995, 17 cases reached the courts. In addition, the Citizens Flag Alliance (1998a) documented 65 flag desecrations between 1994 and 1998. In reviewing those incidents, several key themes are evident, including antiwar and antigovernment messages, commerce, advertising, and patriotism, flag patch controversies, and artistic and cultural expression.

Antiwar and Antigovernment Messages

Violations of the authoritarian aesthetic in the form of flag desecration are viewed commonly by authorities as threats to the social order, prompting efforts to regulate the use of public space by political dissenters. In an incident resembling, *Johnson* and *Eichman*, Paul Dalton and Dane Peterson were charged with receiving stolen property (i.e., the flag) and criminal damage to someone else's property following a demonstration in Oberlin, Ohio, where they staged a flag burning to protest the U.S. invasion of Panama in 1990. "Ever since the Flag Protection Act became law, we viewed flag burning as strictly a tactic, a good tactic," explained Dalton, who also told reporters, "We were very angry at the U.S. invasion of Panama and wanted to protest it in the strongest terms possible. You could equate flag burning with the burning of draft cards during the Vietnam War. It was symbolic protest" (Makalani, 1990: 20). The two dissenters had been investigated previously by the FBI for violating the Flag Protection Act of 1989: says Dalton, "I think the FBI has been instructed to harass flag burners" (Makalani, 1990:20). Eventually, Dalton and Peterson were acquitted of all charges.

In 1990, as the Pentagon was advancing the war effort in the Persian Gulf, Shawn Eichman and Joe Urgo climbed to the roof of the Armed Services Recruiting Station in Times Square (New York City) to voice their opposition to U.S. militarism. Eichman and Urgo posted banners reading "No Blood For Oil", then poured motor oil and a red liquid down the sides of the building; moreover, they lowered a government-owned flag from the station's flag pole and attempted—though unsuccessfully—to ignite it. New York City police observed the incident and scaled the building to apprehend Eichman and Urgo. They were then taken into custody at the Midtown South precinct, where police accused them of condemning the military and trying to burn the Stars and Stripes. Soon federal officials contacted New York City police officials to verify whether the Shawn Eichman they had in custody was the same activist who had recently appeared before the U.S. Supreme Court in the *Eichman* flag-burning case. Local police responded affirmatively. Members of the Federal Bureau of Investigation's Joint-Terrorist Task Force then arrived at the precinct's lockup and transferred Eichman and Urgo to the federal Municipal Correctional Center in lower Manhattan where they were arraigned on charges of damaging government property, felony burglary, and reckless endangerment. U.S. Attorneys also claimed that Eichman and Urgo placed the public in harm's way, saying that the plan to set the flag afire could have caused an uncontrollable inferno; thus, the suspects were charged with felony arson (*U.S. v. Eichman*, 1991). Violations of that federal arson statute are punishable by up to ten years in prison and apply equally to attempting to burn a federal building or a government-owned flag; by contrast, the maximum penalty for flag desecration under the 1968 and 1989 federal statute was one year of incarceration.

All along, Eichman and Urgo said their actions were intended to apprise the public of the impending war in the Persian Gulf, an atrocity that would claim the lives of thousands of innocent people. Conversely, the U.S. Attorneys framed the event in far more ominous terms by insisting that Eichman and Urgo were operating as domestic terrorists. In fact, the heavy weight of the government's argument convinced the U.S. magistrate to detain Eichman and Urgo on unsecured bonds set at the excessive amount of $100,000 each. Activists quickly organized on behalf of Eichman and Urgo. The Free Shawn and Joe Defense Committee generated support from well-known, socially conscious figures, including Fr. Daniel Berrigan of the Catonsville 9, Jon Hendricks of the Judson 3, artists Leon Golub and Nancy Spero, feminist filmmaker Flo Kennedy, and attorney Leonard Weinglass. In preparing for trial, lawyer Ian Weinstein teamed up with co-counsels Ron Kuby and William Kunstler. As a veteran defense attorney whose record of defending protestors include the Chicago 7, Kunstler had seen this type of prosecution many times before; predictably, he resorted to his classic maneuver of using the trial to put the government on trial. The U.S. Attorneys were well-prepared for battle. The presence of the FBI's Joint Terrorist Task Force did not go unnoticed; in fact, on each day of the trial, the agent was reintroduced to the jury. The prosecution boldly presented its case, reiterating its inflammatory claim that Eichman and Urgo were domestic terrorists. Unlike the flag-burning cases that had recently been reviewed by the U.S. Supreme Court, the media virtually ignored this trial; still, notable antiwar activists, including former U.S. Attorney General Ramsey Clark, made conspicuous appearances to show their support for the demonstrators.

Following the five-day trial, the jury deliberated for approximately four hours. Since Eichman and Urgo readily testified that they had indeed climbed on top of the Armed Services Recruiting Center to denounce U.S. military action in the Persian Gulf, it was not surprising that the jury, adhering to its narrow instructions, convicted them of felony arson and depredation of public property. The jury, however, acquitted Eichman and Urgo of reckless endangerment, thus rejecting the prosecution's claim that the protestors imperiled public safety by their actions (McQueen, 1991). Nevertheless, with convictions on two counts, Eichman and Urgo faced sentences of 10 years for felony arson and up to one year for depredation of public property as well as fines reaching $10,000. In the end, Judge Leonard B. Sand sentenced Eichman and Urgo to two years' probation, 200 hours of community service, and a $75 fine—the cost of the flag damaged during the demonstration.

Similarly in 1991, two anti–Gulf War demonstrators who torched Old Glory in St. Louis were arrested for disturbing the peace, but the charges were dismissed after they filed a complaint for false arrest. The St. Louis protestors also accused the police of not intervening when "Rambo" patriots attacked them (*St. Louis Post Dispatch*, March 25, 1991). Also that year, nine high school students in Baltimore were suspended when they burned a flag to protest the Persian Gulf War (*Baltimore Sun*, Jan 18, 1991). At the University of Wisconsin at River Falls, Jeffrey Gerson, a lecturer, burned a flag during an American politics class to illustrate the U.S. Supreme Court rulings on flag desecration and to protest the Gulf War. Students and administrators at the university as well as citizens in the community denounced Gerson for his pedagogical technique while others threatened him with bodily harm. Gerson was not rehired to teach the following semester (*Eau Claire Leader-Telegram*, March 12, 1991).

In Los Angeles, five members of the Revolutionary Communist Youth Brigade were arrested after they burned flags in MacArthur Park in 1990. At one juncture, protesters plopped a bloody head from a butchered pig on the sidewalk where the flag had been, stuck a tiny flag between the nostrils and set it ablaze. In the 1980s and 1990s, MacArthur Park became a common site for demonstrations where the RCYP and its affiliate, La Resistencia, protested the use of police barricades and the operations of a nearby Immigration and Naturalization Service detention center, which opponents call a concentration camp. To embellish their protests, the RCYP distributed flag-burning kits consisting of a tiny paper flag taped to a book of matches. In 1990, several veterans scuffled with protesters in an effort to rescue the flags. "I got three purple hearts for protecting that flag in Vietnam, and I'm not going to stand by and let them burn it," proclaimed Jimmie McAllister (Efron, 1990:B-1). When police intervened they arrested only the protestors, not the veterans who attacked the demonstrators. The protesters were charged with inciting a riot, resisting arrest, and an arson-related offense that prohibits the burning of anything in the park (Efron, 1990).

In Russellville, Alabama, Barry Carpenter, his wife, and their child, armed with chalk, candles, and peace literature, staged an anti-Persian Gulf War demonstration at the post office in 1991. After distributing posters and pamphlets critical of "Desert Storm," Carpenter was arrested for criminal littering and for desecration of a monument (a post office), for chalking antiwar slogans on the sidewalk in front of the building. Carpenter was also charged with endangering the welfare of his child by engaging in unlawful activities that would result in arrest, thus leaving the child unattended—even though his wife was present. While being handcuffed, Carpenter was frisked for weapons when the officer discovered a flag tucked inside Carpenter's pocket. Because the flag was in a "very disorderly" and "wadded condition," Carpenter was charged with desecration of a venerated object for his possession of the soiled and unkempt American flag (*Carpenter v. State*, 1992:758). Under the Alabama penal code, Carpenter was convicted, sentenced to 30 days in jail, and ordered to attend a week of criminal court proceedings to "spend time with the Court each day that week discussing the procedures and the trial of the case, and . . . to write a report [of not less than five pages] of his reaction to his observations and reaction to all that had transpired in court while he [was] there" (*Carpenter* 1992:758).

Although Carpenter was convicted of desecrating the flag, he never voluntarily displayed it during his protest; in fact, the flag was only made visible after the arresting officer removed it from Carpenter's pocket. Appealing his conviction, Carpenter argued that his arrest was based on mere possession of an unkempt flag. In 1992, the Court of Criminal Appeals of Alabama held that "in order to constitute a violation of Alabama Code 1975 . . . the [flag] desecration must have occurred in public or in a public place" (*Carpenter*, 1992:758). The court then reversed the decision, but without addressing the constitutionality of the Alabama antidesecration statute in light of the developments in *Johnson* and *Eichman*. Carpenter later sued the Russellville officials for various violations, including false imprisonment and malicious prosecution, and was awarded an out-of-court settlement.

During the well-publicized Central Park jogger trial in New York City, Donald Payne, one of the numerous activists who routinely gathered outside the courthouse, was arrested for unlawfully setting a fire in public. Payne was arrested when he burned a small cloth flag in front of the courthouse, a demonstration intended to draw attention to racial inequality in the criminal justice system. Payne had engaged in his flag-burning ritual on three prior occasions without being arrested. At his trial, Payne argued that the summonses should be dismissed because the municipal ordinance "precluded him from exercising his constitutionally protected right to burn the flag as a form of political protest" (*People v. Payne*, 1990:35). Citing *Johnson*, the Manhattan Criminal Court judge concurred, noting that Payne's "act of burning the flag was intended to convey a message and therefore was expressive conduct" (*Payne*, 1990:35). The court also expressed concern over the prosecution's motives, pointing out that Payne was not charged with disorderly conduct or criminal nuisance. "It appears that the primary interest in issuing instant summonses was to suppress the defendant's politically charged acts of burning the flag," observed the court (*Payne*, 1990:37). Relying on *Johnson* as the controlling precedent, the court dismissed the charges against Payne.

For protestors who know full well that flag desecration is constitutionally protected, actions by the criminal justice apparatus are viewed as especially repressive. In a case similar to the prosecution of antiwar protestors Shawn Eichman and Joe Urgo, Cheryl Lessin, a supporter of the RCP, was arrested at a 1990 anti-Persian Gulf War demonstration in Cleveland. Lessin was charged with a felony count of inciting to violence when she publicly burned a flag as a "symbol of violence" while denouncing President Bush and the U.S. military. Witnesses testified, however, that the only physical contact seen during the rally was when one of the protesters was slapped in the face by a self-described patriot. Although Lessin was not prosecuted specifically under a flag-desecration statute, the case rested on evidence that her act of burning the flag was central to her arrest, prosecution, and conviction. In a maneuver designed to divert attention from First Amendment violations, the state argued that Lessin was arrested not for burning the flag but for creating an environment conducive to violence. Prosecutors insisted that by screaming statements, "Fuck the United States, I hate this country, Long live the Revolutionary Communist Party" (*State v. Lessin*, 1993:487), Lessin intended to provoke people to commit acts of violence. To corroborate the state's case, arresting officer George Deli testified that he could not have arrested Lessin for her burning of the flag because he was not even aware that a flag had been burned until after the crowd was brought under control. Under cross-examination, however, Officer Deli not only conceded that his previous statement was false, but that he actually said while arresting Lessin, "She burned the flag" (*Lessin*, 1993:489). Lessin was convicted and sentenced to one year in prison.

Adding to the Kafkaesque nature of the trial, Judge Patricia Cleary, in a series of odd rulings, perplexed the defendant and her attorney. During the *voir dire* of the witnesses, Lessin's attorney, Mr. Rossman, asked, "How many of you are aware of recent Supreme Court cases that says [sic] it's okay to burn the flag?" (*Lessin*, 1993:495). The prosecution objected to that question, and the judge concurred, saying: "There has been no Supreme Court case, to my knowledge, that permits under any circumstances that it's okay to burn the flag. That's why the lawyers have been instructed not to discuss the issues of law. And don't do it again" (*Lesssin*, 1993:495). Rossman's request to discuss the matter at sidebar was denied. Because Judge Cleary failed to acknowledge that flag burning is a form of speech protected under the First Amendment, as ruled in *Johnson* and *Eichman*, jury members were not apprised of relevant case law; compounding the problem, Rossman was later held in contempt of Court for pursuing that line of questioning.[1] Despite errors in Lessin's trial, the Court of Appeals affirmed her conviction. It was not until the case reached the Supreme Court of Ohio that sufficient consideration was given to discerning the law. The court recognized that "In this case, the role of the jury instructions was critical in obviating the possibility that each juror would convict on his or her personal prejudices against flag burners and communists" (*Lessin*, 1993:493). The court reversed Lessin's conviction (see *Revolutionary Worker*, November 10, 1991).

In 1990, the "Shut Down the Clamp" coalition publicly challenged Seattle's drug-loitering ordinance which approved the use of Pentagon security for the Goodwill Games. Activist Jerry Edmon Fordyce feared that the policy would degenerate into maintaining detention centers where dissident U.S. citizens, such as himself, would be confined. Tension soon mounted between police and protestors who shouted, "Fuck the police!" "Fight the power!" "Pigs aren't kosher!" and "Police, you can't hide, we charge you with genocide!" (*Fordyce*, 1993:787). Strident speeches calling for revolutionary action were blasted through bullhorns. Emotions escalated when demonstrators burned flags and threw a pig's head wrapped in a flag in the direction of several officers. As Fordyce videotaped the event for a local television production, Judy Worley approached him demanding that he cease recording her and her two nephews, ages 12 and 13. When he refused, Worley angrily lunged at him, apparently to strike him or his camera, and in doing so attracted police attention. After hearing Worley's complaints, the police told Fordyce to stop recording because he was violating a state statute. Asserting that it was a *public* place, Fordyce refused to comply with the order, and was arrested; further, he was detained until the following morning. Evidence corroborating Fordyce's claim that he was falsely arrested was substantiated by videotape; in fact, the alleged taping of Worley and her nephews did not appear on film. In light of the evidence, police eventually dropped the charges against Fordyce, who contends that his arrest stemmed from circumstances other than the dispute with Worley—most notably his political dissent and support for the flag burners who publicly violated the aesthetic of authorities. In a civil action, the U.S. District Court for Western Washington issued declaratory judgment in favor of Fordyce because his recording was not unlawful (*Fordyce*, 1993:791).

Given the military's commitment to outward displays of patriotism, it is understandable that flag etiquette is enforced strictly in the U.S. armed forces. Whereas *Johnson* and *Eichman* afford freedom of political expression to civilians, such protections do not extend to military personnel. Consider the case of Samuel M. Wilson, a military policeman for the U.S. Army, who was charged in 1991 with disobeying a lawful order and dereliction of duty

after he blew his nose on Old Glory while preparing it for flag-raising detail. The incident began when Wilson griped to fellow MPs that the army
and the United States "sucked." In response, another MP told Wilson that
if he didn't like it he should move to a communist country. Wilson then
replied: "[this] is what I think" and blew his nose on the flag, leaving "a
small wet circle." After another brief exchange of words, Wilson completed
the flag-raising detail (*U.S. v. Wilson*, 1991:798). Wilson faced a court-mar-
tial for disobeying a lawful order and dereliction of duty for willfully failing to "ensure that the United States flag was treated with proper respect
by blowing his nose on it when it was his duty as a military policeman on
flag call to safeguard and protect the flag . . . [thus] disrespecting a venerated object (*Wilson*, 1991:798, 799). Under Article 92 of the Uniform Code
of Military Justice, Wilson was sentenced to a bad-conduct discharge, four
months in jail, forfeiture of $482 pay per month for four months, and re-
duction to Private E1.

Contending that his First Amendment right to free speech was violated,
Wilson appealed the decision, but the U.S. District Court of Military Review affirmed his conviction. Even though the court agreed that Wilson's
"statements and his conduct in blowing the nose on American flag when
viewed together are expressive conduct," it did not reverse the previous
ruling (*Wilson*, 1991:798). Instead, the court found that the government's
interest in "promoting the disciplined performance of military duties"
outweighed the need to afford Wilson his constitutional rights (*Wilson*,
1991:800). Because Wilson was in uniform and on duty, the government
was legally allowed to regulate his conduct, according to UCMJ, proscribing dereliction in the course of duty. The court also noted that members of
the U.S. military do in fact have more limited freedom of speech than their
civilian counterparts; thus, "to accomplish its mission the military must
foster instinctive obedience, unity, commitment, and esprit de corps. . . .
The essence of military service is the subordination of the desires and interests of the individual to the needs of the service" (*Wilson*, 1991:799). Citing *Johnson*, the court speculated: "If the accused was a soldier but off duty,
out of uniform, procured a flag, decided to burn it or blow his nose on it
or perhaps spit on it . . . arguably then that expression might be protected"
(*Wilson*, 1991:798).

Commerce, Advertising, and Patriotism

In support of U.S. military action in the Persian Gulf, many Americans
proudly boasted of their patriotism. Andrew Sims shared in the renewed
spirit of nationalism by displaying flag streamers in front of his Buick
dealership in Broadway Heights, Ohio, in 1991. Shortly thereafter, municipal officials ordered Sims to remove the display because it violated a lo-

cal ordinance governing commercial advertising. In what can be viewed as a municipal version of authoritarian aesthetics, the ordinance was created to promote and maintain high-quality residential districts and attractive public facilities. Sims refused to dismantle his patriotic display and asserted his right to freedom of expression, but in court the city prevailed (*Sims v. City of Broadview Heights*, 1994). Similarly, Lawrence H. Dimmitt also challenged the constitutionality of the municipal sign ordinance in Clearwater, Florida, which prohibited a display of 23 flags at his Chevrolet dealership. Clearwater's zoning ordinance specified that only one flag could be placed on any residential property and up to two flags on any nonresidential property. Dimmitt contested the code on the grounds that it interfered with his First Amendment rights, insisting the display was "intended to be expressive and symbolic, in communicating the message of the American flag" (*Dimmitt v. City of Clearwater*, 1991:586). The city of Clearwater responded by arguing that the display was not expressive conduct because one message could not be conveyed that all viewers would understand; furthermore, the rationale of the code was to protect the flag from being commercialized. Moreover, the ordinance "served to avoid visual clutter, preserve the community aesthetics, and prevent distraction to motorists in the city" (*Dimmitt*, 1991:589). In hearing the complaint by Dimmitt, the U.S. District Court for the Middle District of Florida reviewed the case law governing expressive conduct as set forth in *Johnson, Spence,* and *O'Brien*. Complying with these precedents, the court determined that Dimmitt's flag display was expressive conduct requiring First Amendment protection since it communicated an "acceptance of the flag as a symbol of adherence to the government" as well as an "acceptance of the political beliefs for which it stands" (*Dimmitt*, 1991:589; for a similar dispute over local ordinances and flag displays, see Zielbauer, 1999).

Demonstrating the extent to which the government attempts to dictate the "proper" use of the flag, the U.S. Patent Office refused to grant the Old Glory Condom Corporation permission to trademark their products with a flag-like image reading "Worn with Pride, Country-Wide." The U.S. Patent Office rejected Old Glory Condom's application and hinted at moral panic when it characterized the logo as "immoral and scandalous." Maintaining a civil-religious viewpoint, the government proclaimed: "the flag is a sacrosanct symbol whose association with condoms would necessarily give offense" (*In re Old Glory Condom Corp.*, 1993:3). Jay Critchley of Old Glory Condom Corporation said, however, that he was promoting "condoms with a conscience" and explained: "Basically, what they're saying is that condoms are immoral and scandalous and anything to do with sex is dirty. It's really Neanderthal, the whole attitude" (*Boston Globe*, 1991, October 27: 30). On behalf of Old Glory Condom, attorney David Cole, who had served as co-counsel for the defendants in *Johnson* and *Eichman*, filed an appeal with the Patent Office's Trademark Trial and Appeal Board, insisting that the company's rights to free speech and political expression had been violated. Cole noted that the Patent and Trademark Office had approved more than 1000 marks in which the flag appears on products and packaging. For three years, Old Glory Condom litigated, eventually winning the right to register their packaging with the flag emblem along with its pledge to donate a portion of the proceeds to AIDS-related services.

Flag-Patch Controversies

Reminiscent of the flag-patch controversies during the Vietnam War era, several cases surfaced at the height of the military conflict in the Persian Gulf. Sergeant Deiter Troster, a corrections officer for the State Correctional Institution at Greensburg, Pennsylvania, refused to wear the U.S. flag on his uniform. Troster's insubordination violated a new uniform regulation mandating the display of the flag patch on the right sleeve of the uniform shirt. A naturalized citizen who emigrated to the United States in his early twenties, Troster served in the U.S. Army, reaching the rank of major; in 1981, he retired after 20 years of service, including a tour in Vietnam. Troster insisted that "state-compelled display desecrates the flag and debases it [because] . . . the American flag symbolizes freedom from state-coerced political or patriotic speech" (*Troster v. Pennsylvania State Department of Corrections*, 1995:1088). Taking exception to the department's sense of symbolism and aesthetics, Troster also refused to wear the flag patch with its star field to the rear signifying cowardice and retreat from the principles for which the flag stands. For refusing to wear the flag patch, Troster was suspended for five days and faced termination from his job. In 1995, the U.S. Court of Appeals upheld the enforcement of the flag-patch regulation.

In 1990, Jack Dunn, an administrative assistant in the Florissant Valley Fire Protection District (Missouri), sewed a flag patch onto his uniform in support of U.S. troops in the Persian Gulf. Because the flag was not part of the uniform guidelines, however, Dunn was suspended from his job for refusing to remove the flag patch. Dunn replied defiantly: "If he [Chief William Bogue] wants them flags off . . . tell him I'll take them off in front of Channel 2, Channel 4, Channel 5, the American Legion, the VFW, and the DAV, which I'm a life member of" (*Dunn v. Carroll*, 1994:81). Dunn further characterized the order to remove his flag patch as a form of flag desecration. Dunn sued the district and its officials for violating his First Amendment right to free speech, but the U.S. District Court granted summary judgement to the district and its officials. The U.S. Court of Appeals ruled, however, that because Dunn wore the flag patch as a comment on the Persian Gulf War, his action constituted nonverbal conduct intended to express a "particularized message," and therefore, according to *Johnson* was protected speech under the First Amendment (*Dunn*, 1994:293). Also, during the Gulf War, the New York City police department overruled itself and decided that flag patches larger than a lapel pin but no bigger than 1.5 inches by 2 inches would not violate its strict standard (Cottman, 1991a, 1991b; Sachar, 1991; *Time*, 1991). Likewise, the flag controversy penetrated the legal profession, as defense lawyer Kurt Mausert successfully petitioned Queensbury town (New York) to have county prosecutor Michael Muller remove a flag pin he was wearing in court. Mausert argued that Muller's patriotic accessory could prejudice the jury against the defendant. On appeal, State Supreme Court Justice John Dier reversed Mausert's petition and astonishingly ordered that he be banned from representing indigent cases in the county. A panel of New York State's highest court overruled Dier, however, insisting that the trial judge acted appropriately; the panel also rejected penalties against Mausert (*New York Times*, February 14, 1992).

Artistic and Cultural Expression

As strange as it may seem, the orthodoxy of traditional flag aesthetics often leads authorities to dictate the "proper" use of the flag in political, cultural, and artistic expressions, even when the message actually intends to *celebrate* democratic freedoms and patriotism. Consider the uproar beginning in 1991 when students at Elk Grove High School (California) pitted their free-speech rights against the authority of school officials who attempted to control which images were to be painted on campus walls. The controversy emerged innocently enough when school administrators invited student organizations to decorate the walls of the building with murals that reflected their ideas of civics. To depict American freedoms, students from the Model United Nations/Junior Statesmen Club (MUN/JS) decided to paint a mural featuring a burning flag accompanied by statements explaining civil liberties, including a quote from Senator Margaret Chase Smith's 1950 Declaration of Conscience proclaiming the right to independent thought and the right to unpopular belief. Principal Paula Duncan refused to authorize the artwork because she said it could be perceived as an endorsement of flag burning, thereby offending members of the community (Sanders, 1993a).

MUN/JS students took exception to the principal's interpretation, insisting that their mural endorsed American freedoms and taught citizens about the U.S. Constitution. The MUN/JS studied closely the U.S. Supreme Court's rulings in *Johnson* and *Eichman* and believed their mural would enlighten other people about American democracy. MUN/JS vice president Emily Smith reported: "I'd never burn a flag and hopefully no-

body else would. But we have the freedom of speech in this country. Freedom to protest. Freedom to burn a flag. And that freedom is a good thing"
(Sanders, 1993a:A-1). In defense of the MUN/JS, the ACLU filed suit in
Sacramento Superior Court in April 1993, claiming that the school had violated the students' rights of free speech and expression subject to the pro-
tective provisions of the California Education Code. Ann Brick of the
ACLU pointed out that state law keeps student art from being banned simply because some find it objectionable: "The mural's message is that the
First Amendment protects expression we don't like as well as expression
we do like" (Sanders, 1993a:37). "There's tremendous irony here. . . . What
we're intending to promote is discussion of critical issues and freedom of
expression, yet we're not allowed to express ourselves with this mural"
replied Dave Hill, faculty advisor to the MUN/JS (Sanders, 1993a:37). Still,
many students supported the administration's decision. One student
replied, "to see a mural like that would offend me and many others"
(Sanders, 1993b:35; 1993c). Some students viewed the flag-burning mural
as simply another form of graffiti and others suspected that the display
could spark violence (Hoge, 1993b).

The court found that the mural constituted "student speech and expression" protected under California Education Code (*Markgraf v. Elk
Grove Unified School District* 1993). In granting the students a preliminary
injunction, Judge Ronald Robie cited *Johnson* and announced: "The hard
fact is that sometimes we must make decisions we do not like. We make
them because it's right" (Hoge, 1993b:A-1). Principal Duncan's disap-
pointment in the ruling was imbued with moral panic, saying the decision
opens her school's walls "to anything from the Confederate flag to satanic
worship to you name it" (Hoge, 1993b:30). Elk Grove school officials appealed, but the ruling was upheld. In September 1993, the mural was finally painted, prompting intense anger and in some instances violence:
two students were hospitalized after being beaten by six antimural students who had mistakenly thought that a flag had been burned. In an act
of self-proclaimed patriotism, 13-year-old James Hudman slapped white
paint over the mural with a roller brush. Hudman was suspended from
school for five days but defiantly defended his action saying, "I believe I
corrected a wrong. It's not right to paint a burning flag on a school wall.
Too many people died for that flag. . . . If they don't support the American
flag, they should get out of the country." Hudman's father commended his
son for defacing the mural and quipped, "Betsy Ross would turn over in
her grave if she knew about this mural" (Sanders, 1993d:22). Numerous
community residents also publicly supported Hudman, including a World
War II veteran who told reporters: "[The] teenagers who painted the flag-
burning mural artwork deserve a good spanking from their parents"
(Sanders, 1993d:22).

The ultimate act of retaliation against the MUN/JS, however, was carried out by school administrators who later instituted a new policy banning all permanent murals. The day after the policy was passed, 100 Elk Grove High School students left class in protest, and 48 students were suspended for three days when they refused to return to school (Camposeco, 1994). Even though the students had established the right to paint the mural, it was painted over in August 1994 in compliance with the revised policy (Camposeco and Rocha, 1994). Before it was all over, the Elk Grove School District had spent more than $80,000 in legal fees fighting the students' lawsuit (Composeco and Rocha, 1994). In 1995, the students of MUN/JS received a First Amendment Beacon Award for their advancement of freedom of information and expression (*Business Wire*, 1995; Erwin, 1994; Goldstein, 1994, 1996a; *Sacramento Bee*, 1993a, 1993b, 1993c).

In a similar flag case underscoring the authoritarian aesthetic in artistic expression, Lisa Mostoller was charged in 1993 with violating the Pennsylvania state ban on flag desecration. Mostoller, an artist who had recently been recognized as Outstanding Person of the Year by the Somerset County Chamber of Commerce, was accused of flag desecration for partially covering a flag with a black cloth painted with the words "Laurel Arts Pirate Ship" to advertise an annual art festival. Eventually, District Justice Jon Barkman dismissed the charges against Mostoller not on constitutional grounds but rather because he believed that the local artist had not intended to desecrate the flag (Goldstein, 1996b). Several other controversies involving flag art in the post-*Eichman* era emerged across the nation. For instance, the Sacramento Fine Arts Center withdrew an exhibit that featured a burned flag attached to a canvas. In Massachusetts, the Greenfield Community College was the site of contention when a projected video image of a flag on the floor was included in a class installation in the college art gallery (Goldstein, 1994).

In 1996, "Old Glory: the American Flag in Contemporary Art," an exhibit at the Phoenix Art Museum, featured the following art works: Kate Millet's "The American Dream Goes to Pot" in which a flag was stuffed in a toilet; a headless crucifix with the flag in the background created by Hans Burkhardt; a flag made out of human hair and skin by Andrew Krasnow; an image of a man dressed in Ku Klux Klan garb holding a baby painted onto a flag by Ronnie Cutrone; and a flag with a lighter on top with a description that reads, "Now more fun than ever" by Erika Rothberg. The show also included Dread Scott's "What is the Proper Way to Display the U.S. Flag." The "Old Glory" show sparked a national controversy, including demonstrations by thousands of protesters demanding that the show be closed, even though many of the 80 works actually celebrated patriotism in traditional art forms. Despite intense political and community pressure, the museum's director James Ballinger refused to bow to censorship and the exhibit successfully completed its run (Ayres, 1996).

Reminiscent of the Vietnam War era, when citizens were arrested and prosecuted for altering the flag, recent flag alterations similarly have been subjected to repression (see *Koser*, 1993). In 1990, law enforcement officer Jim Sevey was serving a search and arrest warrant (to locate stolen property) on Robert Jimenez in Midland, Texas. While inside the Jimenez residence, Sevey discovered two U.S. flags and two Texas state flags displayed the walls. The flags had been damaged and defaced by obscene writings: on one of the U.S. flags, "Eat Shit" and "Fuck the World" were scrawled along with a pentagram and an inverted cross. The other American flag was defaced with spray-painted initials. One of the Texas state flags had the names "Timothy Dale," "Bobby Jimenez," and "Steve" written on it, along with the words "Hell Awaits," "Suicidal," and a circled letter "A"— which prompted Sevey to observe, "Based on my training and experience, I believed [it] to be the symbol for anarchy (Affidavit of probable cause, trial court No. 52,379, Midland Co., Tx). Officer Sevey charged Jimenez with destruction of a flag, in violation of Section 42.14, Texas Penal Code (*State v. Jimenez*, 1992). At trial, the court cited *Eichman* in ruling that the state statute prohibiting the destruction of a flag was unconstitutional and dismissed the charges against Jimenez.

In a similar example of police intrusion, Pennsylvania State Trooper Brian Travis entered the apartment of Dawn Bricker armed with a traffic warrant for her arrest in 1993. While inside her apartment, Travis noticed a large U.S. flag on the floor. Because the flag was dirty, wrinkled, and had several pairs of shoes on top of it, Travis charged Bricker with desecrating the flag under the Pennsylvania flag-protection law. At her trial, Bricker denied the Commonwealth's claim that she placed the flag on the floor as a doormat. She also denied that the flag's location on the floor was part of any protest or because she was "mad about anything America was doing. . . . It was a decoration for people to see whenever they came in" (*Commonwealth of Pennsylvania v. Bricker*, 1995:3). At trial, the state prevailed: Bricker was convicted under the Pennsylvania state statute prohibiting flag desecration. She appealed, arguing that the state law was an unconstitutional restraint on the First Amendment right to freedom of speech. The Supreme Court of Pennsylvania concurred, reversing her conviction.

Formal and Informal Social Control

Formal mechanisms of social control intended to dictate the *proper* way to display the flag have been embodied in statutes created by legislators, enforced by police powers, prosecuted by the state, and sanctioned by the courts. Although those laws have been invalidated, the post-*Eichman* era continues to feature incidents in which state authorities have taken formal steps to regulate flag use and penalize its misuse. In Courtland, Ohio, Tracy McLellan was arrested for theft, disorderly conduct, criminal trespass, and flag desecration in 1991. Police apprehended McLellan during an incident in which he stripped a church flagpole of its Stars and Stripes and attempted to burn it after dousing it with gasoline. Despite the blatant constitutional violations of punishing an act of flag desecration, McLellan was sentenced to 14 days behind bars (*Warren (Ohio) Tribune-Chronicle*, July 11, 1991). Also in 1991, Mark Cox was convicted of "insult" to the flag for allegedly tearing down three flags from a bridge display and tossing them into a creek amid a heated quarrel with his fiancee in Youngsville, Pennsylvania. In addition to a $500 dollar fine and a jail term of nine to 23-and-a-half months, Judge Robert Wolfe ordered Cox to undergo alcohol counseling and to write a book report on *The Man Without a Country*, a story by Edward Everett Hale (1863) chronicling a man who spends his life at sea after being banished from America. Wolfe said he would review the essay to determine if the exercise "rehabilitates your attitude toward the flag" (*Commonwealth of PA. v. Cox*, 1991). Cox's mother responded bitterly: "It's not right. There's murderers, there's rapers that are out, then there's Mark. I wonder about that" (*Patriot News*, 1991:A-1).

Unlike formal mechanisms of social control, however, informal measures are not officially sanctioned by the state or any other recognized authority. Still, informal retribution in the form of vigilantism is at times more effective than formal sanctions in punishing flag desecration. Months after the *Johnson* ruling in 1989, Grant Speery, a college student in Salt Lake City, was assaulted when Dale H. Osborne, a Vietnam war veteran, unlawfully entered Speery's home. Osborne approached Speery after seeing a newspaper photograph of him burning the flag to protest politicians who wrapped themselves in the flag. Speery gave this account of the assault: "I was sitting in my kitchen talking with some friends when I saw this middle-aged man walk into the back door. He asked me if I was the person who burned the flag." Osborne, a former prisoner of war, barked: "You should die for what you did." Osborne initiated a scuffle, but Speery refused to fight back. Later the police arrived and discovered that Osborne was carrying a concealed and loaded .38-caliber revolver. Osborne was charged with possession of a deadly weapon with the intent to assault, a misdemeanor punishable up to a year in jail (*New York Times*, 1989:15).

On Independence Day 1989, Steven Bruce Dwares suffered serious injuries when beaten by neo-Nazi "skinheads" who repeatedly hit him about the head with a bottle after he verbally supported other protestors who torched the flag in Washington Square Park in New York City. Before unleashing a barrage of blows, the skinheads chanted: "Burn the flag and we'll burn a fag." The skinheads also denounced Abbie Hoffman as an "asshole" and said they would "fuck up anybody who burned the flag" (*Dwares v. City of New York*, 1993; Avni, 1989; Delgado, 1989). After being punched and chased for about 10 minutes by the "skinheads," Dwares finally escaped. With head and face bloodied, Dwares found refuge in a nearby Emergency Medical Services vehicle. The Dwares incident illustrates further that acts of informal social control occasionally transpire in the presence of law enforcement officers. In fact, Dwares filed a complaint alleging that his attacker, Kreitman, conspired with police officers, who allowed him and fellow "skinheads" to assault Dwares in an effort to prevent him from exercising his freedom of speech (*Dwares*, 1993:98).

CONCLUSION

Given the constitutionality of flag desecration, the post-*Eichman* era provides a distinct social context for studying various acts of expression and political dissent. Whereas external social events, such as war, create a context for resistance, dissenters themselves often produce internal themes, scripts, and vocabularies from their personal perceptions, interpretations, and consciousness. Sociologically, it is important that we recognize diverse forms of dissent and the plurality of forms of resistance (Foucault, 1980:95–96; also see Ewick and Silbey, 1992; Ferrell, 1995; Scott, 1990). Consider, for instance, Raymond Peterson, who in 1996 set fire to a flag at a Social Security office in Santa Cruz (California) as a protest over his benefits (CFA, 1998a). In 1995, a high school student in Betwyn, Illinois, burned a flag at his home and brought the remnants to school, where he displayed them in his locker. The student said he burned the flag to make a symbolic expression against slavery, the internment of Japanese-Americans during World War II, and other forms of discrimination (CFA, 1998a). In suburban Detroit, residents were perplexed after numerous flags were stolen and desecrated in 1996. Police believe it was the work of the same individual, who had identified himself in writings left at the scene of the crimes as the "Motor City Magic Man." Some of the flags have been recovered with a black "X" written across them (CFA, 1998a).

One of the more intriguing, though aesthetically vulgar, acts of flag desecration occurred in 1996 in Appleton, Wisconsin, where in a series of related incidents, more than 20 flags were stolen, burned, and defiled. At the Reid Municipal Golf Course, managers replaced a stolen flag. Soon the replacement flag was discovered missing and later located in the clubhouse entrance soiled with human feces. The flag was cleaned and returned to its post but once again was captured by some unknown persons who left a note reading: "The Anarchist Platoon has invaded Appleton, and as long as you [the rich golf club members] put flags up, were (sic) going to burn them" (Pommer, 1998:4-A). After an extensive manhunt, local police apprehended 18-year-old Matthew Janssen, a punk rock band member and self-described anarchist who claimed his act of flag *defecation* was a form of government protest, denouncing the flag as a "symbol of oppression and hatred" (Pommer, 1998:4-A). Prosecutor Vincent Biskupic charged Janssen with theft and felony flag desecration under the Wisconsin flag-protection statute which includes penalties of up to two years in prison. Veterans quickly rallied behind the prosecutor. Bill Remter, past commander of V.F.W. Post 2778 wondered aloud "Why should anyone . . . go out and defecate on it [the flag]? Disrespect it?" (Jones, 1998:1). Janssen's lawyer Eugene Bartman said the case was not over whether defecating on a flag is acceptable or unacceptable: "This case is rather about the power of the government to punish people who express disrespect, in this case disrespect for the government's symbol" (Pommer, 1998:4-A). After much wrangling over the state's antidesecration law, passed in 1919, Outagamie County Circuit Judge John Des Jardins ruled the statute was unconstitutional. Still, Janssen was convicted on two misdemeanor counts of theft and sentenced to nine months in the county jail.

Janssen's flag defecation case sheds additional light on the plurality of resistance against authority, especially in view of its implications to phenomenological criminology. In *Seductions of Crime: Moral and Sensual Attractions of Doing Crime* (1988), sociologist Jack Katz offers a phenomenological interpretation of crime and suggests that many minor offenses, such as theft and vandalism, are merely sneaky thrills. Indeed, punk rocker Matthew Janssen and his friends not only snubbed their noses at authority, but their antics produced for them a certain excitement and adventure as they participated in a *game* of "capture the flag." The particular elements of flag defecation deserve further phenomenological consideration. Katz informs us that occasionally victims of burglary return to find human feces scattered in their homes; the burglar not only leaves behind evidence of intrusion but also a physical and moral stain on the victim's habitation. At a higher level of abstraction, flag defecation goes beyond an act of desecrating a venerated object. Janssen's vulgarity also represents a symbolic attempt to pollute a sacred symbol. Sneaky thrills create euphoria for vandals, thieves, and desecrators, especially when their *offenses* produce intense negative societal reaction in the form of moral outrage and panic.

NOTE

1. Judge Patricia Cleary has often been controversial in her 10 years on the bench. In one incident, she taped shut the mouth of a defendant who was talking back to her. Even more alarming, Cleary sentenced 21-year-old Yuriko Kawaguchi to six months in jail for credit card fraud in a deliberate effort to keep her detained

so that she could not seek an abortion. Cleary had suggested to Kawaguchi that she might be granted probation if she would agree to give birth and put the child up for adoption. When Kawaguchi's lawyer Linda Rocker asked for clarification, Cleary snapped: "I'm saying that she is not having a second-term abortion" (Howlett, 1998:3-A). Rocker and the ACLU said they may push for civil rights charges against Cleary.

1932

GERMANY

1989

U.S.A.

"Whoever publicly profanes the Reich or one of the states incorporated into it, its Constitution, colors or flag or the German armed forces, or maliciously and with premeditation exposes them to contempt, shall be punished by imprisonment."

December 19, 1932, RGB I-I,
Statutory Criminal Law of Germany

"The Congress and the States shall have the power to prohibit the act of desecration of the flag of the United States and to set criminal penalties for that act."

June 22, 1989, H.J. Res. 305
Proposed Amendment to the U.S. Constitution

Figure 1. "1932 GERMANY . . . 1989 U.S.A." ("What's All This Flag Furor." 1989. Emergency Committee to Stop the Flag Amendment and Laws, New York, New York. Reprinted with permission).

Figure 2. "The Politics of Creation" painting by Ron English (Copyright Ron English 1990. Reprinted with permission).

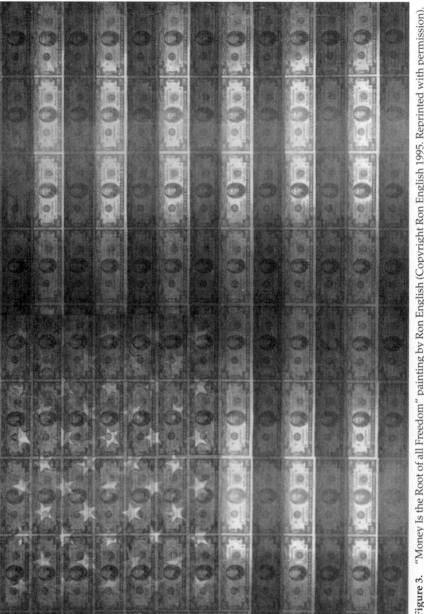

Figure 3. "Money Is the Root of all Freedom" painting by Ron English (Copyright Ron English 1995. Reprinted with permission).

Figure 4. "Piggy Bank" by Ron English on display at the Jesse Helms' Degenerate Art Show at the Black and White Gallery, South Bronx, NY, 1989, curated by Ron English and Shawn Eichman. The pig was stuffed with grant money received from the National Endowment of the Arts (NEA). (Copyright Ron English 1989. Reprinted with permission).

Figure 5. Billboard flag art illegally displayed by Ron English in Austin, Texas (Copyright Ron English 1986. Reprinted with permission).

Figure 6. "Home of the Homeless" placard by Ron English displayed at a protest against censorship at the Statue of Liberty in 1989 (Copyright Ron English 1989. Reprinted with permission).

Figure 7. Rally protesting censorship in New York City in 1989. Among those included in the photograph: Norman Siegel of the New York Civil Liberties Union, poet Allen Ginsberg, and artist Ron English (holding "Piss Helms" sign) (Copyright Ron English 1989. Reprinted with permission).

Figure 8. "What Is the Proper Way to Display a U.S. Flag?" by Dread Scott on display at the School of the Art Institute, Chicago, 1989 (detail of photomontage accompanying Scott's installation for audience participation) (Copyright Dread Scott 1988. Reprinted with permission).

Figure 9. "What Is the Proper Way to Display a U.S. Flag?" by Dread Scott on display at the School of the Art Institute, Chicago, 1989 (installation for audience participation). (Copyright Dread Scott 1988. Reprinted with permission).

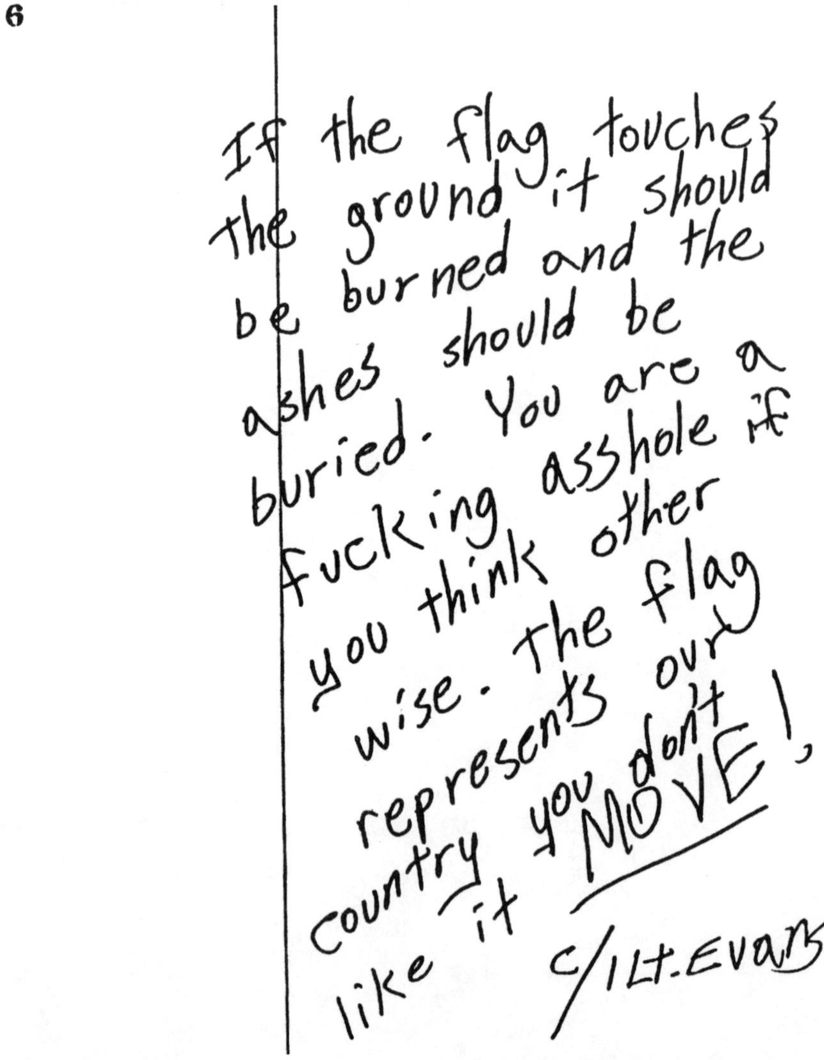
6

If the flag touches the ground it should be burned and the ashes should be buried. You are a fucking asshole if you think otherwise. The flag represents our country if you don't like it MOVE!,

c/1Lt. Evans

Figure 10. Visitors' inscriptions written in the ledger book accompanying "What Is the Proper Way to Display a U.S. Flag" on display at the School of the Art Institute, Chicago, 1989 (Copyright Dread Scott 1989. Reprinted with permission).

3/5 This is becoming an issue of technicalities
Damage of property.
Symbols have become more important
than the issues they stand for.

Does not the flag stand for
freedom of expression?

This smacks of McCarthyism.

3/5
TO MANY PEOPLE HAVE GIVEN THERE
LIVES TO MAKE THIS COUNTRY FREE
THIS IS NOT THE PROPER WAY TO
DISPLAY THE FLAG! IT SHOULD BE
HELD HIGH!

3/5 Shep says you suck shit

3/5 AFTER 2 YEAR 7mo in A Cage I Agree
With my Brother Shep you go Fuck
Your Self   J.W.

3/5 J W said it all Dick R

3/5 I Agear with ABove RA

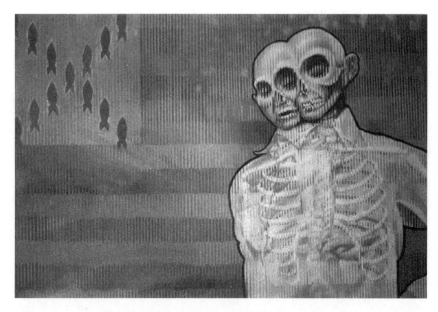

Figure 11. "X-Ray" painting by Ron English (Copyright, Ron English, 1989. Reprinted with permission).

III

Moral Panic Over Flag Desecration

7

Moral Panic and the Social Construction of Flag Desecration

Drugs, crime, and pornography debase our society to an extent that no one would have predicted just two generations ago. . . . There are no limits. Anything goes. . . . We have no monarchy, no state religion, no elite class—hereditary or otherwise representing the Nation and its unity. We have the flag. . . . The American flag forms a unique, common bond among us
—*Senator Orrin Hatch (CR, 1995:S18039-40, S18043, S18282).*

In our neighborhood, we haven't actually had a big flag-burning problem, but there must be places around the country where flag-burning is a menace
—*Humorist Calvin Trillin (1989:6).*

Moral panic has armed sociologists with a potent concept in their efforts to elucidate deviance, social problems, collective behavior, and social movements. Whereas Jock Young is credited with the first use of the term in 1971, the idea of moral panic developed rapidly in the work of Stanley Cohen, who offered its enduring definition. Moral panic has occurred when "A condition, episode, person or group of persons emerges to become defined as a threat to societal values and interest; its nature is presented in a stylized and stereotypical fashion by the mass media; the moral barricades are manned by editors, bishops, politicians, and other right-thinking people" (Cohen, 1972:9). Cohen realized that moral panic was a key component of a moral crusade, an enterprise he discovered while studying societal reaction to youths in England. In his ground-breaking treatise, *Folk Devils and Moral Panics* (1972), Cohen explored the roles of the media and state managers in constructing heightened concern over British youths in the 1964 when the Mods and Rockers were depicted as threats to public peace as well as the social order. Together, the media and members of the political establishment publicized exaggerated claims of the dangers posed by the Mods and Rockers; in turn, such claims were used to justify enhanced police powers and greater investment in the traditional criminal justice apparatus. Since the 1970s, the concept of moral panic has enjoyed growing popularity among sociologists studying the social construction of deviance and crime.[1]

The term moral panic adds considerable weight to this analysis of the flag-desecration phenomenon, especially in light of the defining influence of civil religion. Indeed, a common denominator linking moral panic to civil religion is their shared emphasis on morality, a construct distinguishing right from wrong and good from evil. The purpose of this chapter is to elaborate on moral panic as it pertains to civil religion and the furor over flag desecration, thus developing a theoretical and conceptual framework. In doing so, we shall attend to the criteria of moral panic, the cast of characters in the drama of moral panic, and the four territories of moral panic: deviance, social problems, collective behavior, and social movements. Borrowing from three perspectives of moral panic—the grassroots, interest-group, and elite-engineered models—an eclectic theory is introduced to explain flag desecration as a complex social phenomenon.

CRITERIA OF MORAL PANIC

Moral panic is a sociological concept resting on five prominent social indicators: concern, hostility, consensus, disproportionality, and volatility (Goode and Ben-Yehuda, 1994). In this segment, each of these elements is presented as it relates to the flag-burning controversy, especially in the late 1980s.

Concern

The first component of moral panic is a heightened concern over the behavior of others and the perceived consequences of such conduct on society. Sociologists insist that concern ought to be verifiable in the form of an observed and measurable manifestation (Cohen, 1972; Goode and Ben-Yehuda, 1994; Welch, Fenwick, and Roberts, 1997). The preoccupation with flag burning in the late 1980s provides evidence of moral panic. Public opinion polls showed that citizens were increasingly concerned for the Stars and Stripes and even supported legislation to protect it from desecration. In a national poll conducted shortly after the *Johnson* ruling in 1989, 65 percent of Americans disagreed with the high court and 71 percent supported a constitutional amendment to protect Old Glory as a strategy to undermine the court's decision (*Newsweek*, July 3, 1989). Similarly, a *New York Times*/CBS News poll found that 83 percent of its respondents believed that flag burning should be against the law and 59 percent of those polled endorsed a constitutional amendment (Greenhouse, 1990:B7). Media attention directed at flag burning exploded, resulting in unprecedented levels of news coverage (see Chapter 9). Moral panic over flag burning also was manifested in political debate, culminating in extensive and expensive congressional activity leading to additional laws and penalties designed to punish and deter flag desecration (see Chapter 8). As found throughout this analysis, many supporters of flag protection found refuge in civil religion in putting moral panic in context. Indeed, conservative columnist Cal Thomas likened the *Johnson* decision to "protecting pornography" that "inspires serial killers," "tolerance of marijuana," which had "paved the way for crack cocaine," and even to Elvis Presley, who had "opened the door through which heavy metal and garbage-mouth groups walked" (*New York Daily News*, August 12, 1989: 55).

Hostility

Moral panic also arouses hostility toward an identifiable group or category of people who, in turn, are vilified as social outcasts. Protesters who burn the flag are quickly labeled enemies of respectable society and their conduct is viewed widely as offensive to the majority of Americans who revere the national emblem. Even the *idea* of flag desecration—let alone the act—draws the ire of many patriotic Americans. As mentioned previously, during the "hard hat" demonstrations in 1970, one "hard hat" told a reporter that he would kill his own son with "no compunction" if he "ripped the flag", since flag desecration was "the worst thing" antiwar protestors had ever done (Bogart, 1970: A1). Under certain circumstances, such hostility goes beyond the rhetoric of aggression, manifesting itself in violence and victimization of flag desecrators. Also recall the incidents in which flag burner Grant Speery was beaten in his home by an intruder and Steven Dwares was attacked by neo-Nazi skinheads. Both incidents, occurring in 1989, show the extent to which vigilante justice is driven by intense hostility toward persons who desecrate the Old Glory. In an op-ed article published in *USA Today*, novelist Jesse Hill Ford wrote:

> The current crop of misfits who go schlepping about our streets thinking up new ways and ingenious ways to insult the flag deserve to be arrested, fined and locked up. If handed the key, I will personally throw it away. And believe me, I'm not alone.
>
> A pox on such punks. Who needs them? Are they the living embodiment of free speech? Flag burners deserve to have their heads broken. Prison is simply too good for them, let it be remembered that just because a man is in prison is no reason to assume that he doesn't love his country, too, and revere and respect his flag. But a flag desecrator? There is nothing lower, nothing more disgusting, nothing more insulting and dishonorable—and we must not condone such impiety—not now, not ever. (1989:10A)

Occasionally, vigilante justice is condoned not only by citizens but state managers as well. Consider Pennsylvania's "beat a flag burner" bill in which a fine of one dollar would have replaced the existing penalties of assault and aggravated assault (a 10-year maximum prison sentence and a fine of $25,000). Although the Pennsylvania resolution failed, similar proposals were introduced—albeit unsuccessfully—in Colorado, Georgia, and Tennessee; still, the Louisiana "beat a flag burner" bill passed the House by a 54-39 vote in 1990. The Louisiana measure proposed to lower to $25 the fine for assaulting flag burners, the existing penalty for simple assault is a $500 fine (*New York Times*, July 13, 1990:A-22; *New York Newsday*, 1989, December 16).

In Romeoville, Illinois, municipal leaders passed unanimously their version of a "beat a flag burner" bill, whereby violators would be fined one dollar for physically attacking a flag burner. The measure, however, was repealed when the ACLU threatened to challenge it. "It is outrageous vigilantism, something you wouldn't expect to see in an American city. . . . Romeoville is putting itself in the position of encouraging violence against those who are exercising their right of free speech" said Jay Miller of the ACLU (Zabell, 1990a:13). Mayor John Strobbe defended the resolution, adding that as a kid "if someone burned the flag, you beat the hell out them" (Zabell, 1990a:13). The police chief of Romeoville, Robert Starke, reported that if he saw anyone burning the flag, he would first, "ask them to put it [the flag] down," then try to "grab it away"; if these two efforts failed, "I'd punch them" (Zabell, 1990b:7). Similarly, Trustee Frank Valderrama announced that flag burners be given "a one-way ticket out of this country, never to return" (Zabell 1990b:7). Hostility toward flag desecrators is found in other public statements by political leaders. Miami Beach Mayor Daoud announced, "People who burn the flag should be shot" (*Miami Herald*, July 3, 1989: 1B). Likewise, Louisiana state representative Frank Patti advocated violence along with ostracizing such offenders: "If I saw somebody burning the flag, I would stomp the hell out of him" and "they ought to be deported" (*New Orleans Times-Picayune*, May 29, 1990). What is remarkable about these forms of legislation is that they mark a distinct attempt by state managers to merge formal and informal measures of social control (Welch, 1992; Welch and Bryan, 1998).

Hostility is the product of a dichotomizing process whereby folk devils are distinguished from folk heroes in a morality play of evil versus good (Cohen, 1972; Katz, 1988). Indeed, hostility directed at flag-desecrating villains typically is rationalized by self-righteous, flag-waving Americans who see themselves as good, decent people. Consider the sermon-like quality of a 1989 speech by Pat Buchanan who denounced flag desecration as "moral pollution." Blending moral panic with civil religion, Buchanan justified the use of force in dealing with flag desecrators: "When someone spits in your mother's face, you don't sit them down and 'persuade them they are wrong.' You put a fist in their face. . . . To honor one's parents, to love one's country, to cherish one's flag—these are not options; they are mandated for all men for all time" (1989:31).

Consensus

In becoming a recognizable phenomenon, moral panic requires a certain degree of consensus among members of society. By no means does such agreement need to be universal, or even representative of the majority. Still, there must be a widespread belief that the problem at hand is real, it poses a threat to society, and something should be done to correct it. Patriotism, especially channeled through civil religion, is a deeply shared value among most Americans, and acts deemed disrespectful to the nation's most cherished emblem are viewed commonly as un-American. There is considerable agreement that protestors who torch the flag are seen as different from the rest of society. Even citizens who harbor serious criticisms of the U.S. government generally are unwilling to express their dissent by desecrating Old Glory. As noted previously, public opinion polls serve as persuasive evidence that the vast majority of Americans view flag desecration as a social problem that ought to be remedied by legislation and punishment. Legislative advocates often refer to consensus in describing the putative threat of flag desecration; and in doing so, American society is personified as a *community* with shared values. Testifying in a congressional hearing, Stephen Presser, a Northwestern University law professor, voiced strong support for a constitutional amendment to protect the flag, explaining that such a measure would allow Americans to establish a "baseline of decency, civility, responsibility and order . . . to reconstruct a dangerously fractured sense of community" (*CR*, 1995:S8297). In similar testimony on flag desecration and moral decline, Ken Hamblin criticized liberals who opposed the flag amendment, charging that they were responsible for a "corrosive impact" on "American morality and the principles of basic decency and respect" (*CR*, 1995:S8297).

Disproportionality

Another key element of moral panic is its disproportionality, meaning that the perceived danger is greater than the potential harm. Perhaps by any reasonable circumspection of the flag-burning controversy in 1989, one could conclude that the public anxiety over the issue was excessive. First and foremost, it is crucial to acknowledge that the flag issue is symbolic rather than substantive. Compare the degree of concern over flag desecration with other substantive social problems (poverty, homelessness, inadequate education, inaccessible health care), and the extent of the disproportion is evident.

From an empirical standpoint, concern over the fate of the flag materialized into costly political resources expended in legislation, litigation, and prosecution of violators. During the twelve months between the *Johnson* and *Eichman* decisions, Congress was consumed by the debate over flag protection, taking more time for it than for any other issue. Congress devoted more than 100 hours of floor debate and approximately two weeks of public legislative hearings; lawmakers and their staffs spent thousands of hours in meetings deliberating over the fate of the flag. These activities were entered into the *Congressional Record*, exceeding more than 400 pages at an average cost of $500 per page; in addition, fifteen hundred pages of hearings also were published by U.S. government printing (*CR*, 1990: S8685; see Chapter 8). Remember, those protracted legislative exercises occurred *after* the *Johnson* ruling in 1989; hence, many more costs were accrued after 1984, when Johnson was arrested. In the five years to follow, the defendant would make his way through ascending levels of prosecution and appeal, finally reaching the U.S. Supreme Court. In its wake, *Johnson* generated thousands of pages of trial transcripts, court rulings, and legal briefs, becoming "one of the most expensive legal disputes of all time (Goldstein, 1996a:viii). In the previous chapter we learned that the Elk Grove School District in California spent more than $80,000 in litigation to keep students from displaying their mural, which included a flag-burning scene (Camposeco and Rocha, 1994). Critics of moral panic over flag desecration insist that scarce government resources should have been allocated to the resolution of substantive social problems rather than a mere symbolic one (Goldstein, 1996a; Welch and Bryan, 1998).

Hyperbole over the presumed harmful nature of flag burning exemplifies moral panic; indeed, much of the flag-protection rhetoric serves as tangible evidence that the issue was blown out of proportion. Comparisons of flag burning to violent and truly despicable crimes are examples of how the phenomenon is exaggerated, hyped, and, in the words of Cohen (1972), "stylized." In his dissent in *Johnson*, Chief Justice Rehnquist compared flag burning to murder, and in a similar vein U.S. Solicitor General Kenneth Starr drew parallels between flag burning and child pornography (Oral Arguments before the U.S. Supreme Court, May 4, 1990, in the consolidated case of *U.S. v. Eichman* and *U.S. v. Haggerty*, Nos. 89-1433, and 89-1434). In another popular exaggeration driving moral panic over flag desecration, Representative Ron Marlene characterized the U.S. Supreme Court ruling in *Johnson* as "treasonous" (*CR*, 1989:H3009).

Perhaps the most strained interpretation of flag burning was delivered by state prosecuting attorney Robert Huttash, who supported the Texas flag-protection law, believing fervently in its constitutionality. In filing the state's petition to have the criminal appeals court reconsider its decision in *Johnson*, Huttash contended, "We saw little difference between this law and forbidding Lee Harvey Oswald from shooting President Kennedy to express a political opinion" (Goldstein, 1996a:67). Huttash insisted that the Texas venerated-objects statute was "no more narrowly directed against speech than laws against political assassination, criminal conspiracy, murder, kidnapping, arson and the like, insofar as a person in committing these offenses, also desires to communicate a message." Huttash's preoccupation with presidential assassination continued as he argued that Johnson was not prevented from expressing a political message in other ways, "just as John Wilkes Booth could have expressed his anger against President Lincoln without assassinating him" (Goldstein, 1996a:68). In rationalizing an emotional and visceral response to flag desecration, Huttash's so-called expert remarks escalated moral panic by offering a seemingly plausible theory of law, despite their tortured analogies.

Volatility

In the late 1980s, the flag-burning controversy exploded onto the national scene with blistering intensity as the media and politicians riveted their attention to a Texas case granted an appeal by the U.S. Supreme Court. Although the high court reviewed *Texas v. Johnson*, in 1989, the actual flag-burning incident occurred five years previously at the Republican National Convention in Dallas. The element of volatility suggests that moral panic erupts suddenly even though the issue may have existed for some time. The involvement of the U.S. Supreme Court served to legitimize the issue; further, that major development, compounded by the interest generated by the media and politicians, spurred enormous public anxiety over flag burning. As measured by the extent of media and political attention, the flag-burning phenomenon was more volatile on a larger scale in the late 1980s than in previous historical periods, including the First and Second World Wars and Vietnam War.

Volatility also implies that interest in the putative threat is subject to rapid decline; this feature of moral panic certainly is evident in the contemporary flag-burning controversy. In the summer of 1989, the flag-desecration issue, in the words of a Washington reporter, was "hot as a magnesium flare" but in less than a year, it had become "politically lukewarm" (Goldstein, 1996a: 334). Representative Dennis Eckart, who enthusiastically supported the flag-protection amendment in 1989 conceded that public attention in 1990 was fading: "There is nowhere near the [mail] volume as there was . . . a year ago." Sharing a similar viewpoint, an unnamed Republican source admitted: "This is an issue whose time has come and gone" (Kenworthy, 1990: A14). Whereas the campaign to protect the Stars and Stripes by amending the U.S. Constitution continues to linger in Congress, the issue no longer consumes the media or political institutions as it once did. Simply put, moral panic over the flag has waned along with its volatility.

To reiterate its interconnected criteria (concern, hostility, consensus, disproportion, and volatility), moral panic "locates a 'folk devil,' is shared, is out of synch with the measurable seriousness of the condition that generates it, and varies in intensity over time" (Goode and Ben-Yehuda, 1994:41). Based on our assessment, the flag-burning controversy of the late 1980s undoubtedly conforms to the classic features of moral panic. Still, an in-depth understanding of moral panic requires an examination of its chief actors and institutions.

THE CAST OF CHARACTERS IN THE DRAMA OF MORAL PANIC

Moral panics are complex expressions of fear and anxiety produced by the activities of several formal organizations and their influential players, including the media, the public, agents of social control, lawmakers, politicians, and lobbyists committed to social action (Cohen, 1972; Goode and Ben-Yehuda, 1994). In concert, these participants are the principals in the development of moral panic. To illuminate their particular roles in the social construction process, this section introduces the main characters and their distinct contributions to the reification of flag desecration.

The Media

The media are story-telling institutions geared toward informing and entertaining the audience. Whereas news and entertainment are viewed superficially as separate activities, the lines of demarcation are commonly blurred, thereby producing a form of communication known derisively as infotainment (Bailey and Hale, 1998; Barak, 1994; Fishman and Cavender, 1998; Potter and Kappeler, 1998; Surette, 1998; Welch, Fenwick, and Roberts, 1997). Whereas some examples of infotainment are easily recognized (e.g., television cop shows featuring pursuit-and-arrest footage), other forms of infotainment mask the overtly entertaining elements of programming under the guise of earnest journalism. Media coverage of the flag-desecration controversy of the late 1980s established a serious tone found typically in news programming; still, key components of story telling were evident as the flag-burning furor unfolded according to the standard formula of drama: good versus evil, virtue versus vice, order versus chaos, and heroes versus villains. Adoration for Old Glory was pitted against the reckless iconoclasm of flag desecration, as American patriots committed to nationalism battled political dissidents bent on destroying the country. The tremendous power of the media contributed to the controversy over the Stars and Stripes insofar as the threat of flag desecration was reified, magnified, and exaggerated; in turn, news coverage incited enormous public concern and was used to justify the investment of political resources. The media and their role in the social construction of flag burning are elaborated further in Chapter 9.

The Public

Moral panics are manifestations of a deeper societal concern, and this latent anxiety commonly is unleashed by heightened media attention to a particular social issue—in a manner of speaking, the media hit a public nerve. As in the case of other moral panics, the actual events of flag desecration are not as significant as what they seem to represent (Cohen, 1972; Goode and Ben-Yehuda, 1994). Public reactions to disrespect or desecration of Old Glory go beyond a regard for the nation's most cherished emblem; indeed, such acts are commonly interpreted as threats to American society and culture. Juanita Davis, a retired teacher, said: "People who desecrate the flag show a malicious intent toward our country. We have to bring back respect for the country. And that's all embodied in respect for the flag" (*USA Today*, March 22, 1989:10A). Similarly, Carl von Badinski, member of the Yermo California school board, insisted: "I would fire any teacher who doesn't salute the flag" (*USA Today*, March 22, 1989:10A).

Again, civil religion plays an integral role in defining the putative problem of flag desecration. Acts of antipatriotism were repeatedly interpreted as sacrilegious and as symptoms of deeper moral decline by moral entrepreneurs and politicians during the Reagan and Bush eras. Recall Congressman Applegate's hysterical reaction to the U.S. Supreme Court's ruling in *Johnson*: "What is God's name is going on? . . . Are they going to allow fornication in Times Square at high noon?" (*CR*, June 22, 1989:H3002-04). In a seemingly more populist vein, President Bush declared that flag burning "endangers the fabric of our country" (*Public Papers of the Presidents of the United States*, June 12, 1990:812).

Agents of Social Control

Members of the social-control apparatus, or rule enforcers, play a vital role in the production of moral panics; moreover, their involvement becomes increasingly self-serving, given that their host institutions benefit from enhanced power, authority, and prestige. Law-enforcement campaigns thrive tremendously during moral panics in large part because they are rewarded with greater funding and resources (Hall, et al., 1978; Welch,

Fenwick, and Roberts, 1997). Especially during periods of intense political dissent—for example, World War I and the Vietnam War—the U.S. law-enforcement establishment wielded considerable authority in regulating public protest, particularly in situations in which flags were burned. Correspondingly, police, prosecutors, and judges were granted wide discretion in their efforts to enforce flag-protection statutes, including arresting citizens who altered the flag or accessorized their apparel with flag patches.

Law-enforcement campaigns against those who violate the authoritarian aesthetic by desecrating the flag are bolstered further by another aspect of moral panic—that is, police are encouraged to prevent minor breaches of the peace presumed to have the potential to escalate into large-scale public disorder if left unchecked. Consequently, rule enforcers are given credit—albeit falsely—for maintaining social order in the face of moral panic, an attribution that empowers further the law-enforcement establishment. According to Goode and Ben-Yehuda (1994:27): "The thinking among agents of social control is that 'new situations need new remedies'; a national problem called for a drastic solution, and often, this entailed suspending rights and liberties previously enjoyed" (also see Cohen, 1972). In 1989, Solicitor General Kenneth Starr recommended that the U.S. Supreme Court reconsider its ruling in *Johnson*, arguing that flag burning ought not be viewed as expression protected by First Amendment freedoms. Rather, according to Starr, flag burning is "physical destruction" of a flag "uniquely anathema to the Nation's values" and constituting a "physical, violent assault on the most deeply shared experiences of the American people" (Brief for the United States, in the Supreme Court of the United States, *U.S. v. Eichman*, Nos. 89-1433 and 891434, October Term, 1989).

Lawmakers and Politicians

Rule enforcers are linked systemically to another type of moral entrepreneur, the rule creator. Specifically, lawmakers, politicians, and other inside players involved in the legislation process provide the legal justification for law-enforcement campaigns. Through legislation, rule creators legitimize authority whereby the state increases its power to monitor and regulate the conduct of its citizens. Anti–flag-desecration laws not only intend to protect Old Glory by dispensing punishment, but in doing so they undergird the state's attempt to control political dissent, as unstated and antidemocratic as that agenda may be. Despite mounting pressure from the flag lobby, however, some legislators publicly opposed flag-protection laws, insisting that such legal remedies jeopardize fundamental freedoms. In 1995, Senator Charles S. Robb voted against a flag amendment. "The acid test of a democracy is whether or not we can speak out in peaceful dissent against our government without fear of being arrested, or prosecuted, or punished. . . . And it is precisely those circumstances where the freedom that the flag represents—the basic democracy of this country" (Robb, 1995:1).

Still, many lawmakers who privately resisted flag-protection measures quietly boarded the bandwagon for purposes of securing political cover. Those politicians feared being denounced as unpatriotic and reluctantly voted in favor of proposals for flag statutes and amendments. Indeed, the fear of being stigmatized as unpatriotic serves a compelling function for social control, a form of repression that could hardly survive outside moral panic. As a result, the status quo is reproduced partly because moral panic inhibits the voices of dissent. Looking ahead to Chapter 8, moral entrepreneurs and state managers serve roles vital to the social construction of crime and the criminalizing of protest.

Action Groups

In response to latent anxiety that America is losing ground, as suggested by a perception of waning patriotism, action groups set out to confront the putative threat of national decline. In doing so, formal organizations and their activism enhance and advance the flag-protection movement. During the 1890s, when the Stars and Stripes was being awarded special status, state flag-protection laws were formulated in response to intense lobbying from action groups, including the Sons of the American Revolution, the Daughters of the American Revolution, and the Grand Army of the Republic (Guenter, 1990; O'Leary, 1999). Similarly, the contemporary campaign to protect the flag was initiated and orchestrated by a modern flag lobby, the CFA, a coalition of patriotic organizations spearheaded by the American Legion. According to its mission statement:

> The Citizens Flag Alliance, Inc. is a coalition of organizations, most of which are national in scope, that have come together for one reason: to persuade the Congress of the United States to propose a constitutional amendment to protect the American flag from physical desecration, and send it to the states for ratification.
>
> More than 120 organizations make up the CFA, with collective membership around 20 million. Organized in every state, the individual membership in the CFA is near 20,000 people.
>
> Membership is open to fraternal, ethnic, civic, veteran organizations, corporations, and businesses by application. There is no fee to belong, but it is expected that member organizations would have the endorsement of their governing body; would promote a flag protection amendment among their members and the general public; would allow the publication of their name as a member organization of the CFA; and, that they would participate in leg-

islative activities and grassroots lobbying of The Citizens Flag Alliance, Inc. (CFA, 1998c, February 4)

Much like their predecessors, contemporary flag crusaders operate as moral entrepreneurs whose lobbying activities are inspired by civil religion coupled with a strong sense of authoritarian aesthetics. Indeed, the CFA proudly boasts its reverence to Old Glory in the following proclamation:

> The Citizens Flag Alliance believes the Flag of the United States of America is a national treasure. No statue, no monument, no document, no artifact says "America" so eloquently. No other symbol of our nation has led men and women into battle, been sanctified by the blood of patriots, and then draped—in honored glory—over the caskets of those who gave their last full measure of devotion.
>
> Desecrating the flag of our nation dishonors the memory of those who died defending it.
>
> The American flag represents all that unites us as one nation under God. The American flag is a constant reminder of the ideals we share. Because of its significance, we Americans have always provided our flag some measure of protection from abuse—preferring to hold it above domestic turmoil and political posturing. (CFA, 1998c, February 4)

As an action group, the CFA publicizes its effectiveness in lobbying state and federal legislators, where it has established a notable presence. At many legislative events, some political staffers contemptuously refer to CFA lobbyists as the "hat people" because they wear military hats accessorized with an assortment of patriotic pins and service medals. Projecting a sense of achievement, the CFA claims that their activities influenced 49 state legislatures to pass the Memorial Resolutions, which petitioned Congress to pass a flag-protection amendment and send it to the states for ratification. That number of states is eleven more than are needed to ratify a constitutional amendment; only Vermont has yet to pass a Memorial Resolution. Interestingly, the CFA presents itself less as a lobby than a grassroots movement. Suggesting a growing pool of supporters and resources, the CFA announced that more than three million people have signed petitions asking Congress to pass a flag-protection amendment, and reports that more than 200,000 people have donated money "because they believe in what we are doing, and more people are joining with us as individual citizens everyday" (CFA, 1997: 1).

Its so-called grassroots image is further promoted by the CFA, which states:

> More than 100 organizations, representing millions of Americans, have joined the Citizens Flag Alliance since it was incorporated in June 1994, and

the number of members is growing. This broad-based, single-purpose organization includes ethnic groups, community-based fraternal and veterans organizations, women's groups, businesses and many more. (CFA, 1998d,
February 4)

Despite its claim to be a grassroots movement, however, a huge portion of
CFA's funding stems from a single source, the American Legion, which donated more than $6 million to the coalition. Dan Wheeler, former editor of
the Legion's magazine, is president of the CFA, further evidence of the Legion's dominance. Furthermore, the CFA's initial board of directors was
stocked with high-ranking members of the Legion, and its original office
space was furnished by the Legion (Goldstein, 1996a).

In addition to the media, the public, agents of social control, lawmakers, politicians, and action groups, the drama of moral panic also features
the creation of *folk devils* and the invention of a *disaster mentality* (Cohen,
1972; Goode and Ben-Yehuda, 1994; Hall, et al., 1978). As representations
of evil, flag burners are vilified as folk devils; moreover, rebellious attacks
on Old Glory are construed as an ominous threat to American society and
culture, thus producing a disaster mentality. Civil religion complements
the demonization of flag burners, especially considering that the most visible iconoclasts during the 1980s were supporters of the RCP, depicted by
their detractors as godless enemies of the state. During that time, the shift
to the political right was predicated on the demonizing of communism and
the Soviet Union, which President Reagan referred to as the evil empire.
Indeed, civil religion was promoted fervently by the Christian Right, manifesting itself as a social movement that blends religion with politics and a
commitment to God and country.

Maintaining the moral tone of official condemnation, Chief Justice
Rehnquist demonized flag burners, referring to their protests as "inherently evil and profoundly offensive" (Dissenting opinion in *Texas v. Johnson*, 91, *United States Reports*, 436). A similar form of demonization—
combined with a disaster mentality—emerged during the prosecution of
flag burner Gary Deeds in 1970. Defense attorney Robert Alexander remembered that Deeds was vilified as a "pinko-commie-radical" who "was
going to destroy America." Alexander recalled being confronted by people
in his community who believed that flag desecration not only was "unpatriotic" but also "undermining the country, destroying the family, [and] an-
tireligion" (Goldstein, 1995:170).

TERRITORIES OF MORAL PANIC

Since its inception in the early 1970s, the concept of moral panic has
evolved tremendously, attracting scholarly attention from a wide range of

sociological specialties. Moral panic is a multidimensional construct marking the convergence of four conceptual territories: deviance, social problems, collective behavior, and social movements (Goode and Ben-Yehuda, 1994). The moral aspect of panic stems from conceptions of deviance defined as immoral conduct, thus prompting public concern. Taken a step further, such concern is elevated to a social problem as heightened attention amplifies its perceived seriousness. The volatile nature of the social problem, in turn, triggers collective behavior expressed outwardly as moral outrage. In search of a solution to the social problem, efforts are organized, resources are mobilized, and in the end, a social movement is born. In this section, the four territories of moral panic are discussed, especially as they bear on the flag-burning controversy beginning in the late 1980s.

Deviance, Morality, and Moral Entrepreneurs

The furor over flag burning in 1989 was predicated on notions of deviance filtered through the lens of morality, a construct that distinguishes between right and wrong. Not only is defacing or damaging Old Glory considered wrong by many Americans, but the prevailing reaction to flag desecration takes on a moral tone shaped by civil religion. Disrespecting the flag is known as desecration, thereby implying that the national emblem, an otherwise secular symbol, has been anointed with sacred status. In addition to being stigmatized as un-American, flag burners also are branded immoral and evil; conversely, efforts to shield the flag are hailed as patriotic, a trait imbued with morality and linked to the eternal good.

As a form of deviance, flag desecration draws unforgiving hostility and condemnation; moreover, deviant acts are interpreted as symbolic of a deeper and more despicable form of evil. Deviants are rarely viewed as mere individual violators of the established moral code; rather, they are depicted as belonging to a distinct category of outsiders. Flag burners typically are vilified for desecrating Old Glory *and* for being members of a radical political group (e.g., anarchists, communists, pacifists). Even in instances when a flag desecrator denies membership in any radical organization, suspicion lingers, making the demonization process virtually inescapable. That form of stereotyping streamlines the degradation process whereby protestors, regardless of how legitimate their criticism of government may be, are marginalized as deviants and threats to the social order. Compounding hostility, a chief aspect of moral panic is the denunciation of a particular group that is easy to identify and easy to dislike (Cohen, 1972; Goode and Ben-Yehuda, 1994). In his statements during congressional debate, Representative William Clinger demonized flag burners as "twisted lowlifes" and "pathetic individuals" who engaged in "cheap theatrics" and who are fighting for "sorry causes" (*CR*, 1995:H6433).

Citizens who fail to show proper deference to the flag are easily labeled as folk devils. Particularly during periods of national crisis, those people are made scapegoats, and panic aimed at folk devils diverts attention from the real source of social anxiety (e.g., a depressed economy, a war, a natural disaster) (Best, 1989, 1990). The victimizing of the Jehovah's Witnesses during the Second World War for refusing to salute the flag is a compelling example of scapegoating. As mentioned in previous chapters, many flag desecrators have been beaten by civilians and subjected to harsh treatment by criminal-justice officials. Victimization functions as informal social control intended to instill discipline and conformity among deviants; similarly, the spectacle serves as an emotional outlet whereby public frustrations are vented through spontaneous acts of scapegoating (Welch and Bryan, 1998).

Whereas informal measures of control persist in modern society, over the course of history they have been replaced increasingly by formal mechanisms. Durkheim (1933 [1964]) reminds us that in small societies, informal social control is considered sufficiently effective because personal identities are known publicly, making people susceptible to the pressures of the community's moral center, or collective conscience. In the end, informal social control inhibits deviant behavior and promotes conformity. As societies become larger and more complex, however, the collective conscience weakens as individuals enjoy greater anonymity. To deter deviance in a complex society, state managers must establish formal control whereby punishments are sanctioned officially in an official effort to preserve the social order. Criminal law, police, prosecutors, the courts, and prisons are all products of the shift from informal to formal social control. The formal approach to regulating deviance leads to the criminalizing of undesirable conduct, and precisely which behaviors are criminalized is subject to an array of social forces, most notably politics and morality (Schur, 1980).

It is presumed that criminal law is a reflection of society's moral code, and applying this notion to flag-protection statutes provides another glimpse of civil religion in the formulation of social control. Criminalization is an act of power that imposes a specific symbolic-moral universe on other universes (Ben-Yehuda, 1990; Goode and Ben-Yehuda, 1994; Schur, 1980). Statutes prohibiting flag desecration serve several key functions: first, they legitimize the civil-religious perspective of flag adoration; second, they symbolize the respectability of patriotic Americans; and third, they penalize members of one group for violating an aesthetic established by another.

Whereas civil religion is a cultural condition of American society, it man-

ifests itself in flag protection due to the concerted efforts of moral entrepreneurs. Becker (1963) examines two types of moral entrepreneurs, rule
creators and rule enforcers. Rule creators argue that existing legal codes are
insufficient to combat a persistent evil; therefore, they crusade for the development of additional forms of control. Operating on an absolute ethic,
rule creators impose their fervent self-righteousness onto legislation for
the purpose of stamping out a particular form of evil. Similarly, staunchly
patriotic Americans also hold self-righteous attitudes: recall, for example,
the "my country, right or wrong" sentiment espoused by the hard-hat protestors during the Vietnam War. Flag-desecration laws in many respects resemble formal measures prohibiting alcohol and drugs, insofar as moral
entrepreneurs depict violators as immoral and dangerous (Gusfield, 1963;
Reinarman and Levine, 1997). Still, Becker insists that moral crusaders
aren't simply promoting conformity for its own sake, but rather they believe ardently that their proposed laws are good for all citizens and society as a whole. State legislators echoed the values of flag enthusiasts by
arguing that government held an interest in protecting the flag because
such laws preserved the nation's symbol, which served a unifying purpose
(*Johnson*, 1989).

Rule creators realize that new laws are useless without sufficient enforcement; hence, the role of rule enforcers in the moral enterprise is vital.
Unlike rule creators, enforcers tend to be less self-righteous and exhibit a
more detached and pragmatic understanding of their tasks. The existence
of laws secures jobs for rule enforcers who know intuitively that they risk
their livelihood if they do not carry out their required duties (Becker, 1963).
In sum, moral entrepreneurs express moral panic by influencing legislation that creates new statutes and strengthens the formal social-control apparatus. Likewise, moral panics are maintained on several other fronts,
such as shaping public opinion and convincing other social institutions
that the cause needs their backing, or *moral* support. As part of flag-protection crusades, public-information campaigns alert citizens to the threat
of un-American activities; in fending off that form of evil, social institutions such as schools, and even sporting events, adopt patriotic rituals that
reinforce respect for Old Glory. Indeed, the organizational efforts of the
flag lobby are instrumental in nurturing moral panic into a full-fledged social movement.

Social Problems and Constructionism

The objectivist perspective, a major school of thought in the study of social problems, proposes that society's ills are easily detected since they in-
cur harm that can be verifiably assessed (Manis, 1974, 1976). As a rival to
the objectivist school, however, constructionism (or the subjectivist per-

spective) argues that social problems are the products of collective definitions, determining how issues are perceived by the public. According to
constructionists Spector and Kitsuse, social problems are "activities of individuals or groups making assertions of grievances and claims with respect to some putative conditions" (1977:75; Best, 1987, 1989; Schneider
and Kitsuse, 1984). The subjectivist perspective adds tremendously to our
understanding of the process by which flag desecration was socially constructed. First, the problem of flag desecration was created according to a
collective definition along with several claims-making activities. Second,
demands, particularly in the form of legislation, were put forth to remedy
the problem of flag desecration. Third, public opinion supported the perception that flag desecration was a social problem requiring formal measures of social control. Fourth, the media offered heightened attention to
those developments, thus amplifying moral panic over flag desecration,
contributing to its consensus, disproportionality, and volatility.

Although there is significant overlap between social problems and
moral panic there remain three distinct differences (Goode and Ben-
Yehuda, 1994). First, not all social problems include a folk devil: consider,
for example, an economic depression. Conversely, moral panic, is always
directed at a specific folk devil: a person or group whom moral entrepreneurs can blame and make into a scapegoat for society's troubles. Disproportion marks the second difference between social problems and moral
panic. As noted previously, a key criterion of moral panic is the discrep-
ancy between the degree of concern over the issue and the magnitude of
the putative threat; hence, *panic* stems from the process by which a danger
is blown out of proportion. Social problems, by contrast, do not always
provoke panic, and at times, experts caution against exaggeration so that
the precise nature of the problem can be ascertained, such as environmental issues. Again, moral panic implies volatility resulting in sharp fluctua-
tions of concern: simply put, moral panic *breaks out*. Such vacillation,
however, is not a defining element of social problems. Based on these considerations, the flag-desecration phenomenon of 1989 did not constitute a
bona fide social problem; rather it was manifested as moral panic containing folk devils along with a disproportionate degree of public concern that
changed over time.

Collective Behavior and Persecutions

As another territory of moral panic, collective behavior departs from
activities considered routine in society and involves conduct that is spontaneous, erratic, volatile, and short-lived (Goode, 1992). Collective behavior in 1989 ought to be distinguished from a social movement, which takes
on a more stable, patterned set of organizational objectives. Admittedly,

collective behavior may lead to a social movement, as is the case with flag-protection movements recurring at several points in American history. Collective behavior in the flag-desecration controversy is marked by an erratic and intense public outcry. Such hysteria often is accompanied by intense hostility directed at convenient scapegoats, or folk devils. The Kensington riots of 1844 erupted when Native American Party supporters attacked Irish immigrants, accused of being threats to American nativism and patriotism. The Kensington incident conforms to similar forms of collective behavior, culminating in the victimization of groups labeled un-American. Indeed, collective behavior imbued with hostility and aggression typically leads to the persecution of unpopular persons and groups.

Persecutions exhibit distinct moral tendencies that reproduce moral panic, especially since instigators embark on rabid crusades to root out evil; consider, for example, the witch-hunts of Renaissance Europe and McCarthyism in the United States in the 1950s (Levin, 1971; Rose, 1982). In the realm of flag protection, similar persecutions surfaced during the First and Second World Wars against pacifists and Jehovah's Witnesses, respectively. Likewise, in the post-*Eichman* era, protestors who burned the flag were beaten by skinheads in New York City's Washington Square Park, while other demonstrators were attacked by war veterans in Los Angeles. The persecution of flag desecrators, or even people who refuse to participate in compulsory flag adoration (e.g., Jehovah's Witnesses), exudes a distinct moral connotation shaped significantly by civil religion.

Social Movements and Special Interests

The final territory of moral panic encompasses social movements, an enterprise that harnesses the unbridled energy of the collective conscience and funnels it into organized, coordinated actions aimed at social change rather than merely persecuting undesirable groups. As a result of social movements, moral panic appears less erratic and more formalized. In previous chapters, we explored social movements committed, for instance, to antiwar activities. Here, it is important to note that those same dynamics transpire in other social movements as well, including the campaign to protect the flag. The flag-protection movement first and foremost expresses dissatisfaction with the way things are: specifically, flag crusaders claim that American patriotism is weak, leaving the country vulnerable to immoral and radical forces. Well-publicized incidents of flag burning are cited as evidence by the flag-protection movement to legitimize their claim of moral decline and national threat. To correct the putative problem of flag desecration, depicted as a symptom of larger unpatriotic forces, the flag-protection movement sets out to change society by lobbying lawmakers. As social movements infiltrate legislation, the values of interest, or pressure, groups become increasingly apparent (Useem and Zald, 1982).

When the flag-protection campaign crystallized in the late 1980s, it gained considerable momentum through the acquisition of resources and funds. Armed with the utensils of political influence, the CFA, a coalition functioning as an organ for the American Legion, executed well-planned maneuvers designed to maximize its access to the media, the public, and equally important, policy makers. Due to its persistence and keen organizational skills, the flag lobby emerged as a political insider, not only in Washington, D.C., but in state capitals across the nation where it exerted pressure to legislate against flag desecration.

Not all social movements or interest groups are driven by moral panic. Nevertheless, the flag-protection campaign and the flag lobby are classic examples of how moral panic is manifested in social activism; like all crusades, their activities stem from a basic premise, or claim. The flag lobby argues that flag desecration is wrong and harmful to American society. Further, flag enthusiasts believe that punishing and deterring acts of flag desecration will reverse the inferred decline of American patriotism, a message the flag lobby communicates to the public, the media, and government officials.

Sociologist Erich Goode (1969) insightfully noted that social movements engage in the *politics of reality*. Such activity is situated at the heart of the flag-protection campaign insofar as flag desecration is defined as a threat to American society: moreover, it is depicted as a problem that can be remedied by greater formal social control. To recapitulate, the flag lobby's claim and its proposed solution rest on views of flag desecration shaped enormously by moral panic. Still, the flag-protection movement ought not be interpreted independently of other territories of moral panic. Moral panic over flag desecration is a complex phenomenon that goes beyond a social movement; in fact, it stems from other sociological developments, most notably the social construction of deviance, social problems, and collective behavior. Despite the relevance of these conceptual considerations, we have yet to articulate a precise theory of moral panic, especially in light of the flag-burning controversy of 1989. With this concern in mind, we turn to the truly theoretical underpinnings of moral panic.

THEORIES OF MORAL PANIC

Sociological theories attempting to explain *why* moral panic is constructed must inevitably address the issue of motive; similarly, such frameworks also must *identify* those responsible for the creation of moral panic. Questions of motive typically deal with the benefits that certain people and groups earn from moral panic: whether it be the satisfaction of advancing their own morality, enhancing their power and status, or accruing something more tangible, such as jobs and economic resources. In terms of its

actors, it is important to determine whether moral panic is initiated by organizations at the grassroots level of society, by midrange special-interest
groups, or by high-level elitists (Goode and Ben-Yehuda, 1994). To begin
this theoretical development, we present three theories of moral panic, and
in assembling a framework to understand the flag-desecration phenomenon, an eclectic model borrowing from each theory is proposed.

Grassroots Model

According to the grassroots perspective, moral panic stems from deep-
seated anxieties spawning activities at the bottom rung of the social hierarchy, the masses. Certainly, moral panic is expressed by the media,
special-interest groups, and politicians; still, it manifests itself as a widespread concern originating at the grassroots, where latent fear emanates.
It is assumed that the media and political institutions cannot stir up panic
unless it already exists in the general public (Goode and Ben-Yehuda,
1994). In fact, the media, activist groups, and politicians often *discover* and
expose social problems that are very likely to provoke an emotional public response. The exploitation of hot-button, or third-rail, issues serves the
interests of specific groups; nevertheless, public reaction is real, even if it
is displaced. Consequently, moral panics lead to the production and persecution of folk devils. From the grassroots perspective, scapegoating is
symbolic of the collective conscience, an expression of the will of the people furiously demanding that evil be driven from their midst.

Interest-Group Theory

As a special interest, moral entrepreneurs rely on moral panic to advance their cause; in doing so, they publicize exaggerated claims of a putative social problem, which may lead ultimately to the creation and
enforcement of additional measures of formal social control. Due to the
popular appeal of many moral crusades, interest-group theory is not inconsistent with the grassroots model; yet, according to that model, moral
panic originates at the middle level of the social hierarchy and marshals
support from below. Interest groups become increasingly potent with the
acquisition of resources, which provides them with crucial access to the
media and policy makers. Once these links are established, the group
shapes the image of a problem by imposing its ideology and morality, or
its agenda for status and resources, or a combination of these motives and
interests (Goode and Ben-Yehuda, 1994).

Elite-Engineered Model

The theory of elitism proposes that a group located at the highest step
of the social ladder initiates and orchestrates moral panic. This ruling-class

theory suggests that elites are motivated to preserve their own interests, despite what is good for society as a whole. Moreover, political, economic, or cultural elites create moral panic to divert public attention from other social problems whose solutions would undermine their vested interests. Given their immense power and resources, elites have little difficulty accessing and influencing the media and political institutions; together, their activities contribute to substantive changes in social policy along with the (false) impression that such changes are justified, legitimate, and of overall good for society. Much like the interest-group model, campaigns engineered by elites often benefit from widespread support, even if public opinion is manipulated by the ruling class (Goode and Ben-Yehuda, 1994; Hall et al., 1978).

An Eclectic Theory of Moral Panic Over Flag Desecration

Arguably the most sound approach to moral panic over flag desecration integrates the grassroots, interest-group, and elite-engineered models into a cohesive framework. By doing so, we can attend to an array of motives, interests, and actors in the social construction of the flag-burning controversy beginning in the late 1980s. Consistent with the tenets of the grassroots model, it is assumed that moral panic over flag desecration stems from a deeper anxiety about America's nationhood and its place in the world, regardless of whether that fear is real or imagined. Indeed, sociologist W. I. Thomas, in his famous Thomas theorem (a version of the self-fulfilling prophecy), reminds us of the importance of the definition of the situation: simply stated, what people believe to be real will be real in its consequences (1923; Thomas and Znaniecki, 1927).

Whereas the United States remains a formidable world power, it is a relatively young nation whose identity continues to mature: Perhaps this fragile sense of security explains why a maturing nation feels so threatened by a mere handful of flag burners. In the words of the Senate Judicial Committee:

> We live in a time where standards have eroded. Civility and mutual respect are in decline. . . . Values are considered relative. Rights are cherished and constantly expanded, but responsibilities are shirked and scorned. . . . At the same time, our country grows more and more diverse. . . . The American flag is the one symbol that unites a very diverse people in a way nothing else can, in peace and war. . . . Failure to protect the flag inevitably loosens this bond. (*SJC* Report, 104–48, "Senate Joint Resolution 31" 104th Congress, 1st session, September 27, 1995:24–25)

Political scientist Robert Goldstein concurs with that theory of insecurity: "the public response [to the *Johnson* decision] ultimately reflected extraordinarily deep and widespread insecurities and doubts about the fundamental health of the country" (1996a:364–65). Looking back into history, Goldstein also addresses elements of elitism in his assessment of the 1895 flag-protection movement in which its crusaders were "fearful that their traditional elite roles were about to be swamped by radicalism, immigration, urbanization, and industrialization" (1996b:365; also see Guenter, 1990; O'Leary, 1999).

Underlying anxiety and a false sense of security further explain the degree of vilification of flag burners as folk devils, an essential criterion of moral panic. At the height of the flag frenzy, Johnson and his fellow supporters of the RCP were publicly demonized, routinely facing death threats and other forms of persecution. Whereas the grassroots model of moral panic explains several aspects of the flag fracas, alone it simply does not account for the full range of activity. According to Goode and Ben-Yehuda (1994:141): "While widespread stress or latent public fears almost necessarily preexist moral panics, they do not explain how and why they *find expression* at a particular time. These fears must be articulated; they must be focused, brought to public attention, given a specific outlet. And this almost always entails some form of organization and leadership."

As we segue to the interest-group component of this eclectic model, it important to acknowledge that the flag furor beginning in the late 1980s and early 1990s overlapped with Desert Storm, the first sustained U.S. military action since the Vietnam War. Desert Storm provided a crucial social context in which Americans could boldly project their patriotism and love of country. Nevertheless, concern over flag desecration reached the level of panic in large part due to the activities of special-interest groups, particularly in the form of the flag lobby. As a coalition of several interwoven groups, the CFA continues to operate as a moral entrepreneur committed to increasing public awareness of the so-called *endangered* flag, the *harm* of flag desecration, and the *need* for flag-protection laws. As an interest group, it does not appear that the flag lobby has an agenda for the acquisition of resources or economic gain; rather, it enjoys having its values institutionalized in the form of enhanced patriotism expressed through flag adoration. Thus, the flag lobby's morality—civil religion—constitutes an ideology transmitted through its activism. Whereas the military establishment is a political elite, the flag lobby consists primarily of special-interest activists located in the middle range of the social hierarchy. Admittedly, the military establishment benefits from the activism of the flag lobby, given that respect for the flag also restores the status of soldiers at all levels of service. Recent flag adoration also has enhanced the cultural feature of patriotism insofar as holidays commemorating veterans have renewed appreciation: Veterans Day, Memorial Day, and Pearl Harbor Day.

Unquestionably, the flag lobby as a special-interest group was instrumental in transforming the issue of flag desecration into a "social problem" in the late 1980s, but the flag-protection movement has emerged and reemerged throughout several critical points in American history. The flag-protection campaign was a significant movement during the Civil War, at the turn of the twentieth century, during World Wars I and II, and again in the Vietnam War era. Particularly in its embryonic stages, the flag-protection crusade was engineered by well-established elites, the Daughters of the American Revolution, the Sons of the American Revolution, the Grand Army of the Republic, and the Society of Colonial Wars (Guenter, 1990; O'Leary, 1999). Those organizations, comprised of political, economic, and cultural elites, defined American citizenship and patriotism in highly exclusive and nativist terms, especially in an effort to distinguish themselves from lower socioeconomic groups and recent immigrants. Indeed, past and present nativist movements bristle at so-called hyphenated Americans, including African-Americans, Chinese-Americans, Irish-Americans, Mexican-Americans, etc. Nativists insist that ethnic hyphenation dilutes American culture and patriotism, creating suspicion over divided loyalties and ambiguous identities; in fact, adverse reactions to immigration earlier this century were instrumental in drafting state flag-protection laws and developing patriotic curricula and rituals in public schools. Whereas the contemporary flag lobby draws heavily on the nostalgia of militarism, unlike previous flag-protection movements, the CFA explicitly denounces nativism. Consider the following mission statement:

> Our nation is unique because of our origins. We are mostly a nation of immigrants. We are not a nation of one race, or one religion. We are a nation of many races and many religions, and from our diversity we draw our strength. And that makes us unique in the history of the world. Yet those differences that strengthen us can also destroy us if we are not ever mindful of the values, traditions, and principles that bind us together. (CFA, 1998a, February 4)

The military establishment is more a political elite than a mere special-interest group (Mills, 1956); thus, it stands to benefit from moral panic over flag desecration in two significant ways. In terms of the symbolic rewards, the U.S. military enjoys enhanced status, especially considering that it lost considerable prestige as a result of America's failures in the Vietnam War. As a political elite, the military establishment also is rewarded materially from the wave of renewed patriotism (increased government funding, resources, equipment, and personnel). Arguably, other paramilitary organizations—law enforcement—also benefit symbolically (improved status and prestige) and substantially (greater government funding) from moral panic over flag desecration.

Law-enforcement officers serve a domestic role similar to that of the armed forces insofar as they claim to *serve and protect* the public; taken further, contemporary police agencies increasingly are militarized, in large part due to another moral panic manifesting itself in the war on drugs

(Brownstein, 1996; Chiricos, 1996; Kraska, 1993a, 1993b; Reinarman and Levine, 1997; Welch, Bryan, and Wolff, 1999; Welch, Wolff, and Bryan, 1998). The role of *protecting* society is particularly noteworthy considering that flag panic is a manifestation of a latent fear that American society is in danger (Cohen, 1972; Hall, et al., 1978). As a reminder, the police customarily wear flag patches on their uniforms, and equally important, they have been known to participate in the vilification of flag burners especially by enforcing flag-protection laws.

Politicians obviously constitute the most visible category of elites benefitting from moral panic over flag desecration. By virtue of their exalted position in society, lawmakers already enjoy unobstructed access to the media and benefit personally and professionally from behind-the-scenes state activities. Moral panic over flag desecration bolsters political campaigns, thereby enhancing the careers of elected officials who publicly embrace the flag. For more than a hundred years, politicians at all levels of government have exploited the flag and used it to promote their campaigns. In the late 1980s, the flag flap was manufactured as a calculated maneuver by George Bush's presidential campaign. Similarly, in 1995, the House of Representatives scheduled a vote on the constitutional amendment a few days before Independence Day, while the Senate planned their vote for early December in order to capitalize symbolically on the anniversary of the 1941 Japanese attack on Pearl Harbor.

Consistent with the elite-engineered model, politicians also use moral panic over flag desecration to divert attention from substantive problems that elected officials have difficulty resolving, including wars, military conflicts, and economic woes. And even if politicians could resolve some of those problems, their remedies often would antagonize the interests of the ruling class who benefit from prevailing social and economic conditions (e.g., the narrow distribution of wealth). Diverting attention from substantive problems also averts public outrage that would otherwise be directed at corrupt politicians who endorse unpopular budgetary cuts (e.g., cuts in health-care coverage, education, environmental protection).

Politicians as individuals, and the state as an institution, benefit enormously from moral panic over flag desecration because their proposed remedies (flag-protection laws and a constitutional amendment) restrict freedom of speech. Limiting free speech, especially political criticism expressed by flag desecration, further empowers the state and its managers. With this in mind, Hall, et al. (1978) remind us that moral panic functions as a mechanism for the construction of a version of society that serves the interests of the powerful.

From a Marxian perspective, the dominance of the ruling class extends beyond the ownership and control of the means of *material* production, but also exerts influence over the means of *mental* production. In this vein, civil religion and the need for flag protection are crucial forms of mental production. These mental products are transformed, transmitted, and reproduced according to the imperatives of the dominant ideology, thereby determining what is socially *thinkable*. Likewise, the dominant ideology serves the interests of the ruling class by protecting and reproducing its way of life. Equally important, the dominant ideology also exhibits *universal* qualities that ensure that the elite worldview is shared to some degree by subordinate classes (Marx, 1978; see also Gramsci, 1971; Larrain, 1983; Sahin, 1980; Welch, Fenwick, and Roberts, 1997). In sum, an eclectic theory refines our understanding of the structures and processes shaping moral panic; together, the grassroots, interest-group, and elite-engineered models integrate the varied terrain of the flag-desecration controversy.

CONCLUSION

In this chapter, the conceptual components of moral panic over flag desecration were described in detail. In addition to delineating its criteria, cast of characters, and various territories, moral panic was introduced as the centerpiece of a theoretical framework from which we can interpret reactions to flag desecration at various levels of analysis. The proposed eclectic model enables us to unveil remnants of flag panic at the grassroots, interest-group, and elite strata of the social hierarchy. Overall, the flag panic was rooted in a latent fear that American society and culture is ill-fated. That free-floating anxiety pre-exists among the masses and eventually took the form of a pressing "social problem," as special-interest groups pilloried flag burners as folk devils.

As a key pressure group, the flag lobby benefits from having its values of patriotic flag adoration enforced by formal social control. Similarly, elites also enjoy the windfall from moral panic over flag desecration; moreover, their gains extend beyond symbolism. The ruling class profits in ways that reproduce the status quo, preserving a social order that serves their interests. All along, the flag panic was endowed with a distinct brand of moralism—civil religion, which includes a set of beliefs commonly shared by most members of American society. Moral panic, in conjunction with civil religion, remains an integral concept in the remaining portion of this work.

NOTE

1. The following works illuminate the importance of social constructionism in studying crime and deviance: Best, 1987, 1989, 1990; Chermak, 1997; Chiricos, 1996; Cohen and Young, 1981; Ferrell, 1996; Fishman, 1978; Hall, et al., 1978; Hickman, 1982; Hollywood, 1997; Humphries, 1999; Jenkins, 1992, 1994; McCorkle and Miethe, 1998; Potter and Kappeler, 1998; Surette, 1998; Welch, Fenwick, Roberts, 1998, 1997.

8

Moral Entrepreneurs and the Criminalization of Protest

Maybe we can't stop the glorification of homosexuality. Maybe we can't stop the deterioration of families. But . . . we can draw a line and stand up for one thing in our country, and that is the flag of this country.
—*Rep. Bob Barr (First Amendment Center, 1997:1).*

I am certainly not the best educated Member of this body, nor am I even close to being an expert on our Constitution or Bill of Rights. But through a gift from God, I believe I know what the American people want, and what is right. They want our flag protected.
—*Rep. William Lipinski (CR, June 21, 1990:H4081)*

As is the case with many social movements, the flag-protection crusade serves several functions, some of which are clearly recognizable while others are more subtle. At close range, we can see easily that flag protection satisfies the function of promoting patriotism in the form of respect for Old Glory. Still, there remain latent functions obscured by the flurry of moral panic over flag desecration (see Merton, 1968). Drawing from the eclectic theory of moral panic introduced in the previous chapter, flag protection feeds the interests of grassroots activists, the flag lobby, and political, economic, and cultural elites; indeed, all of these actors enjoy restored status as a result of the flag campaign's success. Moreover, the criminalizing of protest is a significant latent function, given that stifling political dissent reinforces the status quo, benefiting the state, its officials, and, even more important, the ruling class.

In this chapter, moral entrepreneurs who contributed significantly to moral panic over flag desecration are the subjects of discussion—in particular, President Bush and members of Congress. Given that their rhetoric was instrumental in advancing the flag crusade, content analyses were conducted on the *Public Papers of the Presidents* (PPP) and the *Congressional*

Record (*CR*) in an effort to identify key political claims and themes. This chapter shows that political messages serve the manifest function of promoting American patriotism while fulfilling the latent function of criminalizing political protest.[1]

PRESIDENT BUSH AS MORAL ENTREPRENEUR

During his presidency, George Bush delivered 15 speeches containing specific references to Old Glory. Significantly, all were delivered between June 22, 1989, and July 20, 1990, at the height of moral panic over flag burning. Bush spoke publicly about the flag more often than any president in a single term; by comparison, Reagan required two terms to match the number of flag speeches by Bush. Whereas Bush alluded to the Stars and Stripes in the context of American history and the U.S. military, his main focus was on flag desecration and legislation designed to punish and deter such acts of protest. Those remarks, the first of their kind in U.S. presidential history, contributed enormously to moral panic over flag burning; in fact, Bush was the first commander-in-chief to endorse publicly the criminalizing of flag desecration. Departing from Reagan, who embraced civil religion in his flag speeches, Bush expressed himself in more secular terms; moreover, he tended to personalize his crusade for the nation's most cherished emblem. On several occasions, Bush looked inward and said, "I can speak for how strongly I feel about this being the unique symbol of the United States. . . . I believe that the flag should never be the object of desecration" (*PPP*, Bush, 1989:805, 812). On June 22, 1989, Bush shared his thoughts with the audience: "If I might make a very special personal observation before addressing myself to the subject at hand, I want to comment on the Supreme Court decision about our flag. . . . I have to give you my personal, emotional response. Flag burning is wrong—dead wrong" (*PPP*, Bush, 1989:785).

Emulating Reagan, who previewed upcoming Flag Day ceremonies in several speeches, Bush also scattered flag references in a series of addresses, often going out of his way to condemn flag burning. In 1990, Bush injected his plea to protect the flag while speaking at a Republican fundraising banquet for North Carolina Senator Jesse Helms.

> And here, too, I need Jesse Helms's help to keep standing for what's right. . . .
> Forty-eight States had laws protecting the flag against desecration. Forty-eight States. And those laws were effectively struck down when the Supreme Court ruled that flag burning is protected by the Constitution. I honestly can't believe that they [the founding fathers] would condone burning it under the cover of free speech. The constitutional amendment we have proposed is carefully drawn. And here's what it says: "The Congress and the States shall have power to prohibit the physical desecration of the flag of the

United States." I will fight for that amendment, and I am proud to have Jesse Helms at my side. (*PPP*, Bush, 1990:855)

Bush supported a constitutional amendment because he suspected that the Flag Protection Act of 1989 would not survive judicial scrutiny. Such a proposal, however, reveals significant elements of moral panic over flag desecration, since a constitutional amendment, more so than criminal statutes, marks a drastic legislative initiative to protect Old Glory. Indeed, a constitutional amendment that would penalize flag desecration would be a more profound form of criminalization, especially considering the extensive legislative activity needed to satisfy the requirement for amending the U.S. Constitution: a two-thirds majority in the House of Representatives and the Senate before proceeding to state legislatures where a three-quarters majority is required to ratify a constitutional amendment.

After a careful study of the [Supreme] Court's opinion, the Department of Justice concluded that the only way to ensure protection of the flag is through constitutional amendment. Pursuant to that advice, I urged the adoption of such and amendment. After several months of debate about how to protect the flag from desecration, the Congress had forwarded to me H.R. 2978. The bill provides for a prison term of up to 1 year for anyone who 'knowingly mutilates, defaces, physically defiles, burns, maintains on the floor or ground, or tramples upon' any United States flag. When I commend the intentions of those who voted for this bill, I have serious doubts that it can withstand Supreme Court review. (*PPP*, Bush, 1989:1403)

From the standpoint of a moral enterprise, it is revealing that Bush himself referred to the flag campaign as a "crusade to protect that unique symbol of America's honor," adding: "Our flag is too sacred to be abused" (Remarks at the American Legion Annual Convention in Baltimore, September 7, 1989: 1). Moreover, Bush commended other like-minded moral entrepreneurs—the flag lobby—for its efforts: "The American Legion, its men and women, have helped write the story of America and the story of our flag" (Ibid.). Still, criminalization remains a key product of moral panic, and on numerous occasions Bush demanded that a constitutional amendment be passed "making it illegal to desecrate that unique symbol of our liberty" (Ibid.). Similarly, Bush proclaimed his support for an amendment that would "make the burning of the American flag a crime" ("Remarks at a Fundraising Luncheon for Governor Guy Hunt in Huntsville, AL, June 20, 1990:1). In an effort to portray the flag issue as a populist rather than an elitist agenda, Bush tailored his rhetoric to suggest a general consensus. "To the touch, this flag is merely fabric. But to the heart, the flag represents and reflects the fabric of our nation—our dreams, our destiny, our very fiber as a people" (*PPP*, Bush, 1989:832).

During his crusade to amend the constitution, Bush was criticized by civil libertarians for restricting First Amendment freedoms. Likewise, political opponents and the press questioned Bush's motives, since it appeared that the Republicans were making flag protection a partisan issue, insinuating that the Democrats lacked sufficient patriotism to hold public office. During Bush's news conference on June 27, 1989, his exchange with a reporter quickly focused on the issue of partisan politics and Old Glory.

> Question: Mr. President, in light of your renewed concern about the display of proper reverence for the flag, I wonder if you think it helps the situation, sir, for you and other political figures of both parties to make the flag the kind of instrument of partisan politics that it was in your campaign last fall—with a visit to Flag City and the tour of flag factories and flag at all the conventions and so on?
>
> Bush: I don't view that as partisanship. I think respect for the flag transcends political party. And I think what I've said here is American. . . . I just feel very, very strongly about it . . . but I want to take this opportunity to say protest should not extend to desecration of the unique symbol of America, and that is our flag.
>
> Question: You wouldn't dispute, would you, sir, that your visit to Flag City, U.S.A. . . . [was] for the purpose of advancing your political campaign?
>
> Bush: Everything I did last year was the purpose of advancing . . . my election . . . but I didn't put it on the basis that Republicans are for the flag and Democrats are not.
>
> Question: You didn't explain why you went the constitutional route instead of the legislative on flag-burning?
>
> Bush: Because I am told that legislation cannot correct the—in my view— egregious offense; burning the American flag. (*PPP*, Bush, 1989:832)

In sum, Bush's public statements about flag desecration often were delivered with an angry tone coupled with an unmistakable sense of righteousness; each of these qualities are significant to the construction of moral panic given that they stem from emotionally charged proclamations concerning a putative social threat. Again, Bush lamented: "I feel it deep in my heart because the flag and what it means is carried in the hearts of all Americans. . . . It [flag burning] endangers the fabric of our country, and I think it ought to be outlawed" (*PPP*, Bush, 1989:812).

Implications for Moral Panic and Agenda-Setting

President Bush's commitment to flag protection was intensified by his dissatisfaction with the U.S. Supreme Court's decision in *Johnson*. But unlike the Vietnam War era when flag burning reached unprecedented levels, the *Johnson* ruling in 1989 was issued a time when such protests were exceedingly rare, suggesting that the threat of flag desecration was a political invention. Turning attention to other evidence linking presidential rhetoric to claims-making and agenda-setting, Bush's role in the moral panic over flag desecration becomes clearer.

Moral entrepreneurs generate public attention to their crusades by making claims, a process by which rhetoric is carefully crafted so as to shape a particular image of a perceived threat to society. By airing their grievances, moral entrepreneurs create a platform from which policies can be formulated; in the end, they set a public agenda based on their interests and values. To advance their agenda, however, moral entrepreneurs must persuade a significant portion of the public that their claim is legitimate (Beckett, 1994, 1997; Best, 1987, 1989, 1990). Moral entrepreneurs occupying high positions in society contribute tremendously to claims-making and agenda-setting for the simple reason that their visibility attracts media and public attention. Indeed, within the hierarchy of credibility, moral entrepreneurs holding elected office are capable of swaying public opinion since they are viewed by the public as legitimate authorities on social issues (Becker, 1963, 1967; Welch, Fenwick, and Roberts, 1998).

In 1960, Richard Neustadt observed, "Presidential *power* is the power to persuade" (10). Since then, researchers have found consistently that presidents possess profound ability to lead public opinion (Gelderman, 1995; Gonzenbach, 1996; Graber, 1982, 1990; Page and Shapiro, 1992; see also Edelman, 1989, 1971, 1964). Whereas presidents can apprise the public of measurable harms to society (e.g., economic woes), they can also mislead constituents about the precise threat of putative social problems. Beginning in the 1980s, for example, crime declined while fear of crime escalated; in fact, Presidents Reagan, Bush, and Clinton have been criticized for contributing to and exploiting public fear of crime in order to advance their political agendas (Beckett, 1994, 1997; Cohen, 1997, 1994; Gaubatz, 1995; Marion, 1992, 1994a, 1994b; Taylor, 1982; Warr, 1995; Welch, 1999b; Welch, Fenwick, and Roberts, 1998). Much like Reagan and Clinton, Bush remained a staunch advocate of harsher penalties in the wars on crime and drugs; however, his proposal for criminalizing flag desecration constituted a unique form of moral panic when he claimed that flag burning "endangers the fabric of our country" (*PPP*, Bush, 1989:812). Additional findings document the extent to which Bush contributed to public hysteria over flag burning by placing patriotism on the nation's political agenda. In their examination of his term as President, Wanta and Foote (1994) showed that Bush's influence significantly shaped the public perception of flag burning as a social threat. Typical of many elites, Bush utilized his access to the media for the purpose of placing flag protection on the public agenda. By doing so, Bush transformed a mere symbolic issue into a seemingly substantive problem; moreover, he endorsed a criminalization strategy (i.e., a constitutional amendment) designed to punish and ultimately deter flag desecrators.

Bush framed the flag-burning issue in highly emotional terms, prompting scholars to consider the significance of such political rhetoric. Wanta and Foote observed, "It is this type of emotion-laden, symbolic issue where presidents may have the greatest effect on the agenda-building process. It is unlikely that the flag burning issue would ever have pierced the media threshold of importance if it were not for presidential subsidization of the message. To elevate such symbolic issues to national importance requires presidents to tap an underlying emotion or expectation" (1994:446). Smith and Smith (1994:90) agreed: "When the Supreme Court ruled that flag burning is protected by the First Amendment, Bush returned to his 1988 campaign style and gave rallying speeches at a flag factory and in front of the Iwo Jima Memorial. This openly hostile presidential response to the Court's decision played on emotions" (see also Shogan, 1992). Again, it is crucial to note that Bush played a pivotal role in the construction of moral panic over flag desecration insofar as he participated directly in agenda-setting rather than agenda-surfing—an activity in which public figures simply ride the waves of a story within its original news cycle (Wanta and Foote, 1994). Presidential influence on the media and public opinion also extends to Congress (Brace and Hinkley, 1992; Cohen, 1994, 1997). Moreover, if moral panic is to shape public policy and legislation, cooperation between the president and Congress is vital. As we shall see in the next section, moral panic escalated sharply as members of Congress joined the chorus for flag protection.

CONGRESS AND THE CRIMINALIZATION OF FLAG BURNING

In a concerted effort to criminalize flag desecration, Congress, acting as an assembly of moral entrepreneurs, became a key player in moral panic. Indeed, lawmakers condemned flag burning by delivering sermon-like speeches claiming that American society was in steep decline. Consider, for instance, the emotional rhetoric of Representative Henry Hyde:

> I view this as one more struggle in the culture war that has been raging since Vietnam. There are those who hate America and its values and take every opportunity to demean those values. Those who are shocked, revolted and frustrated by the excesses of the counterculture, the pornography and obscenity that inundates our entertainment industry, the drugs, the AIDS explosion, the high abortion rate, view flag burning as one more slap in the face of millions of veterans who found enough values in America to risk their lives in

combat. People resent the vulgarization of their country. (*CR*, House Judiciary Committee, June 19, 1990: 20)

Hyde, like many of members of Congress, crafted his denunciation of flag burning around other social ills he believed were produced by a culture war. The heavy moral tone of Hyde's speech is unmistakable, especially given the type of social issues on his agenda. By lumping together his disdain for the counter-culture of 1960s, pornography, drugs, AIDS, and abortion, Hyde engaged in classic moral panic by professing a deterioration of life in America brought on by liberalism. Moreover, Hyde sanctimoniously praised the virtues of traditional values and military service, components of conservative politics embodied in the Stars and Stripes. As we shall see, the flag crusade is driven by a regressive political undertow that takes aim at social issues associated with liberal lifestyles as shown in the words of Republican James Sensenbrenner: "Why are we so reluctant to amend the Constitution? In a time when perversion is accepted and morality taboo, perhaps this is not asking too much" (Povich, September 13, 1989: 1). In exploring the claims-making activities of moral entrepreneurs in Congress, it is important to examine the political rhetoric they used to justify the criminalizing of protest. Before we embark on that component of the analysis, however, other developments shaping congressional responses to flag desecration are reviewed, including the power of partisan politics, the desire for political cover, and the utility of diversionary political strategies.

Partisan Politics

Certainly, the flag-burning controversy that began in 1989 was a product of earlier posturing by George Bush, who wrapped himself in the flag while running for president in 1988. Old Glory quickly became a symbolic weapon in partisan politics, as Bush questioned the patriotism of Democratic rival Michael Dukakis. An unidentified source in the California Senate told a reporter that Bush was exploiting the national controversy over burning the flag to set a "'death trap' for Democrats" (Ingram, July 14, 1989: 3). At the height of the flag panic, Congressman Tom DeLay boasted: "I think the Republican Party represents what the flag has to offer" (*CR*, June 28, 1989: H3410). Members of Congress understood the crucial nature of establishing ownership of political ideas; in the realm of flag protection, such ownership proved significant: the 1990 proposal to amend the constitution had 160 cosponsors (Holmes, June 22, 1990: 1). Revealing the combative side of partisan politics, Representative Bob Stump voiced his party's support for a constitutional amendment to protect the flag, saying, "We're going to kick some ass today" (Daley, July 21, 1989: 1).

Although initially the flag issue appeared feeble, Democrats had already felt the sharp sting of defeat when voters responded favorably to patriotism in politics. Not to be outflanked again, Democrats were willing to put up a fight over patriotism. Michael McCurry, communications director for the Democratic National Committee, remarked: "They (Republicans) are going to try to do a good cop, bad cop number. It must be astonishingly embarrassing for the minority leader to be turned into a flag-waving bumpkin by the White House. They're perilously close to flag factoryville from the 1988 campaign" (Balz, June 17, 1990: A12). Alluding to the process of social constructionism, Democrat Don Edwards, a staunch opponent of a flag amendment, conceded: "And let's face it, the Republicans have a way of heating this up and getting down to name calling. They have so much more money and more machinery to whip up hysteria" (Holmes, June 14, 1990: 10). Similarly, Democrat Bob Kerrey added: "I consider this [Bush's grandstanding] to be an act of desecration. Desecration to take the American flag and use it to divide us again, desecration to use it to gain some marginal political advantage" (Daley, June 15, 1990: 4).

Paradoxically, Democrats both resisted and participated in the flag furor. Because Republicans had set the flag agenda in Congress, however, they had the privilege of owning the issue. Referring to flag desecration, funding for the arts, and prayer in public schools, Republican Senator Larry Craig agreed with political analysts saying, "They are defining issues. I like to call them bright light issues—issues that show the differences between the two parties" (Chen, May 14, 1997: 16). With the flag phenomenon, the GOP smelled political blood and instructed its membership to attack Democrats on the issue of patriotism. The militancy of the partisanship on the flag issue became increasingly evident when John Yoder (Republican Senate candidate) said that he was warned by the National Republican Senate Committee to support an amendment to protect the flag. More to the point, the Committee threaten to withdraw its support if Yoder didn't "follow their marching orders" (*Washington Post*, June 20, 1990: A28). On a more amusing note, however, *Newsweek* reported that it overheard a slip of the tongue by Republican Congressman Bob McEwen who, during the daily affirmation in House, recited: "I pledge allegiance to the flag of the United States of America, and to the Republicans [sic] for which it stands . . . (October 16, 1998: 23).

Political Cover

As another feature of the flag panic, lawmakers sought refuge from political fallout. Politicians are both astute manipulators and products of public opinion. Legislators are capable of shaping issues that serve their political interests, and at the same time they aware of the dangers of challenging popular opinion. Even though voting against flag protection—

especially on constitutional grounds—makes legislative sense, most politicians dare not risk their careers by being caught on the wrong side of the issue. With this consideration in mind, the vast majority of lawmakers have supported measures to shield the flag from desecration. In short order, the flag-protection crusade crystallized so potently that even elected officials who privately disagreed with flag legislation quietly boarded the bandwagon for fear of persecution, in effect becoming de facto moral entrepreneurs. Congressman Don Edwards acknowledged the prevailing political wind: "It's pretty hard for people to vote against protecting the flag" (Eaton, July 26, 1989: 12). Understandably, few politicians would publicly discuss the nature of political cover; they want voters to believe that their commitment to preserving the dignity of Old Glory is genuine and heartfelt. In 1995, a senior citizen was quoted as saying: "I always vote. And when I get ready to cast my ballot, I'll consider how the candidate voted on the flag amendment" (Goeas, October 10, 1995: 15). The need for political cover stems from the power of moral panic, which reminds dissenters to think twice about provoking the wrath of public hysteria.

Diversionary Politics

In diversionary politics, public concern over substantive problems is redirected to less important issues. As a political tactic, diversion remains a common course of action, especially since many social problems are the result of deep contradictions in the social order which, if they were to be corrected, would require major economic realignments. Recall that in 1985, the city of New York outfitted abandoned buildings in impoverished neighborhoods with imitation windows, complete with paintings of curtains and potted plants. "Window dressing" supplanted the substantive programs necessary to eradicate urban decay (Dubin, 1992). In light of the substantive issues that adversely affect most Americans—including the federal deficit, joblessness, inadequate education, inaccessible health care—the flag debate was a convenient diversion for lawmakers who would rather participate in symbolic politics than deal with troubling social problems. At the peak of the flag panic, columnist Lars-Erik Nelson captured the essence of diversionary politics: "If they put a meter on Congress while it debated whether or not it's constitutional to burn a flag you could track the cost of savings and loan scandal: $31,000 a minute" (1990b: 25; 1990a). Some elected leaders, however, publicly criticized the flag-protection movement, citing political diversion. Senator Patrick Leahy announced to his colleagues in Congress: "Certainly, we've talked more about this flag burner in Texas than we have about the fiscal disaster that we're going to leave the next generation" (Toner, October 5, 1989: Section 2: 12).

Congressional Voting on Flag Protection

Amid moral panic over flag desecration, compounded by partisan politics, political cover, and diversionary politics, Congress was poised to take a stand on defending the Stars and Stripes. Following the *Johnson* ruling in 1989, the House and Senate scrambled furiously to circumvent the high court by formulating new versions of flag-protection laws as well as proposals for a constitutional amendment. On September 12, 1989, the House of Representatives overwhelmingly approved the Flag Protection Act of 1989, 380–38, a measure that would impose criminal penalties for physical desecration of the flag, and on October 5, the Senate finalized passage of Flag Protection Act of 1989, 91–9 (*New York Times*, September 17, 1989: 54; October 8, 1989: 18). The following year, the U.S. Supreme Court invalidated the Flag Protection Act with its ruling in *Eichman*. Still, the flag crusade refused to be demoralized, despite several other setbacks. A proposal to amend the constitution, which won considerable support in the House (254 in favor and 177 against) was 34 votes shy of the two-thirds needed to advance it (*New York Times*, June 24, 1990: 27). Similarly, on June 26, 1990, the Senate failed to pass a constitutional amendment by a margin of 58 (in favor) to 42 (opposed), nine votes short of the two-thirds needed for approval (*New York Times*, June 27, 1990: Section 2: 6).

The flag campaign resurfaced in 1995, only to be turned back by the Senate, which supported a constitutional amendment 63–36, three votes short of the two-thirds necessary for passage (66 votes would have sufficed because there was one absence) (*New York Times*, December 17, 1995: 54). Despite that defeat, the flag lobby remained optimistic and exerted even more energy toward keeping alive the proposal for an amendment. Jim McAvoy, a Washington lobbying consultant, remarked in 1995: "The proposed ban on flag burning is an issue right below the surface. . . . It was an issue that was totally off of Congress' and the media's radar screens, [and] we have to bring it back to the point where people are taking it seriously" (Drew, March 1, 1995: 8). Two years later, the amendment received its largest boost when the House resoundingly passed the measure 310–114 (*New York Times*, June 15, 1997: 30). But later, in 1998, a preliminary count showed that the measure was three votes short in the Senate, and no vote was taken, which allowed the flag lobby to reconfigure its strategy.

On June 24, 1999, after five hours of speeches over two days, the House voted 305–214 to support a constitutional amendment to protect the flag from desecration, well in excess of the two-thirds majority. On March 29, 2000, however, the measure failed in Senate by a margin of four votes (Alvarez, 2000). Polls show that 80 percent of Americans favor the measure. If the initiative ultimately were to pass, it would proceed to the states, where the support of three-quarters of the state legislatures (38) is required for passage. Thus far, 49 states have passed measures expressing support for a flag proposal to become the 27th Amendment to the U.S. Constitution (Vermont is the only dissenting state). In terms of political context, the presence of moral entrepreneurs and civil religion in Congress is unmistakable. A week before the flag debate, lawmakers voted to encourage the display of the Ten Commandments in public schools; later that year, Congress discussed a constitutional amendment that would permit organized prayer in public schools (*New York Times*, June 25, 1999: A-18). As we shall see in an examination of the *Congressional Record*, political rhetoric on flag desecration touches on several social themes; transcending the debate over free speech, patriotism, and militarism, discourse on flag desecration also is imbued with moral and civil religious connotations.

THEMES AND CONTOURS OF THE FLAG DEBATE IN CONGRESS

Concern over the fate of the flag materialized into the expending of costly political resources on legislation, litigation, and prosecution of violators. During the twelve months between the *Johnson* and *Eichman* decisions, Congress was consumed by the debate over flag protection, which absorbed more time than any other issue. Congress devoted in excess of 100 hours of floor debate and approximately two weeks of public legislative hearings; members of Congress and their staffs spent thousands of hours in meetings deliberating over how to shield Old Glory from desecration. Those activities were entered into the *Congressional Record*, more than 400 pages at an average cost of $500 per page; in addition, 1,500 pages of hearings also were published by the federal government (*CR*, 1990, S8685; see Goldstein, 1996a). In an effort to determine the extent of moral panic over flag desecration in Congress, a content analysis (a systematic examination of communication and messages) was introduced to study the *Congressional Record*. By doing so, significant themes of political rhetoric emerged, including justifications for criminalizing flag desecration.

Sample and Procedure

The sample drawn for the content analysis included *all* speeches, addresses, and public remarks delivered by members of Congress during the debate over flag protection and published in the *Congressional Record* between 1989 and 1998.[2] In total, 801 speeches were analyzed according to a coding scheme consisting of nine major themes: First Amendment, patriotism, U.S. military, civil religion, American history, popular consensus, flawed legislation, political diversion, and criminal justice. Moreover, the depth of a particular theme in each speech was measured by the frequency of such statements. Understandably, many statements touched on several themes. For example, a passage referring to the War of 1812 was coded into categories of American history and U.S. military. The chief objective of the analysis was to interpret more accurately the nature of political rhetoric on flag protection expressed by members of Congress.

Findings

The analysis yielded 5,797 total statements falling into nine major themes (Table 8:1). This section presents findings in each thematic category, beginning with the most frequently cited. Accompanying the in-depth examination of the political rhetoric on flag desecration is ample qualitative material that captures the tone of congressional debate.

First Amendment/Freedom of Expression   Since flag protection marks a legislative attempt to limit free speech, it is not surprising to find that issues pertaining to the First Amendment dominated the debate. Of the 801 speeches, 592 (74 percent), contained statements addressing the First Amendment, producing 1,882 total statements on the subject. The vast majority of arguments supported placing limits on free speech for purposes of guarding Old Glory from desecration. In the words of Senator George Mitchell:

> The Supreme Court has both limited and expanded the first amendment's protection. As a limitation, it has imposed restrictions on some forms of speech. In the 1919 case of *Schenk* versus the United States, Justice Oliver Wendell Holmes wrote that "The character of every act depends on the circumstances in which it is done. The most stringent protection of free speech would not protect a man in falsely shouting fire in a theater causing a panic."

Table 8.1.   Findings of Content Analysis: Congressional Record N = 801 Speeches (1989–98)

Themes	Speeches		Statements	
	Frequency	%	Frequency	%
First Amendment	592	74%	1,882	32%
Patriotism	457	57%	1,077	19%
Military	342	43%	615	11%
Civil Religion	280	35%	643	11%
History	251	31%	475	8%
Popular Consensus	166	21%	291	5%
Flawed Legistn.	159	20%	578	10%
Political Diversion	67	8%	127	2%
Criminal Justice	64	8%	109	2%

* Overall, 5,797 statements contained in 801 speeches were analyzed.

Those words represented a commonsense principle of behavior essential to preserve a civil society with free speech. Clearly, no first amendment right would today protect a statement by an airplane passenger that he was about to explode a bomb, even if his purpose was to call attention to his political views. (*CR*, July 18, 1989: S8103)

Congressman Chuck Douglas also supported restrictions on the free speech: "The first amendment rights are not absolute and without limitation. The courts have upheld many exceptions to the great sweep of the first amendment. Thus, one may not express oneself in the following way: (1) incite to riot, (2) criminal solicitation, (3) libel, (4) slander, (5) child pornography, and (6) perjury" (*CR*, July 20, 1989: E2594). Similarly, Senator William S. Cohen drew the following parallel: "It isn't an act of censorship for politicians to criticize music containing lyrics that denigrate women, glorify cop killers as role models, and promote racial divisiveness" (*CR*, December 12, 1995: S18388).

Whereas most lawmakers who spoke publicly in Congress favored circumventing the First Amendment in an effort to shield the flag from desecration, there remained considerable opposition to flag protection: 218 speeches (37 percent in this category) defended the First Amendment, yielding 1,065 such remarks (57 percent in this category). According to Senator Robb: "The acid test of a democracy is whether or not we can speak out in peaceful dissent against our Government without fear of being arrested or prosecuted, or punished. And in this case, the amendment goes directly to the heart of that freedom" (*CR*, December 12, 1995: S18379). "The Members of this body should not risk the desecration of our Constitution simply to express outrage against those who desecrate the flag," said Senator Christopher Dodd (*CR*, December 12, 1995: S18382).

Senator Russell Feingold reminded his colleagues that "this nation was born of dissent, and contrary to the view that it weakens democracy, this nation stands today as the leader of the free world because we tolerate those varying forms of dissent, not because we persecute them" (*CR*, December 8, 1995: S18258). Alluding to the notion that democracy can spiral into a tyranny of the majority, Senator John Glenn argued: "The Supreme Court has held on two separate occasions that no matter how much the majority of us, 99.999 percent of the people of this country disagree [with] that tiny, tiny fractional, misguided minority, still under our Bill of Rights they have the right to their expression. Their expression is looked at as coming under that freedom of speech" (*CR*, December 8, 1995: S18277). Similarly, Senator Joseph Biden opposed a constitutional amendment, insisting, "It cannot apply different rules to Democrats, and Republicans, hippies, yuppies, rich, and poor, black and white, or any other division in this country" (*CR*, December 11, 1995: S18317).

Patriotism The second-most frequently cited theme in the debate over flag protection was patriotism. It ought to be noted that in this category, we distinguish between civilian and militaristic patriotism. Adding to that distinction, Senator Bill Bradley pointed to a form of patriotism shaped by civics and community involvement: "Patriotism—it is like strength. . . . But you don't need a war to show your patriotism. Patriotism is often unpretentious greatness. A patriot goes to work every day to make America a better place—in schools, hospitals, farms, laboratories, factories, offices all across this land" (*CR*, December 12, 1995: S18383). Overall, 457 speeches on flag protection were expressed in terms of (civilian) patriotism, accounting for 57 percent of the sample and producing 1,077 comments; moreover, most of the references to patriotism were used as justification to institute legal protection for the Stars and Stripes. Congressman Christopher Cox spoke fondly of the resurgence of patriotism in the 1980s: "I, of course, had the opportunity to work in the White House with Ronald Reagan. He brought America back. It was morning in America. There was a renewed sense of patriotism. If we remember back in 1984, we were hosting the Olympics, and it was perhaps the high-water mark of patriotism in America for years, and that was the year, 1984, that the Republicans met in Dallas for their national convention" (*CR*, June 18, 1989: H3421). Cox went on to denounce Johnson and supporters of the RCP for attacking American patriotism by burning the flag in downtown Dallas during the GOP convention, an act that he believed should be punished as a crime. Congressman Cliff Stearns concurred: "Flag burning is not political expression, it is an act of patriotic destruction" (*CR*, July 19, 1989: H3889).

Many opponents of flag protection, however, were determined not to be outflanked on the issue of patriotism; in 112 speeches (25 percent), lawmakers challenged efforts to restrict First Amendment protection, specifically referring to American patriotism (224 such statements were found, accounting for 21 percent in this category). Senator Barbara Mikulski offered a conservative worldview, but stood firmly against flag protection: "I am deeply concerned about the desecration of the U.S. flag because of what it says about our culture, our values, and our patriotism. . . . We cannot build a society for the 21st century that advocates permissiveness without responsibility. . . . But I must vote against this amendment" (*CR*, December 12, 1995: S18380).

Military References to soldiers and the U.S. military were found in 342 speeches (43 percent), the third-most common theme, generating 615 such statements. Numerous commentaries visited the significance of flag protection in the American Revolution, the War of 1812, the Civil War, the First and Second World Wars, the Korean War, the war in Vietnam, and Desert Storm. Throughout the flag-protection debate, remarks similar to the one by Congressman Roy Dyson were commonplace: "The desecration of the flag is an insult to [soldiers], what they fought for and all that for which we stand" (*CR*, August 4, 1989: E2941). While commemorating Pearl Harbor Day, Senator Richard Shelby voiced his support for a constitutional amendment to protect the flag from desecration: "The American flag is a national symbol of the values of this country was founded on. Many Americans have fought and died to defend these values and this country. It is an insult to these patriots, their relatives, and all other citizens who hold this country dear, to burn or desecrate the symbol of our Nation and our freedom" (*CR*, December 7, 1995: S18127). Joining the chorus, Senator Pete Wilson criticized the U.S. Supreme Court for its ruling in *Johnson*: "Mr. President, 44 years ago, 6,000 courageous U.S. marines sacrificed their lives in attack upon Iwo Jima which culminated in the raising of the American flag on Mount Suribachi. Just five weeks ago, on June 21, 1989, the U.S. Supreme Court decided by a 5-to-4 vote that those who burn or otherwise desecrate the American flag have a constitutionally protected right under the first amendment to do so. Mr. President, I profoundly and emphatically disagree" (*CR*, July 18, 1989:S8104).

Much like the category of patriotism, many members of Congress who opposed flag protection spoke proudly of the U.S. military; indeed, 22 percent of these speeches (n = 75), containing 119 statements (19 percent of this category), referred specifically to the military in defense of the Bill of Rights. Senator Patty Murray shared her family history in terms of military service: "As an American, and the daughter of a disabled veteran, I take deep pride in our great Nation. . . . For my father's sacrifices, I will vote against this amendment" (*CR*, December 12, 1995: S18379). Drawing on semiotics, Congressman Leon Panetta declared: "Those of us who have served in uniform did not serve to defend a symbol or a piece of cloth, but the liberties and freedoms represented by that flag" (*CR*, June 21, 1990:H4061).

Civil Religion Speeches resonating civil religion had a distinct presence in the debate over flag desecration. Thirty-five percent of all speeches in Congress (n = 280) featured references to civil religion, often alluding to conservative views of morality and what reactionaries consider to be proper conduct by American citizens (overall, 643 statements, comprising 11 percent of the sample, were coded into this category). By drawing attention to civil religion, we are able to discern the degree to which flag burning has been moralized by politicians acting as moral entrepreneurs. Congressman Clarence E. Miller captured the prevailing morality by asking rhetorically: "What could be more offensive to the general public than the burning of that most sacred of American symbols, the American flag?" (*CR*, June 22, 1989:E2291).

Moral condemnation, as a product of civil religion, lends itself to the emergence of moral panic over flag desecration and vilification of protestors. Consider the moral tone expressed by Congressman Donald Lukens: "The ruling of the U.S. Supreme Court is contradictory to the morals and beliefs of a great majority of the American people. To allow anyone to defile and desecrate such a revered symbol is not only foolish, but morally wrong" (CR, June 29, 1989:H3235). With fire and brimstone, Congressman James Cooper angrily pronounced: "I'm all for punishing sinners, flag burners included. . . . Flag burners should be placed in jail" (CR, June 21, 1990:H4065).

In his lengthy, sermon-like speech on the evils of flag desecration, Congressman Gerald Solomon traversed the moral gamut, ranging from imperiled traditional values to the dangers of popular culture:

> If the flag amendment is about anything, it's about holding the line on respect, on the values that you and I risked our lives to preserve. We live in a society that respects little and honors still less. Most, if not all, of today's ills can be traced to a breakdown in respect, for laws, for traditions, for people, for the things held sacred by the great bulk of us. Just as the godless are succeeding at removing God from everyday life, growing numbers of people have come to feel they're not answerable to anything larger than themselves. The message seems to be that nothing takes priority over the needs and desires and "rights" of the individual. Nothing is forbidden. Everything is permissible, from the shockingly vulgar music that urges kids to go out to shoot cops, to "art" that depicts Christ plunging into a vat of urine—to the desecration of a cherished symbol like the U.S. flag. (CR, February 28, 1996:E232)

Similarly, Henry Hyde embraced institutional religion while taking aim at avant-garde art, particularly Dread Scott's art display in Chicago: "[Here is] a sentence for the Book of *Genesis* that came to me as I watched the people stepping carefully around the flag on the floor. 'You meant it for evil, but God meant it for good'" (CR, April 18, 1989:E1274). In another speech, Hyde maintained his civil-religious posture, saying: "the flag is indeed sacred. . . . It is like the sacrament in the Catholic Church. It is like the holy book in other places or religions. We have standards in this country of decency and there are some things you do not do"—flag desecration (CR, June 29, 1989:H3235).

In classic civil-religious form, Congressman Joe Barton demonstrated further that flag burning has been lumped together with other issues shaping public discourse on the separation of church and state: "Look at their [Supreme Court] decision on prayer in schools and public places. They promoted the idea that it was dangerous to allow prayer in schools. Yes, it was dangerous, but not to the American people, only to the Communist party who hates the mere mention of the word God" (CR, July 18,

1989:E2542). Congressman William Lipinski also asserted a sense of sweeping moral authority by announcing: "We the people, choose our Government to protect our God-given rights and to help us make our lives worth living" (*CR*, June 28, 1989:H3383).

Despite the distinctly moral tone in the congressional debate over flag protection, several lawmakers objected strongly to civil religion (comprising 15 percent of the speeches, n = 43, and 19 percent of the statements, n = 120). Congressman Ron Paul, for example, argued: "There are some, I am sure, who would like to equate the state with God. . . . We imply by this amendment that the State is elevated to a religion, a dangerous notion and one the founders feared. Calling flag burning blasphemous is something we should do with great caution" (*CR*, June 10, 1997:H3580). Similarly, Congressman George Brown added: "No human rules over others by divine right. No flag that symbolizes a ruler or state is sacred. To even speak in such terms denies the primacy of God in the world, demeans the spiritual basis of freedom and democracy and smacks of idolatry. The very term 'desecrate' means 'to violate the sanctity of . . .' and sanctity is 'the quality or state of being holy or sacred.' No earthly flag is sacred or holy" (*CR*, June 21, 1990:H4038).

American History Thirty-one percent of the speeches on flag protection contained references to American history (n = 251), producing 475 (8 percent) such statements. Even in arguments against flag protection, historical statements were common, as found in 84 speeches (33 percent of this category) and 179 statements (38 percent). Still, most historical references were used to justify making flag desecration a crime, as if legislation would somehow preserve American history. From that perspective, Senator Dianne Feinstein noted: "In 1782, the Congress of the Confederation chose the same colors for the Great Seal of the United States: Red for hardiness and courage; white for purity and innocence; and blue for vigilance, perseverance, and justice" (*CR*, December 11, 1995:S18337).

References to American history in the flag-protection debate commonly rested on nostalgic reflection. Consider the prose-like quality of Senator Mitch McConnell's speech in which he recalled events of the War of 1812: "But when the dawn came, the bombardment ceased and a dead silence fell over the entire battlescape. Dr. Beanes and Francis Scott Key strained to see any signs of life from the battered ramparts of Fort McHenry. And what they saw brought them incredible joy; despite the brutal onslaught of the night before, the American flag—torn and barely visible in the smoke and mist—still streamed gallantly over Fort McHenry" (*CR*, December 12, 1995: S18377). Numerous other comments on America's history also issued claims for the cultural significance of the Stars and Stripes: "We proclaim that our 'Flag' is a living instrument of our glorious history. It is a living part of what is America" (Congressman Gus Yatron, *CR*, August 2, 1989:E2782). Senator Orrin Hatch intoned "There are symbols and there are Symbols. There are some so rooted in history and custom, and in the heroic imagination of a nation that they transcend the merely symbolic; they become presences" (*CR*, December 6, 1996:S18040). Drawing on notions of history and culture, many lawmakers perpetuated popular American myths and legends. Congressman Christopher H. Smith told his colleagues: "One of the first things our children learn as they enter grade school is reverence for the flag of the United States. They learn the Pledge of Allegiance, and the significance of the Stars and Stripes, as well as the story of Betsy Ross" (*CR*, June 29, 1989:E2397)

Popular Consensus Intent on presenting flag protection as the will of the people, many lawmakers argued that they planned to vote for flag legislation because they believed that it was what their constituents want them to do. A total of 166 speeches (21 percent) relied on such populist reasoning, producing 291 (5 percent) such statements. Senator Bob Dole was among the more vocal supporters of flag protection, often referring to the will of voters whom he portrayed as common folks: "In addition to the letters, there are hundreds of names on the petition. They are just good, hardworking people. They do not take the *Washington Post*. They do not take the *New York Times*. They go to work every day. They attend memorial services. . . . We believe that an amendment to the Constitution should be instituted" (*CR*, July 26, 1989:S8750).

In the debate occurring the day before Pearl Harbor Day in 1996, Senator Hatch referred to his constituents: "Seventy-three percent of my fellow Utahns favor a constitutional amendment to protect the flag" (*CR*, December 6, 1996:S18039). Likewise, Congressman Robert Logomarsino insisted: "The overwhelming number of Americans in this country want for it to be a crime to burn the American flag" (*CR*, June 22, 1989:H3004). Transcending opinion polls, however, many politicians took the opportunity draw broader characterizations of American citizens, depictions which conveniently supported the campaign to criminalize flag desecration. Congressman James T. Walsh pronounced: "The American people want instinctively to protect the flag, as we would any element of our way of life, from those who want to destroy that way of life" (*CR*, June 28, 1989:E2351). By contrast, opponents of flag protection in Congress stayed clear of the populist argument and refrained from mentioning the will of the people.

Flawed Legislation As expected, lawmakers wrangled over the intent and language of flag protection, pointing out multiple contradictions. In 20 percent of the speeches (n = 159, containing 578 such statements, 10 percent), congressmen characterized flag protection as flawed, and in 98 speeches (62 percent of this category) lawmakers voiced their opposition to flag protection on the grounds that it represented self-defeating legislation (421 such statements were made, comprising 73 percent in this category). Alluding to compulsory patriotism in the form of criminalization of protest, Senator Bob Kerrey enlightened his colleagues by saying:

> The respect for the flag is something that is acquired. One makes a choice based upon an understanding of what the flag stands for, and that understanding does not come in some simple fashion. It does not come with a snap of our fingers: Amend the Constitution, pass a law, and thus all of a sudden, young people all across the nation—or adults for that matter—will immediately acquire respect for the flag based upon knowing that they will be punished if they do not. (*CR*, December 12, 1995:S18374)

In another argument opposing flag protection on grounds that it constitutes ineffective legislation, Senator Robb reminded Congress of the problem of redundancy: "We already have in place rules and regulations and statutes that prohibit desecration of our flag under certain circumstances. . . . If the flag is being burned for the purpose of inciting a riot, or anything along those lines, there are already laws in place to prohibit that kind of activity" (December 12, 1995:S18378). At a higher level of abstraction, Senator Carl Levin elaborated on semiotic and ontological elements of flag protection:

> The amendment does not define the flag. Does it cover Jasper John's famous painting of overlapping flags? Does it apply to a T-shirt with a picture of the flag on it? How about wearing a T-shirt with holes in it? Is a 49-star flag a flag of the United States? Does it apply to a flag hung upside down? Would it prohibit the use of the flag in commercial advertisements? These questions, and dozens like them, would be left unanswered. (*CR*, December 12, 1995:S18382)

Interestingly, a significant proportion of lawmakers who cited flaws in flag protection (38 percent) still supported measures to criminalize protest in the form of a statute or an amendment.

Political Diversion Alluding to political diversion, 8 percent of the speeches (n = 67) contained remarks suggesting that flag protection was not an important issue and that Congress ought to direct its attention to more pressing social problems. In the course of the debate, 127 such statements (2 percent) were delivered, most of them (n = 105, 83 percent in this category) issued by opponents of flag protection in 52 speeches (78 percent in this category). Challenging the perception that flag burning endangers American society, Senator John Kerry emerged as one of the more assertive opponents of flag protection; moreover, many of his comments addressed political diversion. "[Flag burning] is not, in my judgment, a great threat to this country. What is a great threat to this country is when 40 percent of our youth do not know what the Cold War was; when 50 percent do not know whether Adolf Hitler was an enemy in the Second World War" (*CR*, December 12, 1995:S18375). Later during the debate, Kerry added:

> This is the ultimate irony. Over the last few months—they [Republicans] have come to this floor with endless speeches about preserving this democracy—their agenda does exactly the opposite. It dishonors veterans with the most destructive budget that I have ever seen in my years here. My Republican colleagues came to the floor with Medicaid cuts this year that would have eliminated coverage for 4,700 Massachusetts veterans—2,300 of them under the age of 65, disabled, and ineligible for Medicare coverage. The remaining 2,400 are over 65 and 1,200 of them are in nursing home.(*CR*, December 12, 1995:S18381)

Bolstering the fight against political diversion, Senator Herb Kohl suggested that: "Instead of focusing on the flag itself, what about the federal deficit (more than $200 billion a year) and the national debt (nearing $5 trillion)? These are far greater threats to Old Glory than some clown with a cigarette lighter at a protest rally." (*CR*, December 11, 1995:S18347) Likewise, Congressman Dave McCurdy pleaded, "We will survive the senseless acts of a few flag burners. America's future is in doubt, instead, because of our huge Federal budget deficit, a decaying infrastructure, a regressive tax policy, increasing illiteracy and declining economic competitiveness. I urge President Bush to turn his leadership responsibilities to these areas which pose genuine threats to our Nation" (*CR*, June 21, 1990:H4063). Ironically, even congressmen who cited political diversion still endorsed flag protection, a tendency found in 22 percent of the speeches in this category.

Criminal Justice Sixty-four speeches (8 percent), contained 109 (2 percent) references to the criminal justice system and its role in flag protection. Cutting to the heart of criminalization, staunch supporters of flag-protection laws favored deploying criminal-justice resources to defend the nation's emblem. Congressman Ike Skelton submitted his endorsement of legal intervention to save the flag: "Thus a constitutional amendment to change this ruling is in order, and I support such an amendment allowing a law to stand that makes it a crime to desecrate Old Glory" (*CR*, June 29, 1989:E2377). Similarly, Congressman William Clinger sarcastically quipped: "I think that if you can punish someone for pulling the label off a mattress under Federal law, you should be able to punish someone for burning a flag" (*CR*, June 21, 1990:H4083). Congressman Gerald Solomon, like many other lawmakers, exaggerated the nature of flag desecration in an effort to criminalize the political protest they deemed offensive: "To that end, burning this blessed symbol is purely a crime against the State" (*CR*, February 13, 1997:E290).

In 25 of these speeches (39 percent), however, opposition to flag protection was expressed in 40 statements (37 percent in this category), most of which argued that relying on criminal-justice personnel to enforce flag-protection laws constituted an egregious misuse of government resources. Once again Senator John Kerry sounded off:

> If the suspicion occurs, under this new constitutional amendment—I assume enabling legislation will occur as a consequence—that somebody, in their home, is desecrating their flag, it will now fall to the police or to the Federal law enforcement officials, I suspect, depending upon how the statute is written, to go into the home to make sure that individual is not desecrating his or her flag. That is the kind of response we are going to have our law enforcement people now charged with the responsibility of making. (*CR*, December 12, 1995:S18374)

Adding to the potential problem of law enforcement, Senator Joseph Biden, in his opposition to the flag amendment, alluded to authoritarian aesthetics dictated by elitism: "[The measure would] permit prosecutors and juries to convict on the basis of whether they like or do not like the defendant. . . . The [Bush] administration wants the States to know whether it is a fringe artist displaying the flag on the floor of an art museum, or whether it is a veteran displaying the flag on the ground in front of a war memorial" (*CR*, June 25, 1990:S8635). Other critics of flag protection reflected on the shifting landscape of social control, including Senator Dale Bumpers: "I was insulted by it, and I did not like it. But I did not want to see anybody there I wanted to send to prison. Is that a legal crime? Why, of course, it is not. . . . So if you had this flag amendment . . . [w]e take freedom away from people and create a class of political prisoners. We will imprison people" (*CR*, December 6, 1995:S18061-2). Congressman Ron Paul reiterated a similar view of the dangers of criminalizing flag desecration: "Will the country actually be improved with this amendment? Will true patriotism thus thrive as the malcontents are legislated into submission? Do we improve the character of angry people because we threaten them with a prison cell better occupied by a rapist? . . . A national flag police can only exist in a totalitarian state" (*CR*, June 10, 1997:H3580-1).

Implications for Authoritarian Aesthetics and Moral Panic

In summarizing these findings, arguments surrounding the flag-protection debate were shaped prominently by themes of free speech and the First Amendment (74 percent), patriotism (57 percent), U.S. military (43 percent), civil religion (35 percent), American history (31 percent), popular consensus (21 percent), flawed legislation (20 percent), political diversion (8 percent), and criminal justice (8 percent). A key benefit of content analysis is that it allows us to quantify various qualitative features of the debate over flag protection, thereby shedding light on how the issue is framed by moral entrepreneurs and their political rhetoric. In addition to these major themes on flag protection, our investigation also reveals implications for authoritarian aesthetics and moral panic. During the debate, Senator Glenn took the opportunity to comment on the proper treatment of the Stars and Stripes.

> I remember back in 1976 we were celebrating the Bicentennial and we had bikinis, flag bikinis advertised in papers. I remember once watching a rock and roll concert that year, and it was quite a spectacle. It was one to make your blood boil, because the lead guitarist, who was bared from the waist up, did not have shirt or anything on, but he is going at it and strumming, and banging away on this thing. Pretty soon his pants started slide down, and lo and behold, you guessed it: He had flag shorts on. The audience went wild. I find that more objectionable than I do some of the things we are talking about, to protect the flag here from burning it. I do not know whether body fluids get spilled on the flag in situations like that, with the bikinis or whatever. But I find that reprehensible. (CR, December 12, 1995:S18389)

Senator Hatch elaborated on flag desecration, placing heavy emphasis on aesthetics and traditional values and symbolism:

> But why can we not ban in the interest of patriotism and honor and values in this country, dispicable, rotten, dirty, conduct against our national symbol? It amazes me that these folks come in here and say how much they support the flag, how wonderful it is, and how terrible it is for people to do these awful things—to smear the flag with excrement, to urinate on it, to tramp on it, to burn it. What do we stand for around here? Have we gotten so bad in this country that no values count? (CR, December 8, 1995:S18281)

Similarly, Senator Chuck Grassley referred to popular consent, suggesting that U.S. citizens want to respect authority: "Why have the American people become so involved in this effort to protect the flag? I believe the answer lies in the rediscovery of core American values, like respect for authority" (CR, December 11, 1995:S18356). Authoritarian aesthetics provide a reactionary foundation for moral panic. Indeed, the flag-protection debate featured claims that American society is permissive and immoral. Senator Hatch pronounced: "I think it would be beneficial to the country to start reexamining some of these things, some of the permissive things, that we have allowed to occur in this society that have really denigrated our society" (*CR*, December 12, 1995:S18390). Congressman Ron Packard concurred: "We live in a liberal, permissive society that appears willing to allow flag burning" (*CR*, June 21, 1990:H4037). "We need this amendment because the soul of our society seems to have been taken over by the tennis-shoe theology of 'just do it.' If it feels good, just do it. Forget about obligation to society. Forget about personal responsibility," added Senator Ron Grams (*CR*, December 6, 1995:S18063).

Operating in the context of moral panic, flag crusaders interpret flag desecration as symptomatic of deeper threats against *decent* society, linking several social ills. "Drugs, crime, and pornography," according to Senator Hatch, "debase our society to an extent that no one would have predicted just two generations ago. The breakdown in the family, the division among our citizens, threaten our progress as one people bound together by common purposes and values" (*CR*, December 6, 1996:S18039). Congressman Owen Pickett added, "With this decision [*Johnson*], the Court cloaks the most offensive behavior as political expression. I submit that burning the flag is not expression. It conveys no real ideas, not political thoughts. It is an act that is designed solely to shock the moral sensibilities and patriotic impulses of our people" (*CR*, June 22, 1989:H2999). In his speech denouncing flag burning, Congressman Newt Gingrich quoted conservative columnist Michael Novak: "In recent years, however, many sensitive scholars have begun to fear that our nation is losing its sense of community. They discern the rapid moral and political atomism" (*CR*, July 21, 1989:E2616). In his support for a constitutional amendment to shield the flag, Senator William Cohen offered a broad assessment of American society: "There is abundant evidence that our civil society is fraying around the edges. People lack faith in the capacity of government to act in the interest of the people" (*CR*, December 12, 1995:S18387). Likewise, Congressman Joseph Bloomfield commented, "The vast majority of Americans believe there are symbols in our civic life that are still sacred. There no longer seem to be any standards for acceptable behavior. I believe my constituents are fed up with social and cultural anarchy and, quite frankly, so am I. I don't believe anarchy is what the framers of the Constitution had in mind. Liberty yes, anarchy no" (*CR*, June 21, 1990:H4082).

In addition to exaggerated claims about the dangers of flag burning, the *Congressional Record* included reactions to moral panic whereby lawmakers resisted perceptions of societal decline. Senator John Kerry insisted that the proposed amendment marks "an extraordinary overreaction to a virtually nonexistent problem. . . . The issue is left over from the dimmest days of the Bush administration when a desperate grasp for symbols masked an abject want of ideas" (*CR*, December 12, 1995:S18381). That perspective was shared by Senator Edward Kennedy who added: "This [flag desecration] is hardly the kind of serious and widespread problem in American life that warrants a loophole in the first amendment. Surely, there is no clear and present danger that warrants such a change" (*CR*, December 11, 1995:S18336–7). Regrettably, arguments against moral panic were limited to a handful of lawmakers. Whether or not they framed the issue in moral terms, the vast majority of politicians participated in moral panic over flag desecration; by simply casting their vote making flag burning a crime, those members of Congress fueled the crusade sponsored by moral entrepreneurs.

CONCLUSION

This chapter examined reactions to flag burning by politicians, many of whom operated as moral entrepreneurs interpreting the desecration of Old Glory as a threat to American society. By reviewing the public statements by U.S. presidents, we confirmed that the flag-burning controversy was invented during the Bush administration, and with the work of Republican opinion-brokers, the issue spread quickly throughout Congress. Although President Clinton has opposed flag protection in the form of a constitutional amendment, the crusade to save the Stars and Stripes endures in Congress. By 1995, evidence of moral panic over flag desecration was still evident as Senator Hatch offered an ominous worldview: "We live in a time where standards have eroded. Civility and mutual respect—preconditions for the robust views in society—are in decline. Individual rights are constantly expanded but responsibilities are shirked and scorned. Absolutes are ridiculed. Values are deemed relative. Nothing is sacred. There are no limits. Anything goes" (*CR*, December 12, 1995:S18391). Such interpretations of American society are drawn from civil religion whereby secular life is channeled through the lens of conservative moralism. As we have seen, 49 of the 50 states are poised to pass a constitutional amendment. Paul Burke, president of the Kansas State Senate, referring to a constitutional amendment to bar desecration of the American flag, quipped: "It would blow through our House and Senate like a thunderstorm through Kansas. I don't think anybody would be opposed" (*New York Times*, 1989, July 4:1). Similarly, Tim Kelly, president of the Alaska Senate, noted that the flag amendment "would pass within 30 days. You're going to have a few liberals whining in the House, but they'll be overwhelmed by the majority of legislators and public opinion" (*New York Times*, July 4, 1989: 1). Moreover, compulsory patriotism abounds, as many state legislatures rely on civil religion to protect the flag as a venerated object. In California, State Senator John Doolittle proposed that the flag be saluted by the senators each time they gather on the floor; ordinarily, the Senate recites the Pledge of Allegiance only on Mondays after a prayer (Ingram, July 2, 1989:3).

Whereas a content analysis of the *Congressional Record* focuses on public manifestations of responses to flag burning, we were mindful of behind-the-scenes activities shaping the debate, particularly efforts by the flag lobby. Indeed, many lawmakers commended such groups as the CFA, the American Legion, and various other veterans organizations for their support in defending Old Glory. Contributing to moral panic, the flag lobby issued the following statement: "The real victims of flag burning are our children. The greatest tragedy in flag mutilation is the disrespect it teaches our children, disrespect for the values it embodies, and disrespect to those who have sacrificed for those values. Disrespect is the genesis of hate, it provokes the dissolution of our unity, a unity which has only one symbol—the flag" (CFA, July 10, 1997: 1). Incidentally, that form of anxiety is consistent with other free-floating fears manifesting as a threat to children, a common manifestation of moral panic (see Best, 1987, 1989, 1990).

In more secular terms, the debate over flag protection centered on First Amendment issues; moreover, most speeches favored curtailing free speech as a remedy for flag burning. Justifying his support for making flag desecration a crime, Congressman Amo Houghton suggested that freedom is a myth: "the essence of freedom is our willingness to give up some it—meaning the more extreme forms. I happen to feel this is one. Desecrating the flag is a freedom we do not need" (*CR*, June 23, 1989:E2304). Despite overwhelming congressional support for flag protection, a few voices of dissent remained committed to the ideals of liberty, and many opponents of an amendment were determined not to be outflagged in the arena of patriotism and support for U.S. troops. In bolstering the campaign against flag protection, a handful of congressmen repeated the impassioned story of James Warner, who survived brutal treatment as a prisoner of war in Vietnam. Even though Warner was tortured by his Communist captors and confined to solitary confinement for 13 months, he later denounced measures to protect the flag on the grounds that it impedes freedom. During a particularly brutal interrogation, the Vietcong showed Warner a photograph of Americans burning a flag as a protest against the war. "There," the officer said. "People in your country protest against your cause. That proves that you are wrong." Warner countered his captor's logic, saying "No . . . . That proves that I am right. In my country we are not afraid of freedom, even if it means that people disagree with us." Warner would become a Reagan administration White House aide, but remained committed to the Bill of Rights and the principles they represent. Amid the flag furor, Warner professed: "Don't be afraid of freedom, it is the best weapon we have" (Warner, July 11, 1989:A21).

NOTES

1. Several research assistants undertook research tasks for this chapter. In particular, Brian Homcy participated in the analysis of the *Public Papers of the President*, and Tom Ehrlich, Jennifer Mennel, Elizabeth Raimondo, Mike Spatola, Armando Patino, and Joseph Fredua-Agyman worked on the *Congressional Record*.

2. Whereas our search for flag protection references reaches back to 1984 (the year Johnson was arrested for flag desecration in Texas), it was not until 1989 that relevant items began to appear in the *Congressional Record*.

9

The Media and Its Contradictions
in the Flag Panic

While last year's event was a major "media event" complete with flags, bunting, and military pageantry, Tuesday's [June 12, 1990] was a small gathering before a handful of reporters and cameras with little advance billing.
—*Journalists David Lauter and Paul Houston* (Los Angeles Times, *June 13, 1990: A-19*)

Politician's self-serving hysteria over flag burning is as much a desecration as a protestor burning the flag. Flag frenzy bestows undeserved attention on flag burners.
—*Editorial*, Chicago Tribune, *June 30, 1989:24*

As mentioned in Chapter 7, the media play a vital role in the drama of moral panic, contributing significantly to the reification of deviance and the reproduction of social anxiety. The construction of flag burning as a social threat in the late 1980s relied heavily on print and electronic journalism; in fact, it is unlikely that moral panic over flag desecration would have emerged without such media coverage. As a constellation of news organizations, the media carried out its duties to inform the public of the controversy over flag desecration. Still, as a story-telling institution, the media presented the flag-burning issue according to a popular formula of drama, featuring good versus evil, virtue versus vice, order versus chaos, and heroes versus villains. Many sources quoted in these news *stories* exaggerated the threat of flag desecration, the virtue of patriotic politicians, and the wickedness of flag burners. Consider the following quotes published in the *New York Times*:

If flag burning is wrong, it is wrong no matter how many times it occurs. In fact, we contend that it is a problem even if no one ever burns another American flag. (William Detweiler, quoted in *New York Times*, June 12, 1995: 14)

I know it sounds corny, but I stayed up and read the biography of Patrick Henry and the Bill of Rights. It was a cultural thing for me. My father was born on the Fourth of July; he was a flag waver, a World War II veteran who taught us how to fold and display it. If my constituents see some guy on television burning the flag, they go psycho. (Raskey, 1990:6)

By burning the flag, they were engaging in acts of mindless nihilism. (Solicitor General Kenneth Starr, quoted in Lewis, May 15, 1990:16)

The power of the media lies in its inherent ability to give birth to an issue; moreover, the furor over flag burning demonstrates the media's unique facility to create a phenomenon that, in a manner of speaking, becomes larger than life. A case in point is the moral panic over flag desecration in 1989.

Whereas the production of news can be viewed as serving the valuable function of informing the public about a particular social issue, such activity also should be understood as fulfilling the economic imperatives of the media. After all, in contemporary culture, news is commodified deliberately in ways that streamline its consumption. Even a passing glance at the media during the flag panic in late 1989 reveals their vested interests. By relentlessly repeating the story's plot—a virtuous, patriotic struggle to protect the Stars and Stripes from despicable revolutionary communists who threaten America's moral fiber—the media generated a form of public attention that translated into profits for news organizations. According to basic economics, more news coverage of flag burning meant more revenue.

Obviously, news coverage of flag burning served the interests of moral entrepreneurs, especially politicians who depend on such exposure to advance their crusade to shield the flag, and by doing so advance their careers in government. Likewise, protestors who torch the flag also enjoy the media's spotlight, since they are granted a public platform to air their grievances against the state. The interests of the media, however, are not without contradictions (see Goldstein, 1996a:138–44). On the one hand, news coverage of flag desecration generates income for news organizations, but on the other, it inflames moral panic to the extent that proposals to criminalize protest ultimately threaten the fundamental freedoms of the press. This dialectical feature of the moral panic over flag desecration suggests that the media engage in activities that appear to "burn the issue at both ends."

This chapter takes a careful look into the inner workings of the media in an effort to understand how they contribute to the social construction of flag desecration—in particular, the process of news sourcing and agenda setting. Similarly, we analyze the press's attempt to reconcile its contradictions by examining editorials that establish newspapers' positions on flag protection and the criminalizing of protest, issues having direct implications for First Amendment freedoms afforded to political dissenters as well as the media.[1]

FRAMING THE FLAG-BURNING ISSUE IN THE MEDIA

Attending to the processes by which the media frame social issues remains a chief concern of scholars studying moral panic. Cohen (1972) reminds us that in the process of elevating putative social problems to the heights of moral panic, the media sensationalizes and stylizes threats to society; by doing so, it produces folk devils, a type of villain demonized by moral crusaders (see also Ferrell, 1996; Jenkins, 1992, 1994). The vilification of folk devils serves the interests of moral entrepreneurs who, in the eyes of the public, appear increasingly virtuous in the face of a social threat, thus empowering their crusade. In a similar vein, Cohen (1972:16) notes that the "media have long operated as agents of moral indignation in their own right," suggesting that their coverage of perceived social problems typically arouses the public by generating concern, or panic. "Less concretely, the media might leave behind a diffuse feeling of anxiety about the situation: 'Something should be done about it,' 'Where will it end?' or 'This sort of thing can't go on for ever'" (Cohen, 1972:17). Mediated images of putative social problems go beyond visual consumption; indeed, they trigger emotional stress among the public that can be manipulated into support for a moral enterprise, resulting in proposals for social change (see Erikson, 1966; Gusfield, 1963; Wilkins, 1965).

Flag protection through making protest a crime is considered by civil libertarians and First Amendment advocates as a regressive, repressive measure of social control insofar as it restricts established freedoms of expression, thereby granting the state enhanced power over its citizens. Why, then, is the public willing to accept additional forms of social control that contribute to repression by the state? In search of answers to this predicament, it is important to recognize that moral entrepreneurs rely on the media to publicize their claims. In this case, flag crusaders claim that flag burning is a harm so great that it constitutes a crime; thus, flag desecration is transformed into a social problem specifically tailored to the criminal-justice apparatus. Consider the following statement by Representative Robert Dornan, who argued that flag burning "is no more a form of protest than the KKK's cross burning. The act of flag burning is not meant to convey a political idea. It is an act that is solely meant to provoke and offend. . . . It is simply an act of cultural and patriotic destruction" (Fritz, June 23, 1989:1). Proposing a constitutional amendment, Dornan declared, "The Congress and the states shall have power to prohibit the act of desecration of the flag of the United States and to set criminal penalties for that act" (Fritz, June 23, 1989:1).

Likewise, moral entrepreneurs favoring the criminalization of protest redefined the nature of flag desecration in ways that were politically self-serving. A 1990 document issued by the National Republican Senatorial Committee reads, "Flag desecration is not free speech. It is an unacceptable and violent assault on the values and institutions that underly [sic] the political and social structure of our country" (*Washington Post*, June 20, 1990:A28). In terms of political proposals designed to punish and deter flag desecration, many politicians defied logic in arguing that such measures would not restrict existing liberties. Representative Lynn Martin reported, "A constitutional amendment is no threat to anyone's right of free speech or expression. We should be willing to support a constitutional amendment for our flag" (Locin, 1990:3).

Turning to the emerging field of newsmaking criminology, additional light is shed on the process by which offensive or deviant behavior becomes criminalized in the news, thereby, paving the way for criminal justice intervention.[2] At its most basic level, crime is "'news' because its treatment evokes threat to, but also reaffirms, the consensual morality of the society: a modern morality play takes place before us in which the 'devil' is both symbolically and physically cast out from the society by its guardians—the police and the judiciary" (Hall et al., 1978:66). Reaching beyond the significance of Durkheimian perspectives on crime news, however, recent research tends to focus on the social-construction processes dictating how crime events become news. Critical investigations have explored the relationship between the media and its sources, particularly the primary definers of crime. In studying mediated versions of street crime, researchers confirm that politicians and law enforcement officials serve as the primary definers and sources for crime news. More significantly, primary definitions are imposed early in the reification of crime news by politicians and state officials whose credibility typically rests on their positions of power and prestige; consequently, their ideological perspectives shape popular images of crime (Barak, 1994; Chermak, 1997; Ericson, Baranek, and Chan, 1991, 1989, 1987; Fishman, 1978; Hall, et al., 1978; Humphries, 1981; Surette, 1998; Welch, Fenwick, and Roberts, 1997, 1998).

Deepening our investigation of the media, we examined sources newspapers relied on in covering the flag-burning controversy. Performing a content analysis on quoted statements attributed to news sources, we explored *how* the press constructs images of flag desecration and from *whose* perspective. Taking a cue from crime-wave critic Mark Fishman, "all knowledge is knowledge from some point of view" (1978:531).

SAMPLE AND METHOD

In an effort to discern patterns of sourcing in the press and their coverage of the flag-burning controversy, we examined the *Chicago Tribune, Los Angeles Times, New York Times*, and *Washington Post*. These newspapers were selected because of their large circulation, their reputation for offering readers national coverage, and because together they contribute to a sense of geographic representation. For each newspaper in our sample, *all* articles on flag desecration were extracted for content analysis, beginning in 1984 (the year of the Dallas flag burning, which led to *Johnson*) through 1998. The purpose of our content analysis was to identify *all* sources quoted in the four newspapers contained in the sample and determine whether those sources supported or opposed flag protection (either in the form of a criminal statute or a constitutional amendment). Further, we delved into the reasons cited by each source to justify its position on the criminalizing of flag desecration.[3]

FINDINGS

Between 1984 and 1998, 147 newspaper articles on flag desecration were published in the *New York Times*, 110 in the *Washington Post*, 102 in the *Chicago Tribune*, and 87 in the *Los Angeles Times*—altogether a total of 446 articles. The greatest number of articles on flag desecration appeared in 1989 when 209 were published, followed by 136 in 1990; during those two years, the 345 articles accounted for 77 percent of the sample. These figures coincide with the emergence of the flag-burning controversy following the U.S. Supreme Court's decision in *Johnson* (1989), prompting the enactment of the Flag Protection Act of 1989, which was invalidated by the high court in *Eichman* (1990). In 1995, 58 articles appeared, as Congress mobilized support for a constitutional amendment to protect the flag; similar congressional activity surfaced again in 1997, as reported in 19 articles (see Figure 9.1).

News Sources and Their Positions on Flag Protection

A content analysis of 446 articles identified 615 news sources whose remarks included their position on flag protection. Overall, 275 sources (45 percent) supported flag protection while 340 (55 percent) opposed such measures. In covering the flag debate, the press relied disproportionately on politicians as news sources; in fact, 363 politicians were quoted, comprising 59 percent of the sample. Their positions on the flag issue were strikingly balanced, as 180 politicians (50 percent) were quoted in support

Flag Desecration Articles: 1984-1998
(n=446)*

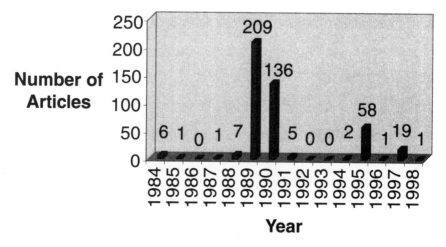

Figure 9:1. Flag Desecration Articles: 1984–1998 (n = 446)*
*Figure combines *New York Times, Washington Post, Chicago Tribune,* and *Los Angeles Times.*

of flag legislation while the same percent opposed flag statutes and proposals for a constitutional amendment (Table 9.1).

Lamenting flag desecration, Senate Minority Leader Bob Dole invoked emotional sentimentalism: "The purpose—the need—for this amendment will not be found in a textbook or in a treatise on constitutional law. No, it will be found in the emotions of the hearts—the emotions deeply rooted in the real-life experiences of millions of Americans—and emotions that are crying out today to give the flag real and lasting protection" (Povich, October 20, 1989:4). Fellow Republicans also framed the flag issue in emotional terms. Wendy DeMocker, spokeswoman for the Republican Senatorial Campaign Committee, reminded the media: "This is a very powerful, very potent, very emotional issue" (Chapman, 1990:25). Armed with such an emotional issue, Republicans opened fire on rival Democrats: "Nothing disgusts me more than liberals who hide behind the 1st Amendment and want to support people who desecrate Old Glory" (Congressman Van Hilleary quoted in Drew, March 1, 1995:8). Congressman Robert Michel also supported making flag burning a crime, embellishing his rhetoric with civil religion: "We are taking this step because it is the only way to protect the flag, given the recent Supreme Court decision. The flag already is con-

Table 9.1.   News Sources and Their Positions on Flag Protection*

Source	Support	%	Oppose	%	Total	%
Politicians	180	(50%)	183	(50%)	363	(59%)
Judges / Justices	28	(33%)	57	(67%)	85	(14%)
Citizens	18	(49%)	19	(51%)	37	(6%)
Military	19	(68%)	9	(32%)	28	(5%)
Editorials	10	(40%)	15	(60%)	25	(4%)
Activists	2	(12%)	15	(88%)	17	(3%)
Law professors	4	(24%)	13	(76%)	17	(3%)
Prosecutors	7	(50%)	7	(50%)	14	(2%)
Defense lawyers	—	—	10	(100%)	10	(2%)
Journalists	4	(40%)	6	(60%)	10	(2%)
Lobbyists	3	(60%)	2	(40%)	5	(1%)
Defendants	—	—	4	(100%)	4	(1%)
Total	275	(45%)	340	(55%)	615	

*Based on 446 articles published in *NY Times* (n = 147) *Washington Post* (n = 110), *Chicago Tribune* (n = 102), and *LA Times* (= 87) between 1984 and 1998.

secrated through 200 years of love and sacrifice and reverence of a special, almost sacred kind" (Getlin, June 30, 1989:16).

Though fully aware of the unpopularity of opposing flag protection, many lawmakers spoke their minds. Contesting a proposed bill that would prohibit the display of the U.S. and Illinois flags on the ground or floor, Illinois State Assemblywoman Barbara Flynn Currie debunked the perception of moral panic: "This is a bad idea. This is an act caused by a perceived but unreal problem. It's in response to the Dread Scott [art exhibit] case. But Scott didn't win the debate. What won were free and open speech, which is what the flag symbolizes" (Marx, September 4, 1989:8). Congressman Ted Weiss also tried to calm his constituents: "There's no rash of flag burning. There's no need to improve the Constitution or the Bill of Rights" (Povich, October 13, 1989:1). Despite sound advice from lawmakers critical of flag protection, the flag crusade surged forward. Mixing metaphors, Senator Dole continued to inflame moral panic: "The right to bear arms, does not give you the right to shoot someone. . . . And the right to free speech does not—or at least should not—mean that American people can desecrate the American flag with impunity" (Fritz, June 23, 1989:1).

The second-largest grouping of news sources were judges and justices, comprising 14 percent of the sample (n = 85). Fifty-seven judges / justices (67 percent) opposed flag protection while 28 (33 percent) favored such prohibitions (Table 9.1). Justice John Paul Stevens argued that flag protection was justified given the sacrifice of U.S. soldiers: "If those ideas are worth fighting for—and our history demonstrates that they are—it cannot be true that the flag that uniquely symbolizes their power is not itself worthy of protection from unnecessary desecration" (Greenhouse, June 22, 1989: 1). On overturning *Johnson*, however, Justice William Brennan said, "Our decision is a reaffirmation of the principles of freedom and inclusiveness that the flag best reflects, and of the conviction that our toleration of criticism such as Johnson's is a sign and source of our strength" (Greenhouse, June 22, 1989:1).

Although the composition of the sample of sources was relatively diverse, consisting of 12 different categories, representation overall was skewed heavily toward politicians and, to a lesser degree, justices. Citizens were the third-most-cited news source (n = 37) but represented only six percent of the sample. Contributing to a pattern of journalistic balance, the views of citizens reached parity; 18 of them (49 percent) supported the criminalization of flag burning while 19 (51 percent) opposed restrictions on free speech. Though relatively few in number, these sources contributed to a spirited debate over flag protection. Diane Guiliani (teacher from Duluth, MN) said: "We should have the right to burn the flag if we want. The flag stands for liberty in and of itself. It's just a physical thing to burn. Who cares about that?" (Dedman and Stevens, 1989, July 5:D1). By contrast, accountant Danny Savage argued: "I don't think anyone should be able to burn a flag. They might as well be able to burn the White House. The flag is not just a piece of material" (Dedman and Stevens, July 5, 1989:D1). Some citizens referred to the larger social picture in expressing their opinions on flag protection. Katie Gannon, a computer operator, wondered aloud: "There are so many issues not being dealt with: racism, the homeless, the economy. We are looking up to the flag in order to forget about the problems right in front of us. There are homeless people sleeping on this very lawn" (Dedman and Stevens, July 5, 1989: D1).

Other news sources were scattered throughout press coverage on flag protection: military figures (n=28, 5 percent), editorials (n=25, 5 percent), activists (n=17, 3 percent), law professors (n=17, 3 percent), prosecutors (n=14, 2 percent), defense lawyers (n=10, 2 percent), journalists (n=10, 2 percent), lobbyists (n=5, 1 percent), and defendants (n=4, 1 percent) (Table 9.1). H. P. Gierke, a veteran and National Commander of the American Legion, lamented: "Many a Gold Star mother cherishes that carefully folded triangular bundle of red, white, and blue as the closest link to a fallen hero son" (Greenhouse, June 22, 1989: 1). Vehemently challenging the popular appeal of civil religion, defense attorney, William Kunstler opined: "The decision forbids the state from making the American flag a religious icon" (Greenhouse, June 22, 1989:1). Newspapers also expanded the debate over flag desecration by publishing syndicated columnists. For instance, humorist Art Buchwald questioned the prevailing flag hysteria: "Have you ever seen anyone burn an American flag? . . . How many flags do you think were burned in the United States last year? . . . There is not a vast pool of flag-burners out there" (*Los Angeles Times*, June 29, 1989:5:2).

Reasons for Supporting Flag Protection

In an effort to ascertain the reasons for supporting flag protection, quoted statements attributed to news sources (n=275) were examined. This facet of content analysis provides a closer look into flag panic by extracting the personal views of those cited in the press (Table 9.2). By an overwhelming margin, the most popular reason for supporting flag legislation was to protect the integrity of the Stars and Stripes (n=226, 82 percent), followed by the belief that people want flag protection (n=34, 13 percent). A small number of news sources supported flag protection as a measure to deter offensive conduct (n=11, 4 percent), while a handful of others contended that U.S. soldiers fought for the flag (n=4, 1 percent).

Taking a nationalistic stance against flag burning, citizen Brian Koelher told a reporter, "If these people don't respect the country they're in, they can at least respect the symbol. It makes me sick to see them do this" (*Los Angeles Times*, October 28, 1989:27). Jeff Crank, a resident of Ft. Collins, broke up a protest at Colorado State University by rubbing out the flames of a burning flag with his bare hands. In explaining his actions, Crank replied: "My father served in World War II. I'm not going to let what he did go by the wayside so that you can burn this flag" (*Los Angeles Times*, October 29, 1989:26). Striving to preserve the integrity of the flag, many legal strategists set out to undermine the spirit of the Bill of Rights. Solicitor General Kenneth Starr argued that flag burning should be treated like "fighting words . . . outside the scope of protected speech under the First Amendment" (Marcus, March 31, 1990: A4). Similarly, Congressman Tom Campbell strained constitutional logic, contending that the Flag Protection Act of 1989 would "not seriously infringe on the First Amendment"

Table 9.2.　Reasons for Supporting Flag Protection*

Reason	Frequency	%
Protect the integrity of the flag	226	(82%)
The people want flag protection	34	(13%)
Deter offensive conduct	11	(4%)
U.S. soldiers fought for the flag	4	(1%)
Total	275	

*Based on 446 articles published in *NY Times* (n = 147) *Washington Post* (n = 110), *Chicago Tribune* (n = 102), and *LA Times* (=87) between 1984 and 1998.

(Phillips, September 13, 1989:A6). Acting as moral entrepreneurs, some news sources believed that criminalizing flag desecration was necessary to deter offensive conduct. Representative Bob Barr maintained a distinctly moral posture in taking aim at politicians who opposed flag protection: "Many of these people believe it is mainstream to recognize homosexual marriages," urging the majority of Congress to "simply stand up and say our flag needs protection" (Clines, June 13, 1997:22).

Reasons for Opposing Flag Protection

The content analysis was also administered to identify reasons for opposing flag protection; in all, 340 news sources and their attributed statements were examined (refer to Table 9.3). By far, the prevailing reason opposing flag protection was to preserve the U.S. Constitution and the right to free speech, a rationale found in 92 percent of the responses (n=312). Despite the dominance of the constitutional argument in opposing the criminalization of flag desecration, other reasons were cited. Three percent of the news sources opposing flag protection (n=10) mentioned that the flag campaign constituted a form of political grandstanding, while 2 percent (n=7) insisted that U.S. soldiers fought for freedom. To a lesser extent, some news sources argued that flag protection was no longer an important issue (n=5, 1 percent) and that politicians should focus on more pressing issues (n=3, 1 percent). Finally, two news sources opposed flag laws as a protest of government while another viewed the Stars and Stripes as a mere symbol undeserving of legal protection.

In defense of freedom of speech, the majority of news sources opposed measures to ban flag desecration. Representative Chuck Douglas denounced his colleagues for passing the Flag Protection Act of 1989: "What we're doing today is both a sham and a shame" (Phillips, September 13, 1989: A6). Senator Danforth confessed that he committed a "mistake of heart" in cosponsoring the flag amendment: "The great thing about the

Table 9.3.   Reasons for Opposing Flag Protection*

Reason	Frequency	%
Protect the constitution / free speech	312	(92%)
Resist political grandstanding	10	(3%)
U.S. soldiers fought for freedom	7	(2%)
No longer an important issue	5	(1%)
Politicians should focus on more pressing issues	3	(1%)
Protest U.S. government	2	(0.6%)
The flag is merely a symbol	1	(0.3%)
Total	340	

*Based on 446 articles published in NY Times (n = 147) Washington Post (n = 110), Chicago Tribune (n = 102), and LA Times (= 87) between 1984 and 1998.

United States of America is that our Constitution protects any crackpot who wants to stand on his soapbox and express any oddball point of view that pops into his mind" (Dewar, October 18, 1989:A5). Danforth's swipe at political dissenters, however, ought not be dismissed as trivial since the vilification of flag desecrators was a common practice during the flag panic. Indeed, Congressman Ben Jones added that amending the Bill of Rights would only be a victory for the "pond scum" who burn flags (Toner, June 17, 1990:1).

Several news sources refused to support flag-protection measures, condemning them as political grandstanding. Senator Gordon Humphrey characterized the flag crusade as "an exercise in silliness . . . a bit of hypocrisy" (Lewis, June 28, 1989:23). Challenging the popular perception that flag desecration threatened the social order, Congressman Ted Weiss proclaimed: "We have nothing to fear from the flag burners" (Toner, July 2, 1989: Section 4:1). The president of the American Bar Association, George E. Bushnell, Jr., also weighed in on the controversy, calling the proposed flag amendment "reckless," adding, "Each young man and woman who has placed themselves in harm's way knows they did so not just to protect the flag. They fought to ensure for their families and for all citizens the fundamental principles upon which this nation was built" (Drew, March 1, 1995: 8). Interestingly, few flag desecrators were quoted as news sources. In a rare interview, flag burner "Jed Outlaw" explained to a reporter: "If it [the flag] stood for freedom, we wouldn't burn it" (Daley, June 15, 1990:4).

While voicing their commitment to constitutionalism, many news sources alluded to moral panic over flag desecration, which had produced unfounded fears and anxiety. N. Lee Cooper, president of the American Bar Association, consoled his organization by reminding its members that Old Glory will survive "rare eruptions of dramatic protest" (*Chicago Tribune*, March 22, 1997:22). Senator Kennedy added: "It is wrong to desecrate the Constitution to prevent desecration of the flag. . . . It would change the flag from a treasured symbol to a government-regulated icon. There is no need to adopt an amendment—or even pass a law merely to express our anger at a single despicable act of flag-burning (Eaton, October 6, 1989:24). Senator Humphrey also lent his support for the Bill of Rights: "Things have gotten blown out of proportion. There are very few instances of flag burning. What are we doing, talking about amending the Constitution to deal with these few cases?" (Gerstenzang, July 28, 1989:14).

SOURCING AND ITS IMPLICATIONS FOR AGENDA SETTING

Data unveiled in our content analysis point to the politicization of flag desecration insofar as the press relied heavily on politicians as news sources. The overwhelming presence of politicians in news coverage suggests that government leaders actively participate in agenda setting through the media, leading to the social construction of flag desecration (see Beckett, 1997, 1994; Best, 1987). Contributing to moral panic, many politicians relied on exaggerated claims of social threat. Recall President Bush, who warned that flag burning "endangers the fabric of our country" (*Washington Post*, June 14, 1989:A22). Such claims set the stage for political agendas and influence the course of policy making, including the criminalization of protest.

Findings from the content analysis fit the general pattern of sourcing in print journalism. Researchers have determined that politicians, or state managers, play pivotal roles in the social construction of crime news. Kasinsky (1994:210–11) reminds us that: "The dominant sources tend to flood the market. Government sources, including local police departments, the Pentagon, and the State Department, can saturate the media with information or disinformation, because information from these sources is considered official and carries with it the assumption of credibility" (see also Ericson et al., 1989; Chermak, 1997; Welch, Fenwick, and Roberts, 1998, 1997). Adding to the redundancy of political sources in stories on flag desecration, many of the exact quotes from elected leaders appeared in several newspapers simultaneously—often the result of press releases issued by political staffers and the reliance on news wire services by journalists.

Despite the huge influx of political sources into the production of news on flag desecration, the coverage on the criminalizing of protest was astonishingly balanced: 50 percent of the political sources cited in our sample supported flag protection and 50 percent opposed such legislation (Table 9.1). These figures create a sense of parity on the issue that is not reflected either in the public opinion polls or congressional voting on flag protection; in fact, citizens and politicians overwhelmingly support measures to make flag desecration a crime. Among the 615 total sources quoted, 55 percent opposed flag protection (n=340) while 45 endorsed criminalizing flag desecration (n=275). These findings certainly are subject to interpretation. On the one hand, it could be argued that the newspapers in our sample are deliberately attempting to show both sides of the debate on flag protection. On the other hand, these newspapers could be exhibiting a bias against flag protection, especially since it could ultimately threaten their own First Amendment freedoms.

Perhaps through citing sources, the media attempted to resolve its contradictory role in the social construction of flag desecration. In covering flag-burning stories, newspapers generate reader interest, which translates into revenue; in doing so, however, they participate in the reification of moral panic, which could curtail the media's freedom of expression in the event that flag desecration is made a crime. As we shall see in the next section, newspapers can express their dissatisfaction with flag protection directly through editorials. Indirectly, however, newspapers can resist the criminalizing of flag desecration by relying on sources who share their views; in fact, researchers have discovered such a bias in the production of crime news, whereby journalists mask their opinions through sources and selective interviewing (Chermak, 1997; Ericson et al., 1991, 1989, 1987; Hall et al., 1978; Kappeler et al., 1996; Kasinsky, 1994; Welch, Fenwick, and Roberts, 1997, 1998). Given that most sources quoted in the newspapers contained in our sample oppose flag protection, it is conceivable that selective interviewing might have occurred, consciously or unconsciously. Consider the following quote by Congressman Thomas Foley: "Speaking personally, I do not feel we should rush into an amendment to the First Amendment to the Constitution. It is a very deeply felt matter and it is also one that touches upon the First Amendment to the Constitution, which is the source of the most sacred personal values of this country—freedom of speech, freedom of religious worship, and freedom of the press" (Toner, June 28, 1989:1).

Finally, social constructionists tend to look at sequences of events in an effort to distinguish causes from effects. Key members of the press bristled at accusations that the media played a role in constructing moral panic over flag burning. Craig Klugman, editor of the *Fort Wayne Journal Gazette* and president of the American Society of Newspaper Editors, "termed such suggestions 'mostly bullshit' because 'the press did not create that furor, the Supreme Court created it'" (Goldstein, 1996a:139–40). Conversely, other members of the press conceded that the media contributed substantially to the rise in popular concern over flag burning: "as soon as the media coverage dropped off after about July 4 [1989], public interest also significantly declined, suggesting that press coverage drove public interest rather than the other way around" (Goldstein, 1996a: 143, 157; see findings reported by the Times Mirror Center for the People and the Press quoted in Rosenstiel, July 13, 1989:6).

NEWSPAPER EDITORIALS AND THEIR RESISTANCE TO FLAG PROTECTION

While the press enjoyed the benefits of the flag-burning controversy, especially in the form of revenue produced by sustained coverage of the issue, the role of newspapers in constructing the phenomenon was clearly contradictory. To reiterate, the press ultimately would have to face the downside of flag panic in the event that restrictions were placed on the First Amendment right to free speech. In a manner of speaking, newspaper editors saw the writing on the wall and quickly used their editorials as a forum to oppose flag protection. Amid the flag panic of 1989, an editorial in the *Washington Post* bolstered its position by citing the American Bar Association: "All through human history, tyrannies have tried to enforce obedience by prohibiting disrespect for the symbols of their power. The American flag commands respect and love because of our country's adherence to its values and its promise of freedom, not because of fiat and criminal law" (*Washington Post*, August 4, 1989:A7).

The potential damage of a flag-protection statute or an amendment to freedom of expression was considered so serious that efforts to derail the flag crusade were organized formally by the American Society of Newspaper Editors (ASNE), an association of one thousand editors of daily newspapers. In 1989 ASNE President Loren F. Ghiglione issued letters to each member of the U.S. Senate and the House of Representatives as well as Speaker of the House Thomas Foley and President Bush. Even though ASNE has a reputation as being politically conservative, Ghiglione cautioned Congress and the president about the dangers of flag legislation: "To give away even a small part of America's great right to free speech would be a historic retrenchment from the basic freedoms that Americans have always enjoyed" (Ghiglione, July 21, 1989). While chairman of ANSE's Freedom of Information Committee, Craig Klugman sent a press alert to each of its member newspapers, urging them to publish editorials opposing measures to ban flag desecration. "The drive for a constitutional amendment, or least new flag-desecration legislation, has taken on a life of its own. . . . By allowing protestors to desecrate the flag, we are reaffirming our belief that the right to dissent is essential to freedom" (Klugman, September 28, 1989). Appealing directly to Congress, Stan Tiner of the ASNE testified against the flag-desecration amendment before a Senate subcommittee: "The impulse to restrict those individual rights is as ancient as the very history of mankind. We are better than that impulse. Just now, we need a few good men and women in the Senate who have the common sense and courage to kill this very bad idea (Tiner, 1998: 3; see also *Editor & Publisher*, 1995; Hernandez, 1995; Ketter, 1995; Osborne, 1990).

Research on the press indicates that editorials on government directives can serve a watchdog or publicist role. Whether newspaper editors oppose or support a particular state policy is important, considering that social scientists have found that the public, during periods of crisis, tends to turn to editorials for guidance on matters of government (see Chiasson, 1991; Gans, 1980). As Congress reinvigorated its campaign to protect Old Glory, the *Detroit News* argued, "A constitutional amendment to outlaw desecration of the U.S. flag breezed through the U.S. House of Representatives this summer. It is now poised for adoption in the Senate. The flag is a revered national symbol, but this amendment is an extremely bad idea" (October

14, 1995: 35). Similarly, the *Chicago Tribune* quoted former Supreme Court Justice Oliver Wendell Holmes, Jr.: "Our devotion to tolerance is permitting 'freedom for the thought we hate'" (February 26, 1995: Section 4:2).

Even though public opinion polls show resounding support for flag protection, we ought not to dismiss the impact that editorials have on the flag-protection movement. Some lawmakers seem to be influenced by what newspaper editors say about flag protection. Senator John B. Breaux (LA), one of several Southern Democrats who cosponsored the flag amendment, confessed, "I'm starting to get some editorials from conservative papers in Louisiana saying we shouldn't do a constitutional amendment" (Toner, October 18, 1989:1). In light of the influence that the press has on the debate on controversial issues, we incorporated into our analysis of the media an examination of editorials on flag protection. This systematic investigation of newspapers helps us understand further how the press, through the use of editorials, attempted to correct its contradictory role in the reification of flag protection.

Sample and Method

For purposes of drawing a representative sample of the nation's newspapers, we set out to identify the four most widely circulated newspapers in each state and the District of Columbia. Overall, 200 newspapers were identified—there are only two newspapers in Delaware as well as in the District of Columbia (*Dow Jones Interactive Publications Library*, 1997). Although many of these newspapers have published several editorials on flag protection over the past ten years, our sample included only their most recent commentary.[4] From the 200 newspapers selected for this study, we retrieved (or received) 148 editorials: a response rate of 74 percent. Each editorial was reviewed to determine the newspaper's stance on flag protection, either supporting or opposing a criminal statute or constitutional amendment prohibiting desecration of the flag.[5]

Findings

Of the 148 newspapers examined, 127 (86 percent) editorials opposed flag protection while eight (5 percent) supported measures to ban flag desecration; 13 (9 percent) reported having no official position on the issue (Table 9.4).

Opposing Flag Protection Editorials on flag protection covered a great deal of subject matter, including First Amendment freedom of speech, partisan politics, political cover, and political diversion. Moreover, some editorials questioned flag protection on the grounds of semiotics, while others criticized civil religion and compulsory patriotism; in a similar vein, sev-

Table 9.4.   Newspaper Editorials on Flag Protection*

Position on Flag Protection	Number	Percent
Oppose	127	86
Support	8	5
No Position	13	9
Total	148	

*Of the 200 newspapers selected for the sample, 148 editorials were received, a response rate of 74 percent.

eral newspapers challenged perceptions of moral panic, insisting that flag burning does not constitute a threat to American society. Concerning free speech, the *Richmond Times-Dispatch* called attention to the contradictions and ironic effects of flag protection: "The flag protection amendment they are thinking about putting into law will set a precedent for giving our government the power to abridge the First Amendment of the Bill of Rights—in effect, reducing our unalienable right to freedom of speech. Isn't that ironic, or is it moronic?" (September 24, 1998:A-18). Likewise, the *Baltimore Sun* weighed in on the controversy: "It's a mistake to elevate a symbol to a position of greater importance than what it represents. Clearly at the very heart of the rights that the flag symbolizes is the notion that unpopular—even objectionable, misguided and obnoxious—speech is deserving of protection, too" (*Baltimore Sun*, April 10, 1999:10A). Other newspapers commented on the importance of free expression in a democracy, noting that "The country can tolerate the desperate, misguided burning of the flag more than it can tolerate erosion of free, unfettered political speech" (*Seattle Times*, May 20, 1999:B4), and that "Democracies by definition are more lenient on such things than dictators" (*Commercial Appeal* [Memphis], June 16, 1997:A6). Countering the argument by flag enthusiasts who cite militaristic reasons for flag protection, the *Detroit News* pointed out, "those soldiers died defending the values represented by the flag, not the flag itself. One of those values is expressed in the First Amendment, which guarantees freedom of speech—not just for people we agree with, but for people with whom we profoundly disagree" (*Detroit News*, April 11, 1998:C7).

Several editors criticized Congress for using the flag issue for purposes of partisan politics and political cover. "Part of the debate over this amendment is pure politics. The public overwhelmingly supports the amendment, so protecting the flag comes just after honoring motherhood on the congressional care-o-meter. Members of Congress who would not seek this amendment on their own are forced to take a position that, if they say yes, will get them votes, and if they say no, will get them angry mail. Many would like to avoid the angry mail" (*Bangor Daily News* [Maine], July 10, 1998:22). "There's nothing coincidental about '92, '94 and '98 being election years. Supporters of the flag amendment hope to time the debate and vote in the Senate to just before the election day, forcing those on the fence to go their way" (*Standard Examiner* [Ogden, Utah], May 29, 1998:24). Similarly, numerous editors detected political diversion within the flag controversy: "Pick an issue: Social Security. Medicare. Relations with China. The bombing of Kosovo. Urban revitalization. Train and plane safety. Entrenched poverty. Pollution. With all these issues and more confronting Congress, you'd think members would be too busy to waste time on frivolous legislation. You'd be mistaken. . . . Congress should forget the flag desecration amendment. They have plenty of real problems to fix" (*Dallas Morning News*, April 20, 1999:10A).

Examining the semiotic and ontological dimensions of flag protection, some editors insisted that the lack of precise definitions would lead to an unfair enforcement of the law. "Just what does 'desecration' mean? Who gets to decide? What about a dusty bumper sticker or dirty patch on a police officer's uniform? The flag motif is used on all sorts of goods from garments to lampshades. Freedom of expression is as important an ideal to preserve as someone's arbitrary definition of patriotism. We don't need to be jailing flag burners. Too many others deserve the space more" (*Macon Telegraph*, April 30, 1999:10). *New York Newsday* also expressed semiotic and political concerns, concluding that flag protection would be aimed at unpopular dissent. "Supporters argue there's a national consensus to protect the flag. But how would it work? Would it ban the stars-and-stripes motif on paper napkins and boxer shorts? Probably not. It would, in all likelihood, punish acts of protest the majority finds offensive" (June 14, 1995:A34).

Given the prominent role of civil religion in shaping flag protection, some editorials took a hard look at the religious implications of antidesecration laws. "Some religious groups regard saluting the flag as idolatry. This amendment suggests they may have a point. Just using the word 'desecrate' transfers a religious aspect to a secular object. Enforcing any orthodoxy by law is un-American (*Greensboro News and Record*, July 2, 1998:A15). Similarly, the editor at the *Las Vegas Review-Journal* wrote: "Frankly, I've wondered about the use of the term 'desecration,' with its roots in religion. Doesn't it bother backers of the constitutional amendment that this smacks just a bit of melting down earrings to create a golden calf idol?" (*Las Vegas Review-Journal*, May 9, 1999:2D).

Addressing another form of orthodoxy, several editorials explored the danger of compulsory patriotism. The *Greensboro News & Record* reminded readers that compulsory flag adoration is at odds with a free society. "It's easy to play to emotion and patriotic pride by wrapping oneself in the flag. . . . I feel that emotion, too. Just this week I took a flag away from my 6-year old son because he has not yet learned to treat it with proper respect. But teaching respect and mandating it by law are very different things" (July 2, 1998:A15; *Portland Press Herald*, Maine, December 14, 1995:15A). "If Americans are forced to pay homage to a symbol, then their basic rights are diminished," noted the *Kansas City Star* (July 7, 1995:C5), and, according to the *Boston Globe*, "The amendment would open the way for zealotry of its own kind, inviting competition among legislators to see who could come up with the most stringent methods of enforcement and the stiffest penalties for outrages against the flag—to be enforced by local police with wide range of practice" (June 26, 1998:A22).

The *Tulsa World* chastised state lawmakers for devoting so much time to flag protection while neglecting important legislative business; moreover, the game of patriotic oneupmanship seemed to never end. One state representative proposed that schools teach the "history and etiquette" of the flag, while another added that "President Clinton and others in his generation burned flags when they were students," even though there is "no evidence that Clinton ever participated in flag burning." The state legislature passed a measure requiring that "all public school students recite the Pledge of Allegiance everyday, unless they didn't want to." In a similar manner, the body passed a bill "requiring all supervisors in state agencies to lead their employees in the Pledge of Allegiance each day" (*Tulsa World*, March 1, 1997:A12).

Finally, editorials opposing bans on flag desecration also took the opportunity to challenge the perception that flag burning endangers American society. Taking direct aim at the construction of moral panic, the *Providence Journal-Bulletin* opined:

> After the amendment's defeat, the American Legion lobbied heavily to have the question revisited, and evidently succeeded. "If burning the flag is wrong," said the American Legion's William Detweiler, "it is wrong no matter how many times it occurs. In fact, we contend it is a problem even if no one ever burns another flag." The American Legion considers a nonevent a problem? How many other monsters are under the bed? We would declare this a classic case of borrowing trouble. (June 14, 1995:B-8)

Insinuating that Senator Orrin Hatch was contributing to moral panic, the *New York Times* stated flatly: "Having no epidemic of flag desecration to point to since the Court spoke, Judiciary Committee chairman Orrin Hatch, the amendment's leading Senate sponsor, ought to drop this destructive effort to weaken the Bill of Rights" (May 7, 1999:A-26).

Supporting Flag Protection In our sample, only eight newspapers (5 percent) publicly supported flag-protection legislation (Table 9.4). Given the apparent contradiction of a member of the media endorsing a measure that would restrict the First Amendment freedom of speech, a closer look at such editorials is warranted. The *Omaha World-Herald* took exception to the semiotic and ontological criticisms of flag protection, arguing that for war veterans,

> To see their flag intentionally desecrated causes an anguish that is almost physical. It is as though a member of the family were being harassed and they were not permitted to come to the person's defense. . . . The opponents too often argue by deconstruction. What's desecration, they ask. What about a wiseacre protester who fashions an 11-stripe flag with 57 stars and burns that? Surely that's not an American flag. What about another wiseacre who burns a green, gray and yellow version of the Stars and Stripes and demands to be arrested? What about a flag on a pair of undershorts? Would burning the garment constitute a violation of the law? What about red, white and blue bunting? Or a photograph of a flag? Those are silly, frivolous questions. If an amendment passed, they could be addressed by careful legislating and, if necessary, litigation. (June 27, 1999:24a)

In an earlier editorial, the same newspaper projected a smug sense of elitism while ridiculing protestors: "The deterioration of political discourse into street theater continues. . . . Dramatics have now replaced ideas in some of what passes for political discourse. Certainly, flag-burning is not an idea. It is an act, the principal purpose of which is to shock and offend" (June 13, 1990:26). Also challenging the high court's view of flag burning as free speech, another editor asked rhetorically: "Why is it okay to desecrate the American Flag, the one true symbol of our country, but it is a crime to burn a cross? We wonder if the Founding Fathers knew that their references to free speech in the First Amendment was [sic] going to one day be turned into a defense of those whose main means of expression seems to be just this side of a two-year-old gorialla's [sic]" (*Union Leader* [NH], June 27, 1999:18). Offering unswerving support for the flag crusade, the paper continued: "Adoption of the amendment that would do so would not limit free speech one whit. It ought to become a national cause for the new century." Voicing similar support for a constitutional amendment, the *Knoxville News-Sentinel* quoted veteran Ralph Reel, a member of the CFA, who insisted, "'This won't take anyone's free speech rights away from them.' . . . Needless to say, we hope Reel's campaign meets with real success" (June 11, 1995:F2; see also *Augusta Chronicle* [GA], April 29, 1999:A4).

In several editorials favoring an amendment to shield Old Glory, condemnation of flag burning took on a decidedly moral tone.

> Flag-burning isn't speech. It's an act. It is a kind of behavior that, like public nudity or the display of anti-Semitic symbols, deeply offends a lot of people. . . . What [William] Kuntsler [sic] and others are demanding now, in effect, is a constitutional right to perform just about any act that comes into their minds and call it speech. Their crusade reflects the devaluation of ideas that can occur when theater-of-the-streets demonstrations are substituted for rational debate. (*Omaha World-Herald*, February 25, 1990:24a)

Likewise, another editor argued: "We think that, if anything, free speech is weakened when the courts insist on applying the principle to flag-burning, nude dancing, or anything else that takes their fancy. So far as we can remember, this country was not a police state when 48 states had laws against flag desecration on their books (*The Capital* [Annapolis, MD], June 14, 1999: A8). Alluding to informal social control by way of vigilante justice, the *Daily Oklahoman* boldly remarked: "Decades ago such an amendment wasn't needed. Respect for the values of the flag represents and for the blood of patriots who defended them was greater than it is now. Miscreants who dared defiling Old Glory risked an old-fashioned throttling by those who knew better" (June 15, 1998:6).[6]

To summarize, editorials opposing flag protection can be interpreted as a conscious attempt by the press to reconcile its contradiction in the flag-burning controversy; by criticizing formal measures that place limits on the First Amendment, newspaper editors preserve their own right to free speech. Such editorials also challenged perceptions of moral panic by arguing that flag burning does not pose a threat to American society. That form of dissent is important, considering the moral overtone of editorials favoring flag protection. The *Portland Press Herald* [Maine] wrote, "Despite bleatings about free speech, that's not what's at stake: If the Supreme Court were serious about protecting speech, it would permit schools to set aside time for voluntary student prayer. No, there's another agenda at work here, one that values wholesome patriotism much less than it does the increasingly common and highly destructive rootless selfishness that so permeates our culture" (October 7, 1996:7A). Interestingly, the *Press Herald* exhibited few qualms about joining the flag crusade, enthusiastically chiming, "Let's get this amendment passed, and begin to reclaim our nation's honor. . . . (Those wanting to help can reach the Citizens Flag Alliance at 1-800-424-FLAG)" (Ibid.). Based on our analysis, it is difficult to determine precisely the impact editorials have had on the flag-protection campaign. Still, there is evidence suggesting that lawmakers paid close attention to what the press had to say about Congress and its attempt to amend the constitution. After the flag measure failed in 1990, Sonny Montgomery, the leading Democratic House amendment sponsor and the chairman of the Veterans Committee, lamented, "The newspaper editors just killed us" (Goldstein, 1996a:332).

CONCLUSION

That the world has become a global village is a sobering reminder of the media's impact on modern culture (McLuhan, 1964). With its technological prowess, the media can project images of social problems in ways that amplify and exaggerate a perceived threat, and at key historical moments these messages can contribute to a growing sense that public disorder is imminent (Gamson, et al., 1992). Media coverage of the flag-burning controversy in 1989 and 1990 contributed to the notion that America was losing ground to iconoclastic revolutionaries. In particular, our investigation found evidence of moral panic over flag desecration in newspaper articles in which many politicians, operating as moral entrepreneurs, defined flag burning in terms of morality. Representative Henry J. Hyde said:

> I view this as one more struggle in the culture war that has been raging since Vietnam. Those who are shocked, revolted and frustrated by the excesses of the counterculture—the pornography and obscenity that inundates our entertainment industry, the drugs, the AIDS explosion, the high abortion rate— view flag burning as one more slap in the face of the millions of veterans who found enough values in America to risk their lives in combat. (Kenworthy, June 20, 1990:A14)

The sweeping nature of Congressman Hyde's condemnation of flag desecration exhibits a classic feature of moral panic: lumping several social problems into a moral quagmire. Other moral entrepreneurs were more succinct in denouncing flag burning. While endorsing the criminalizing of flag desecration, Senator Orrin G. Hatch stated flatly, "We want to ban offensive behavior" (Sleelye, March 22, 1995:16).

Despite the preponderance of statements undergirding moral panic, the newspapers in this study also published quotes from sources that criticized making flag desecration a crime. Indeed, such comments were directed squarely at preserving the First Amendment freedom of speech, denouncing civil religion, and challenging the perception that flag desecration threatens the social order. Representative Gary Ackerman addressed each of those concerns: "Some of us have mistaken the flag as a religious icon to be worshiped. They would diminish the Constitution by changing it needlessly." Ackerman added that he would hate to see the flag burned in protest but quickly conceded that such "behavior poses no danger to the nation" (Fulwood, 1997:27). Similarly, other sources looked deeply into the regressive forces driving the campaign to protect the flag. Law Professor David Cole mused, "We seem to be in an era where the right wing is pushing and succeeding in cutting away 1st Amendment freedoms in the name of morality, in the name of tradition, family tradition. They are grasping for symbolic fights. They feel very threatened by the changes that are occurring (Madigan, 1990:1). By publishing observations by Professor Cole and others like him, the press serves a sociological function in resisting moral panic over flag burning. Moreover, these keen insights properly place the moral crusade to protect Old Glory in the context of other struggles over morality in a modern democratic society (see Dubin, 1992).

To reiterate, the production of news of flag desecration conforms to the general pattern of sourcing insofar as journalists rely on politicians who, given their elevated position in the power structure, provide credibility for the news coverage. The press benefits from these privileged sources—but so do the elected leaders who exploit media exposure to advance their political and moral crusades as well as their careers in government. The findings of our content analysis, however, depart significantly from journalism's tendency of supporting government initiatives on criminalization. For years researchers have been uncovering evidence that the media contribute enormously to moral panic over street crime and drugs, leading to massive state investment in the criminal-justice apparatus and coercive social control over citizens (Beckett, 1997, 1994; Chermak, 1997; Fishman, 1978; Hall et al., 1978; Tunnell, 1992; Welch, Fenwick, Roberts, 1997, 1998). Conversely, the newspaper articles studied here tended to challenge the criminalizing process. Such resistance by the press emerged *directly* through the publication of editorials and *indirectly* through selective quoting of sources who opposed limiting freedom of expression. In doing so, newspapers in this sample apparently attempted to resolve their contradictory position in the flag-desecration controversy: the media fueled moral panic over flag burning with extensive news coverage, an activity that put freedom of the press at risk in the event that political dissent were to be made a crime. Whereas conservative politicians set the agenda for criminalizing flag desecration, our findings suggest that the press established its own agenda aimed at resisting legislation that would curb free expression. The media thus appeared to have its cake and eat it too: It benefited economically by covering—thus, contributing to—the flag frenzy, and at least for the time being, has averted the negative consequences of flag protection, government regulation of political dissent.

As a final note on the contradictions of the press, it is important to acknowledge that while the media hyped the flag panic in 1989, it neglected to pay sufficient attention to the resurrection of the flag crusade, beginning in the mid-1990s. The campaigns to amend the U.S. Constitution in 1995, 1997, and again in 1999 received scant press coverage. In those roll calls, the House of Representatives approved the flag proposal overwhelmingly; in the Senate the measure failed by three votes. Goldstein adds, "If the press went overboard in covering the flag desecration controversy in 1989, in 1995 large segments of the press went to the other extreme . . . leaving much of the American public ignorant of the fact that the First Amendment was in grave danger of being altered for the first time in American history" (1996a:376–77). Clearly, the role of the media in the social construction of moral panic over flag desecration was unique given its polarizing contradictions—still, other ironies abound.

NOTES

1. Whereas televised and radio news programs contributed tremendously to moral panic over flag desecration, the scope of this analysis remains on the press rather than the electronic media.

2. "Newsmaking criminology presupposes that there is no such thing as 'objective' news reporting and interpreting: The presentation of crime and violence in the mass media, for example, cannot be disconnected from the prevailing ideologies of the day" (Barak 1994:261; also see Fishman and Cavender, 1998; Greek 1994; Henry 1994).

3. Several of my research assistants from 1997 to 1999 were instrumental in administering a content analysis on the newspapers: John Sassi, Allyson McDonough, and Elizabeth Raimondo. In addition, the following research assistants retrieved data for this study: Eric Price, Kristin Mortellito, Kevin Tunney, Joseph Fredua-Agyman, Lisa Steiner, and Sheri McKay.

4. Most newspapers are linked to the *Dow Jones Interactive Publications Library*, making their retrieval simple by downloading the editorial. Some newspapers, however, were not in the *Dow Jones* system; therefore, we resorted to a survey method of contacting editors by electronic mail and telephone.

5. Kristin Mortellito and Laura Niedermayer, serving as my research assistants at Rutgers University in 1998 and 1999, were instrumental in retrieving and analyzing editorials.

6. It should be mentioned that except for the *Manchester Union Leader*, all newspapers favoring flag protection are members of ASNE, which urged its membership to publish editorials opposing bans on flag desecration.

10

Resisting the Criminalization of Protest

The flag is not a religious icon. It's not a religious symbol. It is the symbol of the United States. It's a symbol of good and it is a symbol of bad, and people ought to be able to use it to protest the bad.
—*William Kunstler, Attorney for Gregory Johnson and the D.C. 4 (Savage, 1990a: 29).*

Burn, baby, burn. Stop the fascist flag law!
—*Members of the D.C. 4, chanting while burning flags on the steps of the U.S. Capitol in 1989 (Ross, 1989: 4).*

Earlier in this book, we were reminded that the history of free speech in the United States stems from political activism by Radical Whigs who battled for civil liberties in seventeenth-century England. Of particular significance, radical Whigs succeeded in legislating the right to criticize government publicly, a freedom that would become a centerpiece of the U.S. Constitution. Many Americans in the new republic, however, thought the state had gone too far by allowing citizens the right to political protest, but in the end, First-Amendment advocates won the debate (Finkelman, 1992; Mayer, 1991; Schwartz, 1971). Despite the right to freedom of speech explicitly spelled out in the Bill of Rights, from time to time, the state was able to impose restrictions; indeed, the Sedition Act of 1789 is a sobering reminder of how political protest had been criminalized. Eventually, the act expired—during the Jefferson presidency—only to resurface during World War I, when thousands of radicals, anarchists, and pacifists who publicly criticized the U.S. military were arrested, prosecuted, and imprisoned for violating the Sedition Act of 1918 (Goldstein, 1978; Rabban, 1997; Walker, 1990). The state's crackdown on antiwar demonstrators during the Vietnam War marked a key period of political repression as thousands of dissenters were arrested under flag-desecration statutes. Although the history of free speech in America is marred by numerous intrusions by the state, especially during times of war, the enduring principle of political dissent has generally prevailed. In fact, First-Amendment strategists have relied on the power of political protest in defending the Bill of Rights, a struggle that continues today. In 1999, the House of Representatives overwhelmingly approved a constitution amendment that would make political dissent in the form of flag desecration a crime; in March 2000, however, the measure failed by only four votes in the Senate (Alvarez, 2000). In light of the ongoing push for flag protection, civil libertarians warn us that the right to political dissent ought not be taken for granted (see Dye and Zeigler, 1993).

Social movements aimed at restricting free speech have particular relevance to sociology, given that many such crusades are propelled by moral panic. Recall the 1990 prosecution of the rap group "2 Live Crew" on obscenity charges for their sexually charged album "Nasty as They Want To Be." The campaign was initiated by the fundamentalist Reverend Wildmon, who persuaded law enforcement to join the cause. In due course, a U.S. District Judge in Florida ruled the music obscene, paving the way for prosecutors to target record-store owners who sold the album. Charles Freeman, a businessman in Ft. Lauderdale, was arrested, prosecuted, and convicted on obscenity charges for selling 2 Live Crew's album; he was fined $1,000 and court costs. Eventually, the performers themselves faced trial but were acquitted; still, other prosecutions against rap artists surfaced in Texas and Louisiana (Dubin, 1992; Rimer, 1990; Steinfels, 1990; Stepp, 1990). Regressive flag-protection campaigns not only restrict political dissent, but promote civil religion and reinforce the authoritarian aesthetic, key values embraced by reactionaries in proclaiming their American patriotism.

Other citizens, however, express their patriotism by defending American constitutionalism—after all, they point out, the nation was founded on the principle of political protest. At the center of the flag-desecration controversy stands resistance, a phenomenon emerging in two forms. First, flag burners publicly criticize and resist various government actions, including civil rights violations and U.S. military policies. Second, as the state tries to censor or repress political dissent, resistance is expressed through the defense of First Amendment freedoms. This mutually reinforcing loop of repression and resistance remains an integral dynamic produced by the ironies of social control; that is, efforts to criminalize protest merely incite the behavior that authorities hope to deter. Kathleen Taylor of the ACLU concurs: "The [flag desecration] law encourages the very action it is intended to discourage. . . . There were no incidents of public flag burning in Seattle until Congress enacted the prohibition. Liberty needs special protection, not its symbol, the flag" (*Los Angeles Times*, 1989: 26).

In this closing chapter, paradoxes inherent in the criminalizing of protest are explored, particularly in light of their tendency to escalate re-sistance against the state. Special attention is aimed at the contemporary civil rights movement devoted to protecting free speech, a liberty currently jeopardized by the crusade to amend the constitution with a flag provision.

FLAG PROTECTION AND THE IRONIES OF SOCIAL CONTROL

As a social phenomenon, rule breaking often is analyzed without tak-ing into account the crucial role of authorities who unintentionally escalate (or even cause) the very behavior they set out to control. Contributing to the idea of escalation, sociologist Gary Marx (1981) points out that social control can be ironic and self-defeating since it has the potential to produce, worsen, or escalate a putative problem rather than resolve it. Arguing against the view that an absence of social control promotes deviance, Marx joins a perspective of sociology arguing that the presence of social control also contributes to rule breaking (Becker, 1963; Cohen 1972; Welch, 1999b; Wilkins, 1965; Young, 1982). Marx contends that authorities manufacture crime and deviance by "defining some of the wide range of behavior as il-legal, using their discretion about which laws will then be most actively enforced, and singling out some of those who violate these laws for pro-cessing by the criminal justice system" (1981: 222).

As authorities deploy law enforcement against dissenters, they con-tribute to escalation by inadvertently triggering and encouraging rule breaking. In fact, the flag-burning controversy of the late 1980s was an es-calation of a single—and virtually unpublicized—act of protest, *Texas v. Johnson*. The chronology of *Johnson* demonstrates a snowball effect, esca-lated further by a growing cast of authorities.

Johnson was arrested and charged with desecration of a venerated ob-ject after a U.S. flag was burned by a crowd of protesters in 1984. Under the Texas Law of the Parties, Johnson was convicted and sentenced to one year in jail and fined $2,000. The Texas Court of Appeals overturned John-son's conviction, maintaining that the state could not essentially license the flag solely for the promotion of the status quo (*Johnson*, 1988). Texas cam-paigned to reinstate Johnson's conviction and persuaded the U.S. Supreme Court to hear the case in 1989, thus escalating the flag issue to an even higher level of controversy. To the dismay of moral entrepreneurs advo-cating the criminalizing of flag burning, the U.S. Supreme Court over-turned Johnson's conviction. In the wake of Johnson, political leaders, veterans' organizations, and other moral entrepreneurs denounced the court's ruling, pumping new life into an otherwise dying issue. In a move designed to legitimize state symbolism and preserve the authoritarian aes-thetic, Congress passed the Flag Protection Act of 1989.

As a formal mechanism of social control, the Flag Protection Act of 1989 did not deter flag desecration; ironically, it precipitated flag burnings specifically planned to challenge the newly enacted law. Demonstrators in two separate incidents were arrested under the revised federal statute, but federal district judges dismissed the charges (*U.S. v. Eichman*, 1989; *U.S. v. Haggerty*, 1989). The prosecutions were resurrected by U.S. attorneys, however, who appealed both decisions directly to the U.S. Supreme Court for expedited review (*U.S. v. Eichman*, 1990). In what turned out to be a repeat of the *Johnson* ruling, the high court held that the prosecution of the defendants under the Flag Protection Act of 1989 violated the First Amendment. Still, the escalation process continues; currently, moral entrepreneurs continue to lobby federal lawmakers, hoping to generate sufficient support to advance their proposal for a constitutional amendment intended to shield Old Glory.

Rather than deter flag desecration, however, formal measures of social control tend to incite protest against the state; moreover, the conflict escalates when dissenters are unjustly treated by the criminal-justice apparatus. As an irony of social control, many protestors wear their punishment not as a stigma, but as a badge of honor. Flag burners Johnson, Eichman, Scott, Blalock, and Joe Urgo have all testified that being arrested, manhandled, and accosted by aggressive police officers, as well intimidated by prosecutors, is a punishing and humiliating experience. Nonetheless, demonization is the price some activists are willing to pay for social change. Demonstrators commonly point to their harsh treatment as evidence of a vengeful government and an unjust criminal-justice system bent on stifling political dissent. Reflecting on his arrest with the D.C. 4, David Blalock, a Vietnam War veteran, described the detention experience:

> The cops are yelling. They took us down below the Capitol building, and we were manacled to a wall for six hours, while they're trying to get us to tell them information. But we were all silent so they finally took us to Washington, D.C.'s lockup. This is a big, big jail, basically full of Black people. And they stuck me and Joey in a cell together and Dread was in the cell next to us by himself. And I hear a Black guy yelling, "What you white boys doing in here?" And Joey was, "Hey we just burned the flag on the steps of the Capitol!" And he plunked his whole speech out. And cheers went up throughout the prison. Then it got all quiet, and this other guy says, "How come you stopped with the flag?" After a day in official Washington, I felt like I was at home. (Blalock, 1990: 6)

One can merely speculate how many protestors would challenge a prohibition on flag desecration in the event that a constitutional amendment passed. Compounding the symbiotic relationship between rule enforcers and rule breakers, many civil libertarians and attorneys are eager to defend protestors targeted by police and prosecutors. The pattern is clear. Repression does not always contribute to conformity; ironically, coercive social control tends to produce the opposite—resistance. As we shall see in the next section, many activists and organizations who are committed to preserving freedoms guaranteed by the Bill of Rights, enthusiastically join forces of resistance, even if they do not necessarily endorse the ideology of the dissenters they represent.

IN DEFENSE OF DISSENT

The most recent flag-burning controversy, beginning with the 1984 protest in Dallas and escalating into a political firestorm and media frenzy by 1989, was the culmination of several different social movements. As discussed previously, the Reagan Revolution boasted a conservative worldview, setting the stage for notable confrontations with communism and its godless "Evil Empire." That regressive social movement looked fondly on nostalgia, recalling days when the Stars and Stripes was revered by citizens proud to blend their religion with their politics. In 1986, Harvard Law Professor Alan Dershowitz noted, "There is a campaign afoot to return us to those not-so-glorious days when the states were free to establish and support a particular religion. . . . We live in a society where religion and government seem locked together in an incestuous embrace" (Dershowitz, 1986: 20). Transcending civil religion, however, the emergence of the Religious Right and a renewed sense of American nationalism in the 1980s were products of a regressive social movement taking aim at liberalism, a political philosophy derisively characterized by reactionaries as morally corrupt and un-American.

Against that social, cultural, and political backdrop, Johnson, virtually unknown beyond radical circles, was arrested for flag burning at a protest staged outside the 1984 Republican National Convention, where President Reagan accepted his party's nomination on his way to serving a second term. While Johnson's case gained attention as it spiraled upward through the courts, so did his celebrity status; indeed, Johnson's exploding visibility pumped unprecedented energy into the RCP's otherwise bantam resistance to the state. Because several RCP supporters had been arrested for flag desecration over the years, the membership viewed itself as targeted by the government, convinced that prosecutions against them for flag burning were politically motivated. Nevertheless, the RCP was no match for the state, the Republican party, or any other sector of the establishment. As a result of escalation, however, prosecuting flag burners attracted other like-minded radicals to the RCP as well as to other leftist causes, leading to greater public defiance of the state. And, as right-wing government officials clamped down on protestors, civil libertarians took careful note, embarking on their own campaign to protect First Amendment freedoms. By the time the Supreme Court agreed to review *Johnson*, a significant social movement organized by civil libertarians was in full stride.

In the 1980s, conservatives had dominated the American political climate, shown by moral crusades against homosexuality, abortion, and avant-garde art; by the end of the decade, however, their ability to dictate public policy was reaching its limits, especially in the realm of free speech (see Dubin, 1992). In the late 1980s, resistance had finally established itself as a formidable opponent against a monolithic enterprise engineered by right-wing politicians and special-interest groups as well as many citizens who espoused conservatism, nostalgia, and civil religion. Whereas flag protection was merely a symbolic social movement, resistance to it was driven by substantive concerns over restricting freedom of expression.

Resistance to criminalizing political protest was grounded firmly in the efforts of an intricate network of social activists and civil libertarians. That coalition expanded rapidly in the late 1980s, as several established civil-rights groups were joined by a handful of grassroots and ad hoc committees organized to defeat legislation designed to criminalize flag desecration. Specifically, the First Amendment coalition included the ACLU, People for the American Way (PAW), the Center for Constitutional Rights, the Emergency Committee on the Supreme Court Flag Burning Case (ECSCFC), the Emergency Committee Against the Flag Amendment and Laws (ECAFAL), the Emergency Committee to Defend the First Amendment (ECDFA), and a direct action group known as Refuse & Resist.

When the U.S. Supreme Court granted certiorari to the state of Texas in 1988, civil libertarians feared that the court was poised to uphold Johnson's conviction, a ruling that would restrict political dissent. In more alarming language, Joe Cook of the Dallas Civil Liberties Union depicted the court's willingness to review Johnson as "a part of the creeping fascism" of the times (*Village Voice*, April 4, 1989: 27; see also Garbus, 1989: 369–70). Because one of its more vocal and visible supporters was at the epicenter of the flag quake, the RCP was eager to have Johnson reviewed by the Supreme Court. Essentially, the RCP could not lose: if Johnson's conviction was upheld, the high court would be viewed as a tool of the ruling class; if Johnson were acquitted, however, the state would be seen as yielding to resistance. The RCP announced that "a bold and broad political and legal battle" around the case could "strengthen the pole of revolutionary communism in society" by uniting "broadly people who themselves would not burn the flag but who will defend the right to do so [for many different reasons]" (*RW*, December 5, 1988: 5). Not only did the Emergency Committee on the Supreme Court Flag Burning Case (ECSCFC) serve as an ad hoc defense group for Johnson, it set out to raise public awareness of the larger constitutional implications of the case. By muting some of its RCP influence, the ECSCFC appealed widely to civil libertarians, even those who did not necessarily share a communist or revolutionary vision.[1]

When the Supreme Court overruled Johnson's conviction, Congress wasted little time drafting two key pieces of legislation, the Flag Protection Act of 1989 (FPA) and a proposal for a constitutional amendment that would prohibit flag desecration. In response, the ECSCFC reorganized to challenge congressional flag protection, renaming itself the Emergency Committee Against the Flag Amendment and Laws (ECAFAL). Like its predecessor, ECAFAL operated with a distinct RCP nuance: in the *Revolutionary Worker*, the group accused Congress of playing good cop/bad cop, with the Democrats supporting the FPA as an alternative—and lesser evil—to the Republican-sponsored constitutional amendment (see *RW*, August 12, 1990; November 10, 1991; December 22, 1991, January 6, 1992).

Other constitutional-rights organizations were equally distressed by congressional efforts to criminalize flag desecration. In the nation's capital, Morton Halperin of the ACLU and John Gomberts of the PAW would become key political lobbyists committed to persuading lawmakers not to tamper with First Amendment freedoms. Still, the "lesser evil" predicament would hound these civil liberties organizations. One month following the *Johnson* ruling, members of Congress were polarized either into the statute or amendment camps; in fact, few lawmakers were willing to risk political suicide by standing in front of the flag-protection juggernaut. With only two realistic options, the ACLU, PAW, and other constitutional lobbyists advised—albeit reluctantly—legislators to vote for the proposed flag statute rather than a constitutional amendment. As the debate between a statute or an amendment deepened, external pressure on the legislative process intensified. An ad hoc group calling itself the Constitutional Law Professors against a Constitutional Amendment generated support from 511 such academics representing 158 law schools from 46 states and urged Congress to oppose the amendment "as unwise and inconsistent with the basic premises of the Bill of Rights," especially since the core purpose of the First Amendment is to protect "unpopular speech from suppression of the majority" (Goldstein, 1996a: 202). Adding political weight to the expanding civil liberties coalition, the Emergency Committee to Defend the First Amendment, a group comprising elite university presidents, former high-ranking state officials, and prominent attorneys, also advised Congress not to criminalize symbolic speech. While the coalition continued to marshal support from key constitutional-rights organizations, the campaign to defeat the proposed amendment benefited tremendously from the efforts of two notable law professors. Laurence Tribe of Harvard Law School and Duke University's Walter Dellinger drew support from more than 100 of their peers in preparing eloquent statements in defense of political dissent.

By endorsing a flag statute as a lesser evil, civil-liberties pressure groups, including the ACLU and PAW, realized that members of Congress could both save face with their constituents and preserve the Bill of Rights since they doubted the Flag Protection Act (FPA) of 1989 would pass constitutional muster. In the end, their political instincts proved correct, Democrats garnered sufficient votes to pass the FPA, which blocked the Republican proposal for a constitutional amendment. In less than a year, the Supreme Court surged forward with an expedited review to consider the constitutionality of the FPA. Despite the ultimate victory for civil liberties in 1989, the equivocal lobbying strategy of the ACLU and PAW annoyed First Amendment purists committed to resisting all forms of governmental intrusion into constitutional freedoms (Taylor, 1990; Tiefer, 1992). Oddly, the only two mainline professional organizations to take an uncompromising stand against the FPA and the proposed amendment were the American Bar Association (ABA) and the American Society of Newspapers (ASNE), both of which had a conservative rather than liberal reputation (see Goldstein, 1996a: 202–12). Still, liberal voices of resistance were heard from the editorial cartoonist Paul Conrad, director Oliver Stone, painter Jasper Johns, the American Jewish Congress, the National Association for the Advancement of Colored People (NAACP), the Association of Art Museum Directors, and the Modern Language Association, all of whom filed amicus briefs to the Supreme Court in an effort to invalidate the FPA on constitutional grounds (see Goldstein, 1996a: 272–76).

While lobbying efforts by Morton Halperin (ACLU) and John Gomberts (PAW) proved essential for defeating flag protection, other key individual contributions ought not be forgotten, particularly the work of liberal attorneys William Kunstler and David Cole, as well as conservative Washington insider Charles Fried. Unlike many of their peers who favored the FPA as a maneuver to undermine a constitutional amendment, Kunstler, Cole, and Fried never equivocated on the right to political dissent.

Before elaborating on the work of Kunstler and Cole, it is fitting that we acknowledge briefly Charles Fried and his courageous—albeit unpopular—defense of dissent. Given his background as Reagan's solicitor general, Fried seems to have been an uncommon defender of political protest. As congressional battle lines were drawn between supporting the FPA or a constitutional amendment, Fried proposed a principled third strategy: "bravely do nothing." In 1989, Fried, a recent addition to the faculty of Harvard Law School, testified before Congress: "Though I do not often agree with Justice Brennan, I agree with him entirely that our disdainful tolerance of the likes of Gregory Johnson only honors the flag he sought so ineffectively to dishonor" (*Statutory and Constitutional Responses to the Supreme Court Decision in Texas v. Johnson, Hearings before the Subcommittee on Civil and Constitutional Rights of the House Committee of the Judiciary*, 101st Congress, 1st session, 1989, serial no. 24, 222). In opposing both the FPA and an amendment, Fried replied: "I agree with the judgment that whatever the technicalities, the evident purpose of such a statute would still be to punish acts of expression, acts that do no harm as they express political convictions—mistaken and sordid as those convictions are" (Ibid., see also Goldstein, 1996a: 93–94, 273–74; 1996b: 198–99; Wicker, 1989). Most members of Congress ignored Fried's "bravely do nothing" option, placing their support behind either the FPA or a constitutional amendment, both of which were designed to criminalize protest. Still, a few voices of dissent could be heard on Capitol Hill. Representative David E. Skaggs explained that his father left Germany in the 1930s when the government began locking people up for burning the Nazi flag, and he didn't want to see that happen again: "Of course, this isn't Nazi Germany. But it is a question of a symbol of the state becoming an object of criminal sanctions" (Phillips, 1989: A4).

Also defending principles of freedom and the right to dissent during the flag panic were William Kunstler and David Cole of the Center for Constitutional Rights. Kunstler and Cole served as lead defense attorneys in *Johnson* and *Eichman* when both cases reached the Supreme Court in 1989 and 1990, respectively. Together, Kunstler and Cole presented arguments challenging the constitutionality of the Texas flag-desecration statute (*Johnson*) and the FPA (*Eichman*). Reminding the high court of the constitutional rationale supporting right to political protest, Kunstler in *Johnson* spoke passionately: "I sense that it goes to the heart of the First Amendment, to hear or to see things that we hate test the First Amendment more than seeing or hearing things that we like. It wasn't designed for things we like" (Oral argument before the U.S. Supreme Court, March 21, 1989, in the case of *Texas v. Johnson*). Similarly in *Eichman*, Kunstler added: "To criminalize flag burning is to deny what the First Amendment stands for [and to] make the American flag, a political symbol, cherished as it is by many people, into a golden image" (Oral argument before the U.S. Supreme Court, May 4, 1990, in the consolidated case of *U.S. v. Eichman* and *U.S. v. Haggerty*, Nos. 89-1433 and 89-1434).

Kunstler's courtroom flair was complemented by the sound legal analysis of Cole, then a 30-year-old Yale Law School graduate who prepared many of the main briefs submitted to the Supreme Court. Kunstler agreed that as author of the briefs, Cole was "the intellectual architect of the courtroom victories" (Margolick, 1990: B-5). While astutely revealing the technical flaws in flag-protection legislation, Cole consistently kept his sites on the larger principles of political dissent:

The United States seeks to do in these cases precisely what this Court barred the State of Texas from doing in *Texas v. Johnson*: "criminally punish a person for burning a flag as a means of political protest." . . . To permit the government to incarcerate individuals merely for expressing opposition to its most political symbol would have grave consequences for the meaning of freedom of expression. (Brief for Appellees in the consolidated case of *U.S. v. Eichman* and *U.S. v. Haggerty*, Nos. 89-1433 and 89-1434, in the Supreme Court of the United States, October term, 1989)

Kunstler not only defended the protestors' constitutional right to political dissent, he admired their courage. When politicians and the media mocked his clients, Kunstler fired back. In a letter published in the *New York Times*, Kunstler reacted angrily to an editorial titled "The Flag and a Few Punks" (April 11, 1990: A-24) in which his clients were referred to as "small-minded dissidents." Kunstler elaborated:

The obvious purpose of this unfortunate and unjustified vitriol was to tout the fervor of your brand of patriotism while playing the "liberal" role by criticizing the Bush Administration for its "demagoguery." . . . These flag burners, whom I am privileged to represent, hardly deserve such epithets. They were willing to jeopardize their liberty to test the validity of the new flag law, which you criticize as the result of an "ignoble" Congress. . . . [They] were acting in the best tradition of American protestors. Like so many before them, they provided by direct and peaceful confrontation the basis for a legal attack on a hasty statute that unconstitutionally inhibited symbolic speech (Kunstler, 1990: 22; see also Kunstler, 1989).

Prior to forging an illustrious career in law, Kunstler was awarded a Bronze Star in the Philippines during the World War II. Later, armed with a law degree from Columbia University, Kunstler found his niche representing civil rights workers in the 1960s, but eventually he became best known for this defense of radicals, political outcasts, defiant protestors, and flag burners. Forever known as a radical lawyer, Kunstler died in 1995, leaving an impressive legacy of civil rights achievements. Among his high-profile clients were Martin Luther King, Jr., Malcolm X, Stokely Carmichael, and Lenny Bruce; Abbie Hoffman, Jerry Ruben, Tom Hayden, and the other members of the Chicago 7; members of the Black Panther party; Leonard Peltier and members of the American Indian Movement; Fr. Daniel Berrigan and members of the Catonsville 9; and Attica inmates in the aftermath of the prison riot. Though commonly known for his prime-time persona, which attracted self-serving media attention, Kunstler also defended the civil rights of hundreds of other citizens who did not enjoy celebrity status, powerless people truly in need of legal counsel in resisting government repression (Kunstler, 1994; see Hentoff, 1999).

Whereas the legal expertise of Kunstler, Cole, and Fried, coupled with the organizational acuity of the civil liberties coalition, contributed tremendously to the demise of flag protection in 1989 and 1990, the crusade to save Old Glory from desecration marches forward. By the mid-1990s, the flag lobby had mobilized enormous support in Congress, even among Democrats, to advance a proposal for a constitutional amendment. Civil libertarian organizations and the press appear to have been asleep at the switch as the House of Representatives passed overwhelmingly constitutional amendments banning flag desecration in 1995, 1997, and 1999. Unquestionably, the flag lobby has successfully penetrated Congress, an achievement that could result in diminishing freedom of political dissent. The campaign to criminalize political protest remains very much alive in today's volatile world of politics, and civil libertarians face a much steeper hill to climb in the event that a constitutional amendment meets its legislative requirements. If the constitutional scenario does play out, most certainly we can expect another round of raucous defiance, escalated by prosecution, and countered by the defense of dissent, a chain of events that illuminates the symbiotic relationship between rule makers and rule breakers prolonged by repression and resistance.

CONCLUSION

Taking into account the conceptual underpinnings of flag desecration and measures designed to repress that particular form of political expression, we refine our comprehension of the ironies of social control; indeed, such incidents of escalation demonstrate the symbiotic relationship between rule makers and rule breakers. Moreover, the controversy over flag burning is compounded by the actions of First Amendment advocates who staunchly defend protestors' constitutional right to political dissent. Former U.S. Attorney General Ramsey Clark adheres to the principles of civil libertarianism by insisting, "A right is not what someone gives you; it's what no one can take from you" (1970: x). Flag protectionists obviously disagree with the notion that the right to political protest is inalienable; nevertheless, their crusade to prohibit flag burning is fraught with futility, contributing further to the paradox of social control. Questioning the merits of the flag-protection movement, Senator Bob Kerrey asked, "Where does it lead? When you are all done arguing, what have you got? Have you built a house? Have you helped somebody? Have you created a better world? Have you fought a battle worth fighting? Or are you banging into shadows on the wall of a cave? It seems to me there's nothing produced from it and you've divided the nation" (Toner, 1989: A13).

Attending to elements of civil religion, nostalgia, and the authoritarian aesthetic, this work explored the emergence of moral panic over flag desecration, culminating in the crusade to criminalize protest. In shoring up this observation, evidence of flag panic was presented throughout this book. Consider the words of conservative Phyllis Schlafly, who supports flag protection to "help give us a national identity" given that "so many demonstrators trample on patriotism, religion, family, decency, Western Civilization and U.S. traditions" (*New York Post*, July 2, 1989: 26). Despite the compelling forces of flag panic, especially in 1989 and 1990, there remained voices of dissent that challenged the putative threat of desecration. Stuart Comstock-Gay of the ACLU warned us that impulsive reactions to acts of protest perceived as offensive could undermine the very foundation of American democracy: "Our emotions tell us we should stop flag burners . . . but freedom of expression is no good at all if it doesn't protect the ideas we hate" (Shen, 1990: B8). Similarly, Arthur J. Kropp, president of PAW, argued, "As a nation we are strong enough to withstand the pain of seeing our flag burned. What we could not withstand is seeing the First Amendment cast aside out of a misguided sense of nationalism" (Greenhouse, 1989: 1).

In closing, this work unveiled the sociological significance of the flag-protection campaign—regrettably, a phenomenon ignored by other sociologists and criminologists.

NOTE

1. From an organizational standpoint, the ECSCFC benefited tremendously from the work of Bruce Bentley, Nancy Kent, and Shawn Eichman.

References

"A Test for Old Glory." 1967. *Life*, March 3: 18–25.

Abrams, H. 1991. *"Degenerate Art": The Fate of the Avant-Garde in Nazi Germany*. Los Angeles: Los Angeles Museum of Art.

Adams, L. 1976. *Art on Trial: From Whistler to Rothko*. New York: Walker & Co.

Alpert, H. 1939. *Emile Durkheim and His Sociology*. New York: Columbia University Press.

Alvarez, L. 2000. "Measure to Ban Flag Burning Fall 4 Votes Short in Senate." *New York Times*, March 30: A24.

American Civil Liberties Union. 1997. "Three Cheers for the Red, White, and Blue?" *Civil Liberties*, November: 7–8.

———. 1970. "Flag Laws Still Wave." *Civil Liberties*, September: 1.

———. 1971. "Flag Desecration." *Civil Liberties*, May: 5.

Andersen, W. 1940–41. "Constitutional Law—Due Process—Freedom of Religion and Conscience—Compulsory Flag Salute." *Michigan Law Review*, 39, 149–52.

Andrews, E. B. 1890. "Patriotism and the Public Schools." *Arena*, 3: 71.

Anthony, D., and T. Robbins. 1982. "Spiritual Innovation and the Crisis of American Civil Religion." *Daedalus*, 111, 1: 215–34.

Augusta Chronicle [Georgia]. 1999. "Protect Old Glory." April 29: A4.

Aronowitz, S., and W. DiFazio. 1994. *The Jobless Future*. Minneapolis: University of Minnesota Press.

Arrigo, B. A. 1995. "The Peripheral Core of Law and Criminology: On Postmodern Social Theory and Conceptual Integration." *Justice Quarterly*, 12, 3: 447–72.

Avni, B. 1989. "The Flag, Free Speech Take a Beating in Washington Square." *New York Times*, July 8: 23.

Ayres, B. D. 1996. "Art or Trash? Arizona Exhibit on American Flag Unleashes a Controversy." *New York Times*, June 8: 6.

Bailey, F., and D. Hale. 1998. *Popular Culture, Crime and Justice*. Belmont, CA: Wadsworth.

Baker, J. 1977. *Ambivalent Americans: the Know-Nothing Party in Maryland*. Baltimore: Johns Hopkins University Press.

Balch, G. 1898. *Methods of Teaching Patriotism in the Public Schools*. New York: D. Van Nostrand.

Baldwin, C. 1974. "Art and the Law: The Flag in Court Again." *Art in America*, May/June: 50–54.

Baltimore Sun. 1991. January 18: B2.

———. 1999. "Burning Issue: Constitutional Ban." April 10: 10A.

Balz, D. 1990. "The President and Politics of the Flag." *Washington Post,* June 17, A12.

Bangor Daily News [Maine]. 1998. "Rights of the Flag." July 10: 22.

Barak, G. 1994. *Media, Process, and the Social Construction of Crime.* New York: Garland Publishing, Inc.

Barber, H. W. 1947. "Religious Liberty v. the Police Power: Jehovah's Witnesses." *American Political Science Review,* XLI: 226–47.

Barry, J. W. 1924. *Masonry and the Flag.* Washington, D.C.: Masonic Service Association of the United States.

Barthes, R. 1967. *Elements of Semiology* (translated by A. Lavers). New York: Hill and Wang.

Baudrillard, J. 1983. *Simulations.* New York: Semiotext.

Becker, H. S. 1963. *Outsiders: Studies in the Sociology of Deviance.* New York: Free Press.

———. 1967. "Whose Side Are We On?" *Social Problems,* 14: 239–47.

Beckett, K. 1994. "Setting the Public Agenda: 'Street Crime' and Drug Use in American Politics." *Social Problems,* 41, 3: 425–47.

———. 1997. *Making Crime Pay: Law and Order in Contemporary American Politics.* New York: Oxford University Press.

Bellah, R. 1967. "Civil religion in America." *Daedalus,* 96, 1–21.

———. 1970. *Beyond Belief.* New York: Harper & Row.

———. 1975. *The Broken Covenant.* New York: Seabury.

———. 1978. "Religion and Legitimation in the American Republic." *Society,* 15, 4: 16–23.

———. 1988. "Civil Religion in America." *Daedalus,* 117, 3: 97–118.

Ben-Yehuda, N. 1990. *The Politics and Morality of Deviance: Moral Panics, Drug Abuses, and Reversed Stigmatization.* Albany: State University of New York Press.

Berkman, Alexander. 1916. "The Sacred Rag." *The Blast,* July 1: 5.

Best, J. 1987. "Rhetoric in Claims-Making." *Social Problems,* 24, 2: 101–21.

———. 1989. *Images of Issues: Typifying Contemporary Social Problems.* New York: Aldine de Gruyter.

———. 1990. *Threatened Children: Rhetoric and Concern About Child Victims.* Chicago: University of Chicago Press.

Blalock, D. 1990. "Vietnam Memories: Lessons for Burning the Flag." *Revolutionary Worker,* May 6: 6–7, 14.

Blanchard, M. 1986. *Exporting the First Amendment: The Press-Government Crusade of 1945–1952.* New York: Longman.

———. 1992. *Revolutionary Sparks: Freedom of Expression in Modern America.* New York: Oxford University Press.

Bloom, L. 1990. "*Barnette* and *Johnson*: A Tale of Two Opinions." *Iowa Law Review,* 75: 417–32.

Blumenthal, S. 1990. "Symbolic Logic." *New Republic,* July 9 and 16: 13.

Blumer, H. 1974. "Social Movements." In R. S. Denisoff ed. *The Sociology of Dissent,* 4–20. New York: Harcourt Brace Jovanovich.

Bogart, H. 1970. "Thousands in City March to Assail Lindsay on War." *New York Times,* May 16: A1.

Bonner, R. 1984. *Weakness and Deceit: U.S. Policy and El Salvador.* New York: Times Books.

Boston Globe. 1991. "US Finds No Glory in Red, White and Blue Condoms." October 27: 30

———. 1998. "Flag Waving." June 26: A22.

Bourdieu, P. 1989, "Social Space and Symbolic Power." *Sociological Theory,* 7, 1: 14–26;

———. 1983. *Distinction: A Social Critique of the Judgement of Taste.* Cambridge: Harvard University Press.

Brace, P., and B. Hinckley. 1992. *Follow the Leader: Opinion Polls and the Modern Presidents.* New York: Basic Books.

Brinkley, A. 1990. "Old Glory: The Saga of a National Love Affair." *New York Times,* July 1: E-1.

Broad, D. 1998. "New World Order Versus Just World Order." *Social Justice,* 25, 2: 6–15.

Broder, D., 1990, "Trivial Issues" *Washington Post,* June 17: D7.

Brownstein, H. 1996. *The Rise and Fall of a Violent Crime Wave: Crack Cocaine and the Social Construction of a Crime Problem.* New York: Harrow and Heston.

Buchanan, P. 1989, "Congress Can Write Law to Protect the Flag." *San Antonio Express News,* June 24: 31.

———. 1996. Speech delivered at the Heritage Foundation, Washington, D.C., January 29. Federal Document Clearing House, Inc.

Burawoy, M. 1991. *Ethnography Unbound: Power to Resistance in the Modern Metropolis.* Berkeley: University of California Press.

Business Wire. 1995. "First Amendment Heroes to be Saluted at Conference Coming to Oakland." September 14: 1–4.

Calavita, K., H. Pontell, and R. Tillman. 1997. *Big Money Crime: Fraud and Politics in the Savings and Loan Crisis.* Berkeley: University of California Press.

Camposeco, M. 1994. "48 Students Suspended After Mural Ban Protest." *Fresno Bee,* February 24: A-4.

———, and E. Rocha. 1994. "Elk Grove Trustees Vote to Ban All Murals From Schools." *Sacramento Bee,* February 23: B-1.

Capital. 1999. "This Year, Let's Make Old Glory's Protection a Priority." June 14: A8.

Cembalist, R. 1993. "The Flag on the Floor." *ARTnews,* March: 35.

Chafee, Z. 1941. *Free Speech in the United States.* New York: Antheneum.

———. 1919. "Freedom of Speech in War Time." *Harvard Law Review,* 32: 932–78.

Chalmers, D. 1981. *Hooded Americanism: The History of the Ku Klux Klan.* New York: Franklin Watts.

Chapman, S., 1990, "Republicans Seize a Star-Spangled Political Issue." *Chicago Tribune,* June 14: 25.

Chen, Edwin. 1997. "Congress Braces for Renewed Salvos in 'Culture War.'" *Los Angeles Times,* May 14: 16.

Chermak, S. 1997. "The Presentation of Crime in the News Media: The News Sources Involved in the Construction of Social Problems." *Justice Quarterly,* 14 4: 687–718.

Chiasson, L. 1991. "Japanese-American Relocation During World War II: A Study of California Editorial Reactions." *Journalism Quarterly,* 68, 1–2: 263–68.

Chicago Tribune. 1989. "Flag desecration on Capitol Hill." June 30: 24.

———. 1995. "Clinton Against Amendment to Ban Burning U.S. Flag." June 6: Section: Evening, 1.

———. 1995. "Crazy For the Red, White and Blue." February 26: Section 4: 2.

———. 1997. "Flags and Rights." March 22: 22.

Chiricos, T. 1996. "Moral Panic as Ideology: Drugs, Violence, Race, and Punishment in America." In M. Lynch and E. Patterson, eds., *Justice With Prejudice: Race and Criminal Justice,* 19–48. New York: Harrow and Heston.

Christian Science Monitor. 1973. "Flag Desecration in the Courts." May 15: 1.

Chomsky, N. 1970. *Trials of the Resistance.* New York: Vintage.

Ciolli, Rita. 1990. "Flag-burning Debate Unfurling." *New York Newsday,* May 15: 31.

Citizens Flag Alliance. 1997. "July 4th Weekend Flag Desecration Underscores Need for Flag Protection Amendment." July 10, Press Release, Indianapolis, IN: Citizens Flag Alliance, Inc.

———. 1997. "Significant Campaign Events." December 12, p. 1. Indianapolis, IN: Citizens Flag Alliance, Inc.

———. 1998a. *Flag Desecration Acts.* Posted on the World Wide Web.

———. 1998b. "Protestors Torch Flag at White House: American Outraged by Dishonorable Act." Press Release on February 24: Indianapolis, IN.

———. 1998c. "Who We Are." February 4. Indianapolis, IN: Citizens Flag Alliance, Inc. Webmaster at dbrannon@legion.org.

———. 1998d. "Message Points." February 4. Indianapolis, IN: Citizens Flag Alliance, Inc. Webmaster at dbrannon@legion.org.

Clark, R. 1970. *Crime in America: Observations on Its Nature, Causes, Prevention and Control.* New York: Simon and Schuster.

Cleveland Plain Dealer. 1990. "Oberlin Student, Friend Admit They Burned Flag." January 26: 12.

Clines, F. 1997. "Flag Measure Stirs Lawmakers Blood." *New York Times,* June 13: 22.

Cohen, J. E. 1994. "Presidential Rhetoric and the Public Agenda." *American Journal of Political Science,* 39: 87–107.

———. *Presidential Responsiveness and Public Policy-Making: The Public and the Policies that Presidents Choose.* Ann Arbor: University of Michigan Press.

Cohen, S. 1972. *Folk Devils and Moral Panics.* London: Macgibbon and Kee.

———. 1979. "The Punitive City: Notes on the Dispersal of Social Control." *Contemporary Crisis,* 3: 339–63.

———, and J. Young. 1981. *The Manufacture of News: Deviance, Social Problems and the Mass Media.* London: Constable.

Colgrove, C. 1896–97. "Patriotism in our Public Schools." *American Magazine of Civics,* 9: 124–26.

Collins, R. 1991. "The Constitutionality of Flag Burning: Can Neutral Values Protect First Amendment Principles?" *American Criminal Law Review,* 28, 4: 887–927.

Commercial Appeal [Memphis, TN]. 1997. "Freedom Issue Spare Constitution on Flag-Burning Ban." June 16: A6.

Congressional Record. Washington, DC: U.S. Government Printing.

Cottman, M. 1991a. "Police Union Takes Flag Flap to Court." *New York Newsday*, January 24: 31.

———. 1991b. "A Special Meaning in Patch." *New York Newsday*, January 26: 6.

Craig, B. J. 1996. *American Patriotism in a Global Society*. Albany: State University of New York Press.

Crow, T. 1996. *Modern Art in Common Culture*. New Haven: Yale University Press.

Curti, M. 1968. *The Roots of the American Loyalty*. New York: Columbia University Press.

Curtis, M. K. 1993a. *The Constitution and the Flag: Volume 1, The Flag Burning Cases*. New York: Garland Publishing, Inc.

———. 1993b. *The Constitution and the Flag: Volume 2, The Flag Salute Cases*. New York: Garland Publishing, Inc.

Daily Oklahoman. 1998. "Do the Right Thing." July 15: 6.

Daley, S. 1989. "Lawmakers Amending Plans on Flag Measure." *Chicago Tribune*, July 21: 1.

———. 1990. "Amendment Friends, Foes Rally" *Chicago Tribune*, June 15: 4.

Dallas Morning News. 1999. "Flag Desecration: An Overkill Solution to a Nonexistent Problem." April 20: 10A.

Danzig, R. 1993a. "How Questions Begot Answers in Felix Frankfurter's First Flag Salute Opinion." In M. Curtis, ed., *The Constitution and the Flag: The Flag Salute Cases*, 77–94. New York: Garland.

———. 1993b "Justice Frankfurter's Opinion in the Flag Salute Cases: Blending Logic and Psychology in Constitutional Decisionmaking." In M. Curtis, ed., *The Constitution and the Flag: The Flag Salute Cases*, 239–87. New York: Garland.

Daughters of the American Revolution Flag Committee. 1899. *American Monthly Magazine* (April) *1903 National Year Book*. National Society of the Sons of the American Revolution.

Dedman, B. and A. Stevens. 1989. "Flag Burning Issue Inflames Passions at the Mall." *Washington Post*, July 5: D1.

Defense Campaign for the War Parade 18. No Date. *Hands Off The War Parade 18!*. New York: Stop the U.S. War Machine Action Network.

"Degenerate Art." 1993. Aired April 16. New York City: Public Broadcasting System.

Delgado, K. 1989. "Stars and Stripes Forever." *Village Voice*, July 18: 11.

Demerath, N. J., III, and R. H. Williams. 1985. "Civil Religion in an Uncivil Society." *Annals of the American Academy of Political and Social Science*, 480: 154–66.

Denisoff, R. S. 1974. *The Sociology of Dissent*. New York: Harcourt Brace Jovanovich.

Derrida, J. 1976. *Of Grammatology* (translated by G. C. Spivak). Baltimore: Johns Hopkins University Press.

Dershowitz, A. 1986. "Justice." *Penthouse*, August: 20.

Detroit News. 1995. "Save the Constitution," October 14: 35.

———. 1998. "Constitutional Vandalism." April 11: C7.

Devroy, A., 1995. "Entering Fray, Administration to Announce Opposition to Flag-Burning Amendment." *Washington Post*, June 6: A4.

Dewar, H., 1989, "Flag Protection Amendment Set Back as 2 Sponsors Switch." *Washington Post*, October 18: A5.

Dickey, C. 1985. *With the Contras.* New York: Simon & Schuster.

Dillon, S. 1991. *Commandos: The CIA and Nicaragua's Contra Rebels.* New York: Henry Holt.

Donner, F. 1990. *Protectors of Privilege: Red Squads and Police Repression in Urban America.* Los Angeles: University of California Press.

Dow Jones Interactive Publications Library. 1997. New York: Dow Jones & Co., Inc.

Drew, C. 1995. "Anti-Flag Burning Drive Begins." *Chicago Tribune,* March 1: 8.

Dubin, S. 1982. "Paying the Piper: The Public Funding of Artists." Unpublished Ph.D. dissertation. University of Chicago.

———. 1990. "Visual Onomatopoeia." *Symbolic Interaction,* 13, 2: 185–216.

———. 1992. *Arresting Images: Impolitic Art and Uncivil Actions.* New York: Routledge.

Durkheim, E. 1912 [1954]. *The Elementary Forms of Religious Life* (translated by J. Swain). New York: The Free Press.

Durkheim, E. 1933 [1964]. *The Division of Labor in Society.* New York: The Free Press.

Dye, T., and H. Ziegler. 1993. *The Irony of Democracy: An Uncommon Introduction to American Politics.* Belmont, CA: Wadsworth.

Eaton, W. J. 1989. "Flag Bill on Fast Track to Exclude Amendment." *Los Angeles Times,* July 26: 12.

———. 1989. "Senate Passes Ban on Burning U.S. Flag, 91 to 9." *Los Angeles Times,* October 6: 24.

Eau Claire Leader-Telegram, March 12, 1991: 3.

Eco, U. 1976. *A Theory of Semiotics.* Bloomington: Indiana University Press.

Edelman, M. 1964. *The Symbolic Uses of Politics.* Urbana: University of Illinois Press.

———. 1971. *Politics as Symbolic Actor: Mass Arousal and Quiescence.* New York: Academic Press.

———. 1989. *Constructing the Political Spectacle.* Chicago: University of Chicago Press.

Editor & Publisher. 1995. "Flag Amendment Opposed by ASNE." July 8: 36.

Efron, S. 1990. "5 Arrested After Flags are Burned." *Los Angeles Times.* July 9: B-1.

Eggenberger, D. 1964. *Flags of the United States of America.* New York: Crowell.

Emergency Committee to Stop the Flag Amendment and Laws. 1989. Document in author's possession.

English, R., and S. Eichman. 1989. "Curatorial Statement." *Helms' Degenerate Art Show.*

Ericson, R. V. 1995. *Crime and the Media.* Aldershot, VT: Dartmouth.

Ericson, R. V., P. M. Baranek, and J. B. L. Chan. 1987. *Visualizing Deviance: A Study of News Organizations.* Toronto: University of Toronto Press.

———. 1989. *Negotiating Control: A Study of News Sources.* Toronto: University of Toronto Press.

———. 1991. *Representing Order: Crime, Law, and Justice in the News Media.* Toronto: University of Toronto Press.

Erikson, K. 1966. *Wayward Puritans: A Study in the Sociology of Deviance.* New York: John Wiley.

Erwin, D. 1994. "Students, Don't Let District Discourage You." *Sacramento Bee,* February 8: A-2.

Ewick, P. and S. Silbey. 1992. "Conformity, Contestation, and Resistance: An Account of Legal Consciousness." *New England Law Review*, 26: 731–49.

Faigman, D. 1990. "By What Authority?: Reflections on the Constitutionality and Wisdom of the Flag Protection Act of 1989." *Hastings Constitutional Law Quarterly*, 17: 353–67.

Feeley, M. 1979. *The Process is the Punishment: Handling Cases in a Lower Criminal Court*. New York: Russell Sage Foundation.

Fennell, W. 1941. "The 'Reconstructed Court' and Religious Freedom: The Gobitis case in Retrospect." *New York University Law Quarterly Review*, 19, 31–48.

Ferrell, J. 1994. "Confronting the Agenda of Authority: Critical Criminology, Anarchism, and Urban Graffiti." In Gregg Barak, ed., *Varieties of Criminology: Readings From a Dynamic Discipline*, 161–78. Westport, CT.: Praeger.

———. 1995. "Urban Graffiti: Crime, Control, and Resistance." *Youth & Society*, 27: 1: 73–92.

———. 1996. *Crimes of Style: Urban Graffiti and the Politics of Criminality*. Boston: Northeastern University Press.

———. 1997a. "Against the Law: Anarchist Criminology." In B. MacLean and D. Milovanovic, eds., *Thinking Critically About Crime*, 146–54. Vancouver: Collective Press.

———. 1997b. "Youth, Crime, and Cultural Space." *Social Justice*, 24, 4: 21–38;

———. 1998a. "Stumbling Toward a Critical Criminology: And Into the Anarchy and Imagery of Postmodernism." In J. Ross, ed., *Cutting the Edge: Current Perspectives in Critical Criminology*, 63–76. Westport, CT.: Praeger.

———. 1998b. "Freight Train Graffiti: Subculture, Crime, and Dislocation." *Justice Quarterly*, 15, 4: 587–627.

Finkelman, P. 1992. "The First Ten Amendments as a Declaration of Rights." *Southern Illinois Law Journal*, 351.

Finley, L. 1989. "2,000 Unfurl Flag Protest." *Chicago Sun-Times*, March 13: 1.

First Amendment Center. 1997. "House Holds Hearing on Flag-Desecration Amendment." page 1: First Amendment Center Homepage, web at fac.org.

Fishman, M. 1978. "Crime Waves as Ideology." *Social Problems*, 25: 531–43.

Fishman, M., and G. Cavender. 1998. *Entertaining Crime: Television Reality Programs*. New York: Aldine de Gruyter.

"Flag Exhibit Upheld in Chicago." 1989. *New York Times*, March 3: A-16.

Ford, J. H. 1989. "We Need Tough Laws to Protect Our Flag." *USA Today*, March 22: 10A.

Foucault, M. 1979. *Discipline and Punish*. New York: Vintage.

———. 1980. *The History of Sexuality*. New York: Vintage.

Friedrichs, D. 1996. *Trusted Criminals: White Collar Crime in Contemporary Society*. Belmont, CA: Wadsworth.

Frisbie, R. 1971. "What So Proudly We Hailed." *U.S. Catholic and Jubilee*. February: 2.

Fritz, S. 1989. "Angry Congressmen Vow New Laws to Protect Flag." *Los Angeles Times*, June 23: 1.

Frohnmayer, J. 1993. *Leaving Town Alive: Confessions of an Arts Warrior*. Boston: Houghton Mifflin.

Fulton, J., and B. Seaman. 1989. "The Flag Fracas." *New Art Examiner*, May: 30–31.

Fulwood, S. 1997. "House Again Approves Ban on Burning American Flag." *Los Angeles Times*, June 13: 27.

Gallup, G. 1992. "Poll on Flag Protection." *The Gallup Poll*. Princeton, NJ: Gallup Organization, Inc.

Gamoran, A. 1990. "Civil Religion in American Schools." *Sociological Analysis*, 51, 3: 235–56.

Gamson, W., D. Croteau, W. Hoynes, and T. Sasson. 1992. "Media Images and the Social Construction of Reality." *Annual Review of Sociology*, 18: 373–93.

Gans, H. 1980. *Deciding What's News*. New York: Vintage.

Garbus, M. 1989. "The 'Crime' of Flag Burning." *Nation*, March 20: 369–70.

Gaubatz, M. 1995. *Crime in the Public Mind*. Ann Arbor: University of Michigan Press.

Gelderman, C. W. 1995. "All the President's Words." *Wilson Quarterly*, 19: 68–79.

Gerstenzang, J. 1989. "Bush Asks Ban on Flag Desecration." *Los Angeles Times*, July 28: 14.

Getlin, J. 1989, "Constitutional Protection for Flag Launched in House." *Los Angeles Times*, June 30: 16.

Ghiglione, L. 1989. Letters to President George Bush, U.S. Senate, and U.S. House of Representatives. July 21. Washington, DC: American Society of Newspaper Editors.

Gibbs, N. 1991. "America's Holy War.", *Time*, December 9: 60–68.

Gibson, M. 1986. "The Supreme Court and Freedom of Expression from 1791 to 1917." *Fordham Law Review*, 55, 263–86.

Gilkey, R. C. 1957. "Mr. Justice Frankfurter and Civil Liberties as Manifested in, and Suggested by, the Compulsory Flag-Salute Controversy." Unpublished Ph.D. Dissertation, University of Minnesota.

Gitlin, T. 1987. *The Sixties: Years of Hope, Days of Rage*. New York: Bantam.

Glasser, I. 1989. "Bush Lowers the Flag." *The New York Times*, June 28: A-23.

Glowen, R. 1992. "The Big Chill Comes to Alaska." *Artweek*, December 3: 3, 28.

Goeas, E. 1995. "Majority of Public Supports Flag Amendment." *Chicago Tribune*, October 10: 15.

Goffman, E. 1959. *The Presentation of Self in Everyday Life*. New York: Doubleday Anchor Books.

Goldstein, R. J. 1978. *Political Repression in Modern America: From 1870 to the Present*. Cambridge, MA.: Schenkman Publishing Company, Inc.

———. 1990. "The Great 1989–1990 Flag Flap: An Historical, Political, and Legal Analysis." *University of Miami Law Review*, 45: 19–106.

———. 1993. "The Vietnam War Flag Flap." *Flag Bulletin*, 150: 142–75.

———. 1994. "This Flag Is Not For Burning." *Nation*, July 18, 84–86.

———. 1995. *Saving "Old Glory": The History of the American Flag Desecration Controversy*. Boulder, CO: Westview.

———. 1996a. *Burning the Flag: The Great 1989–1990 American Flag Desecration Controversy*. Kent, OH: Kent State University Press.

———. 1996b. *Desecrating the American Flag: Key Documents of the Controversy from the Civil War to 1995*. Syracuse, NY: Syracuse University Press.

Gonzenbach, W. 1996. *The Media, the President, and Public Opinion: A Longitudinal Analysis of the Drug Issue, 1984–1991*. Mahwah, NJ: Lawrence Erlbaum Associates.

Goode, E. 1969. "Marijuana and the Politics of Reality." *Journal of Health and Social Behavior*, 10: 83–94.

———. 1978. *Deviant Behavior: An Interactionist Perspective*. Englewood Cliffs, NJ: Prentice-Hall.

———. 1992. *Collective Behavior*. Fort Worth, TX: Harcourt, Brace, Jovanovich.

———. 1993. *Drugs in American Society*. 4th Edition. New York: McGraw-Hill.

———, and N. Ben-Yehuda. 1994. *Moral Panics: The Social Construction of Deviance*. Cambridge, MA.: Blackwell

Goodwyn, L. 1978. *The Populist Movement*. New York: Oxford University Press.

Gottdiener, M. 1995. *Postmodern Semiotics: Material Culture and the Forms of Postmodern Life*. Cambridge, MA: Blackwell Books.

Graber, D. A. 1982. *The President and the Public*. Philadelphia: Institute for the Study of Human Issues.

———. 1990. *Media Power in Politics*. Washington, DC: Congressional Quarterly Press.

Graham, F. 1971. "The Supreme Court and the Flag." *Art in America*, March 1971: 27.

Gramsci, A. 1971. *Selections from the Prison Notebooks*. New York: International.

Greek, C. 1994. "Becoming a Media Criminologist: Is 'Newsmaking Criminology' Possible?" In G. Barak, ed., *Media, Process, and the Social Construction of Crime*, 265–86. New York: Garland Publishing, Inc.

Green, M. 1988. *New York 1913: The Armory Show and the Paterson Strike Pageant*. New York: Charles Scribner's Sons.

Greenawalt, K. 1990. "O'er the Land of the Free: Flag Burning as Speech." *UCLA Law Review*, 37: 925–47.

Greenberg, J., J. Porteus, L. Simon, T. Pyszczynski, and S. Solomon. 1995. "Evidence of a Terror Management Function of Cultural Icons: The Effects of Mortality Salience on the Inappropriate Use of Cherished Cultural Symbols." *Personality and Social Psychology Bulletin*, 21, 1221–28.

Greenhouse, L. 1989, "Justices, 5–4, Back Protestors' Right to Burn the Flag." *New York Times*, June 22, 1989: 1.

———. 1990. "Supreme Court Voids Flag Law." *New York Times*, June 12: A-1, B-7.

———. 1998. "The Fight Over God's Place in America's Legacy." *New York Times*, November 1: B-10.

Greensboro News & Record. 1998. "Burning Flag is Bad, But not a Crime." July 2: A15.

Grinnell, F. 1939. "Children, the Bill of Rights, and the American Flag." *Massachusetts Law Quarterly*, 24, 1–7.

Guenter, S. 1989. "The Hippies and the Hardhats: The Struggle for Semiotic Control of the Flag of the United States." *Flag Bulletin*, 130–36.

———. 1990. *The American Flag, 1777–1924: Cultural Shifts from Creation to Codification*. Rutherford, NJ: Fairleigh Dickinson University Press.

Gusfield, J. 1963. *Symbolic Crusade: Status Politics and the American Temperance Movement*. Urbana: University of Illinois Press.

———. 1967. "Moral Passage: The Symbolic Process in Public Designations of Deviance." *Social Problems*, 15: 175–88.

———. 1981. *The Culture of Public Problems: Drinking-Driving and the Symbolic Order*. Chicago: University of Chicago Press.

Guthrie, W. 1918. *The Religion of Old Glory*. New York: George H. Doran.

Hale, E. 1863. "The Man Without A Country." *Atlantic Monthly*, December: 665–79

Hall, S., and T. Jefferson. 1976. *Resistance Through Rituals*. London: Hutchison.

Hall, S., C. Critcher, T. Jefferson, J. Clarke, and B. Roberts. 1978. *Policing the Crisis: Mugging, the State and Law and Order*. New York: Holmes and Meiser.

Hammond, P. E. 1976. "The Sociology of American Civil Religion: A Bibliographic Essay." *Sociological Analysis*, 37, 2: 169–82.

Harrington, M. 1989. *Socialism Past and Future*. New York: Arcade Publishing.

Harvin, A. 1991. "College Player Quits, Citing Threats Over Flag." *New York Times*, February 14: D-23.

Hayes, C. 1960. *Nationalism: A Religion*. New York: Macmillan.

Henderson, R. 1998. "Lasorda Bleeds Red, White & Blue." *Orange County Register*, July 12: 22.

Hendricks, J., and J. Toche. 1978. *G.A.A.G.: The Guerrilla Art Action Group*. New York, Printed Matter, Inc.: Section 12

Henry, S. 1994. "Newsmaking Criminology as Replacement Discourse." In G. Barak, ed., *Media, Process, and the Social Construction of Crime*, 287–318. New York: Garland Publishing, Inc.

Hentoff, N. 1995. "The Ultimate Desecration of the Flag." *Village Voice*, July 18: 20–21.

———. 1996. "The Teachings of Mahmoud Abdul-Rauf." *Village Voice*, April 30: 10.

———. 1997. "Who Speaks for the Village Voice?" *Village Voice*, June 24, 1997.

———. 1999. "A Free-Speech Warrior." *Village Voice*, September 28: 33.

Herman, E. H., and N. Chomsky. 1988. *Manufacturing Consent: The Political Economy of the Mass Media*. New York: Pantheon.

Hernandez, D. G. 1995. "Dodging a Bullet." *Editor & Publisher*, December 23: 13, 31.

Hertzberg, H. 1989. "Flagellation." *New Republic*, July 17: 4–5.

Hess, E. 1989. "Capture the Flag: Is Dread Scott's Flag-piece Art, Treason or Both?" *Village Voice*, April 4, 25–31.

———. 1990. "Gutter Politics." *Village Voice*, July 3: 89.

Hickman, M. 1982. "Crime in the Streets—a Moral Panic: Understanding 'Get Tough' Policies in the Criminal Justice System." *Southern Journal of Criminal Justice*, 8: 7–22.

History of the American Civil Liberties Union. 1998. Documentary aired October 27. New York City: Public Broadcasting System.

Hitchens, C. 1997. "Waving the Flag." *Nation*, July 21: 8

Hochfield, S. 1989. "Flag Furor." *ARTnews*. Summer: 43–47.

Hoffman, A. 1989. *The Best of Abbie Hoffman*. New York: Four Walls Eight Windows.

Hoge, P. 1993a. "Elk Grove Students Sue School." *Sacramento Bee*, April 17: B-1.

———. 1993b. "Students Win Fight to Lift Ban on Mural." *Sacramento Bee*, May 20: A-1.

Hollywood, B. 1997. "Dancing in the Dark: Ecstasy, the Dance Culture, and Moral Panic in Post Ceasefire Northern Ireland." *Critical Criminology: An International Journal*, 8, 1: 62–77.

Holmes, S. A. 1990. "House Flag-Burning Amendment Advances on Subcommittee Vote." *New York Times*, June 14: 10.

————. 1990. "Amendment to Bar Flag Desecration Fails in the House." *New York Times*, June 22: 1.

Hopkins, W. 1991. "Flag Desecration as Seditious Libel." *Journalism Quarterly*, 68, 4: 814–22.

House of Representatives, *To Prevent Desecration of the United States Flag*. 51st Congress, 1st session, 1890. Report accompanying H.R. 10475 (subsequently passed by the House of Representatives in 1890 [*Congressional Record*, 10697].

House Judiciary Committee Subcommittee No. 1, *To Preserve the Purity of the Flag*. 62nd Congress, 2nd session, 1918.

Houston, P. 1990. "Flag Amendment Faces Uphill Fight." *Los Angeles Times*, June 15: 4.

————. 1990, "Amendment to Protect the Flag Rejected by House." *Los Angeles Times*, June 22: 1.

Howlett, D. 1998. "Pregnant Woman Free to Choose, But Hasn't Yet." *USA Today*, October 15: 3-A.

Hoy, T. 1974. "Albert Camus: The Nature of Political Rebellion." In R. S. Denisoff, ed. *The Sociology of Dissent*. New York: Harcourt Brace Jovanovich, 364–71.

Hughes, R. 1997. "American Visions." *Time*. Special Issue, Spring: 84.

Hughey, M. 1983. *Civil Religion and Moral Order: Theoretical and Historical Dimensions*. Westport, CT: Greenwood Press.

Humphries, D. 1981. "Serious Crime, News Coverage, and Ideology." *Crime and Delinquency*, 27: 191–205.

————. 1999. *Crack Mothers: Pregnancy, Drugs, and the Media*. Columbus: Ohio State University Press.

Ingram, C. 1989. "Protect-the-Flag Fervor Spreads to State Capitol." *Los Angeles Times*, July 2: 3.

————. 1989. "State Senate Jumps on Bandwagon for the Flag." *Los Angeles Times*, July 14, 1989: 3.

In These Times. 1989. "Tread on Dread." April 5–11: 4.

Irons, P. 1993. *May It Please the Court*. New York: Free Press.

————. 1997. *May It Please the Court: The First Amendment*. New York: Free Press.

Jaffe, J. 1972. *Crusade Against Radicalism: New York During the Red Scare*. Port Washington, NY: Kennikat.

Jenkins, P. 1992. *Intimate Enemies: Moral Panics in Contemporary Great Britain*. New York: Aldine de Gruyter.

————. 1994. *Using Murder: The Social Construction of Serial Murder*. New York: Aldine de Gruyter.

Johns, C. 1991. "The War on Drugs: Why the Administration Continues to Pursue a Policy of Criminalization and Enforcement." *Social Justice*, 18: 147–65.

————. 1996. *Operation Just Cause: The War on Drugs and the Invasion of Panama*. New York: Praeger.

Johnson, J. E. 1923. *Ku Klux Klan, The Reference Shelf*. New York: H. Wilson.

Johnson, R. 1989. "Anti-Helms Art Show in the Bronx." *New York Post*, December 9: 6.

Johnson, W. 1930. *The National Flag: A History*. Boston: Houghton Mifflin.

Jones, R. 1998, "High Court Asked to Save Flag Desecration Law: Judges Asked to

Revive Century-Old Statute in Outagamie County Case." *Milwaukee Journal Sentinel*, April 19: 1

Jones, S. 1984. *The Presidential Election of 1896*. Madison: University of Wisconsin Press.

Journal-Star (Peoria, IL). 1989. "Hotline." March 20: 2.

Judson, H. F. 1997. "Waving Our Freedom." *New York Times*, June 16: A-15;

Kahn, R. 1996. *Other People's Blood: U.S. Immigration Prisons in the Reagan Decade*. Boulder, CO: Westview Press.

Kansas City Star. 1995. "Constitution in More Peril than Old Glory." July 7: C5.

Kappeler, V. E., M. Blumberg, and G. W. Potter. 1996. *The Mythology of Crime and Criminal Justice*. 2nd edition. Prospect Heights, IL: Waveland Press, Inc.

Kasinsky, R. G. 1994. "Patrolling the Facts: Media, Cops, and Crime." In G. Barak, ed., *Media, Process, and the Social Construction of Crime*, 203–360. New York: Garland Publishing, Inc.

Katz, J. 1988. *Seductions of Crime: Moral and Sensual Attractions in Doing Evil*. New York: Basic Books.

Kazin, M. 1989. "The New Historians Recapture the Flag." *New York Times Book Review*, June 2: 1, 19, 21.

Kenworthy, T. 1990. "Flag Amendment Sent to House Floor." *Washington Post*, June 20: A14.

Ketter, W. B. 1995. "Getting Tough on Flag-Burners in Communist Asia and Democratic U.S." *American Editor*, September: 2, 43.

Kevelson, R. 1990. *Law and Semiotics*. New York: Plenum.

Kidd-Hewitt, D., and R. Osborne. 1995. *Crime and the Media: The Postmodern Spectacle*. East Haven, CT: Pluto Press.

Kilborn, P. T. 1984. "As Ireland Visit Ends, 5,000 Protestors March." *New York Times*, June 5: 12.

Kimmelman, M. 1991. "Exhibition of Works By Those the Nazis Hounded and Scorned." *New York Times*, February 25: C-11.

Kittrie, N., and E. Wedlock. 1986. *The Tree of Liberty: A Documentary History of Rebellion and Political Crime in America*. Baltimore: Johns Hopkins University Press.

Klehr, H. 1988. *Far Left of Center: The American Radical Left Today*. New Brunswick, NJ: Transaction Books.

Klugman, C. 1989. *Press Alert to ASNE Members, RE: FLAG-BURNING PROPOSALS*. September 28. Washington, DC: American Society of Newspaper Editors.

Kmiec, D. 1990a. "In the Aftermath of *Johnson* and *Eichman*: The Constitutional Need Not Be Mutilated to Preserve the Government's Speech and Property Interests in the Flag." *Brigham Young University Law Review*, 2: 577–638.

———. 1990b "A Case for Protecting the Flag as Public Property." *Chicago Tribune*, February 26: 11.

Knoxville News-Sentinel. 1995. "Campaign Closes in on Flag Amendment." June 11: F2.

Kramer, H. 1967. "Herman Rose's New York." *New York Times*, May 21: 2-B.

———. 1967. "Mixing the Media." *New York Times*, October 29: 4-B.

———. 1970. "A Case of Artistic Freedom." *New York Times*, March 1: 3-B.

Kraska, P. 1993a. *Altered States of Mind: Critical Observations of the Drug War.* New York: Garland Publishing, Inc.

———. 1993b. "Militarizing the Drug War: A Sign of the Times." In P. Kraska, ed., *Altered States of Mind: Critical Observations of the Drug War,* 159–206. New York: Garland Publishing.

Kunstler, W. 1989. "What Shocked Me Most About the Flag Decision." *New York Times,* August 5: 25.

———. 1990. "Praise Those Who Test the Flag Burning Law." *New York Times,* May 1: 22.

———. 1994. *My Life as a Radical Lawyer.* Secaucus, NJ: Carol Publications.

Larrain, J. 1983. *Marxism and Ideology.* London: MacMillan Press.

Las Vegas Review-Journal. 1999. "Go With Head, Not Heart, on Flag Burning. May 9: 2D.

Lauter, David, and P. Houston. 1990. "Bush Urges Flag Amendment But Does So With Less Fanfare." *Los Angeles Times,* June 13: A-19.

Lawson, C. 1984. "Patriotism Stirs Business for Flag Manufacturers." *Chicago Tribune,* July 4, Section 5: 4.

Lefcourt, J. 1989. Public statements at the Memorial Service for Abbie Hoffman. June 17. New York, NY.

Lerner, M. 1937. "Constitution and Court as Symbols." *Yale Law Journal,* 46, 1290–1324.

Lesieur, H., and M. Welch. 1991. "Vice, Public Disorder and Social Control." In J. Sheley, ed., *Handbook of Contemporary Criminology,* 175–217. Belmont, CA: Wadsworth.

———. 1995. "Vice Crimes: Individual Choices and Social Controls." In J. Sheley, ed., *Handbook of Contemporary Criminology,* 201–29. 2nd edition. Belmont, CA: Wadsworth.

———. 2000. "Vice Crimes: Personal Autonomy Versus Societal Dictates." In J. Sheley, ed., *Handbook of Contemporary Criminology,* 233–63. 3rd edition. Belmont, CA: Wadsworth.

Levi-Strauss, C. 1963. *Structural Anthropology.* C. Jacobson and B. Schoepf, trans. New York: Basic Books.

Levin, M. 1971. *Political Hysteria in America: The Democratic Capacity for Repression.* New York: Basic Books.

Lewis, Anthony. 1989. "What is America?" *New York Times,* June 28: 23.

Lewis, A. 1991. *Make No Law: The Sullivan Case and the First Amendment.* New York: Vintage Books.

Lewis, N. A. 1990. "Arguments on Flag Burning Heard." *New York Times,* May 15: 16.

Lilla, M. 1998. "Still Living with '68." *New York Times Magazine,* August, 16: 34–37.

Lippard, L. 1972. "Flagged Down: The Judson Three and Friends." *Art in America,* May: 48–53.

Lipsyte, R. 1993. "Silent Salute, Ringing Impact: Two Small Gloved Fists, One Large Revolution." *New York Times,* Section 8: 1, 11.

Locin, M. 1990. "Flag Ruling Provides Martin an Issue in Race." *Chicago Tribune,* June 14: Section 2: 3.

Loewy, A. 1989. "The Flag-Burning Case: Freedom of Speech When We Need It Most." *North Carolina Law Review*, 68: 165–75.

Lofland, J., B. Colwell, and S. Johnson. 1990. "Theories of Change Among Peace Activists." In S. Marullo and J. Lofland, eds. *Peace Action in the Eighties*, 87–105. New Brunswick, NJ: Rutgers University Press.

Los Angeles Times. 1989. "Saluting the Star-Spangled Burner.". June 29: Section 5: 2.

———. 1989. "Flags Burned During Protest at UC Berkeley." October 28: 27.

———. 1989. "Protestors Defy New Anti-Desecration Law, Burn Flags." October 29: 26.

Lynch, M., and W. B. Groves. 1989. *A Primer in Radical Criminology*. 2nd edition. New York: Harrow and Heston.

MacLean, B., and D. Milovanovic. 1997. *Thinking Critically About Crime*. Vancouver: Collective Press.

Macon Telegraph. [Georgia]. 1999. "Well-Meaning Flag Amendment Bad Idea." April 30: 10.

Madigan, C. 1990. "Battles of Symbolism: Flag, Arts Dispute Reveal a Queasiness over Self-Expression." *Chicago Tribune*, June 17: 1.

Makalani, M. 1990. "To Burn or Not to Burn." *In These Times*, February 21: 20.

Manis, J. 1974. "The Concept of Social Problems: Vox Populi and Sociological Analysis." *Social Problems*, 21: 305–15.

———. 1976. *Analyzing Social Problems*. New York: Praeger.

Mann, M. 1984. *International Encyclopedia of Sociology*. New York: Continuum.

Manwaring, D. 1962. *Render Unto Caesar: The Flag Salute Controversy*. Chicago: University of Chicago Press.

Marcus, R. 1990a. "Justices Expedite Flag-Burning Case [Supreme Court Schedules Unusual May Session to Hear Argument]." *Washington Post*, March 31, A4.

———. 1990b. "'Old Glory' May Wave In Fall Campaign Winds." *Washington Post*, May 14: A4.

Margolick, D., 1984. "Student's Allegiance Lies in Independence." *Chicago Tribune*, December 7: 35.

———. 1990. "The Lawyer Who Helped Set the Flag Debate Aflame Calmly Prepares to Move On." *New York Times*, June 22, 1990: B-5.

Marion, N. 1992. "Presidential Agenda Setting in Crime Control." *Criminal Justice Policy Review*, 6: 159–84.

———. 1994a. *A History of Federal Crime Control Initiatives, 1960–1993*. Westport, CT: Praeger.

———. 1994b. "Symbolism and Federal Crime Control Legislation, 1960–1990." *Journal of Crime and Justice*, 17: 69–91.

Markoff, J., and D. Regan. 1981. "The Rise and Fall of Civil Religion: Comparative Perspectives." *Sociological Analysis*, 42, 4: 333–52.

Marwick, A. 1997. *Cultural Revolution in Britain, France, Italy, and the United States*. New York: Oxford University Press.

Marx, Gary. 1989. "Thompson Alters Flag Desecration Bill." *Chicago Tribune*, September 4: 8.

Marx, Gary T. 1981. "Ironies of Social Control: Authorities as Contributors to Deviance through Escalation, Nonenforcement and Covert Facilitation." *Social Problems*, 28: 221–46.

———. 1988. *Undercover: Police Surveillance in America*. Berkeley: University of California.

Marx, K. 1867 [1967]. *Capital*. New York: International Publishers.

———. 1978. "The German Ideology." In R. D. Tucker, ed., *The Marx-Engels Reader*, 146–200. 2nd edition. New York: Norton.

Massey, C. 1990. "Pure Symbols and the First Amendment." *Hastings Constitutional Law Quarterly*, 17: 369–82.

Mastai, B., and M. L. D'Otrange Mastai. 1973. *The Stars and Stripes: The American Flag as Art and as History from the Birth of the Republic to the Present*. New York: Alfred A. Knopf.

Mathisen, J. A. 1989. "Twenty Years After Bellah: Whatever Happened to American Civil Religion?" *Sociological Analysis*, 50: 2: 129–46.

Mauss, A. 1974. "On Being Strangled by the Stars and Stripes: The New Left, the Old Left, and the Natural History of American Radical Movements." In R. S. Denisoff, ed., *The Sociology of Dissent*, 144–60. New York: Harcourt Brace Jovanovich.

Mayer, D. 1991. "The English Radical Whig Origins of American Constitutionalism." *Washington University Law Quarterly*, 70, 131–63.

McCorkle, R., and T. Miethe. 1998. "The Political and Organizational Response to Gangs: An Examination of a 'Moral Panic' in Nevada." *Justice Quarterly*, 15, 1: 41–64.

McLuhan, M. 1964. *Understanding Media: The Extensions of Man*. New York: New American Library.

McPherson, J. 1989. *Battle Cry of Freedom: The Civil War Era*. New York: Ballantine.

McQueen, M. P. 1991. "Guilty in Flag Burning." *New York Newsday*, March 26: 37.

Mehan, H., and H. Wood. 1975. *The Reality of Ethnomethodology*. New York: Wiley and Sons.

Meier, B. 1989. "Decision A Victory For 1 Man. *New York Newsday*, June 22: 5, 29.

Merton, R. 1968. *Social Theory and Social Structure*. 2nd edition. New York: Free Press.

Miami Herald. 1989. "Daoud: Constitution Defends Flag from Fire." July 3: 1B.

Michalowski, R. J. 1996. "Critical Criminology and the Critique of Domination: The Story of an Intellectual Movement." *Critical Criminology: An International Journal*, 7, 1: 9–16.

Michelman, F. 1990. "Saving Old Glory: On Constitution Iconography." *Stanford Law Review*, 42, 6: 1337–64.

Miller, C. K. 1898. "Desecration of the American Flag and Prohibitive Legislation." Address delivered an Illinois SAR banquet, Chicago, November 2. Pamphlet.

———. 1901. "The United States Flag Dishonored and Disgraced in America, Cuba, and the Philippines." Pamphlet.

Miller, M. V., and S. Gilmore. 1965. *Revolution at Berkeley*. New York: Dell.

Million, E. 1940–41. "Red Flags and the Flag." *Rocky Mountain Law Review*, 13, 47–60.

Mills, C. W. 1956. *The Power Elite*. New York: Oxford University Press.

———. 1959. *The Sociological Imagination*. New York: Oxford University Press.

Milovanovic, D. 1988. *A Primer in the Sociology of Law*. New York: Harrow and Heston.

Morey, G. K. 1924. *Mystic Americanism*. East Aurora, NY: Eastern Star Publishing.

Mullins, M. 1989. "That 'Burning' Flag Issue: Is It Finally Resolved in *Texas v. Johnson?*" *Ohio Northern University Law Review*, 16: 103–10.

Murphy, P. 1972. *The Constitution in Crisis Times, 1918–1969*. New York: Harper & Row Publishers.

Murray, R. 1955. *Red Scare*. New York: McGraw-Hill.

Nahmod, S. 1991. "The Sacred Flag and the First Amendment." *Indiana Law Journal*, 66, 511–48.

Nation. 1990. "Patriotic Bore." July 2: 1.

———. 1998. "Truth on El Salvador." April 27: 3–4.

National Gallup Poll. 1992. *National Gallup Poll of Americans' Opinions on the Flag Burning Issue*. January 3.

National Observer, June 1, 1970: 1.

Neitzche, F. 1967. *Birth of Tragedy and the Case of Wagner*. W. Kaufman, trans. New York: Random House.

Nelson, L. 1990a. "Flagging the Ripoff in S&L Scandal." *New York Daily News*, June 25: 25.

———. 1990b. "Apple Pie, Mom, & that Other Crisis." *New York Daily News*, June 13: 31.

Neustadt, R. E. 1960. *Presidential Power*. New York: John Wiley.

New Orleans Times-Picayune. 1990. "La. Flag Burners Take a Beating in House Bill." May 29: A1.

New Republic. 1990. "Get Serious." July 9, 16: 7–8.

New York Daily News. 1998. "Flag Can Take the Heat." July 20: 24.

———. 1989. August 12: 55.

New York Newsday. June 5, 1989: 5, 29.

———. 1989. "Beat a Flag Burner, Pay $1." December 16: 9.

———. 1989. June 5: 5, 29.

———. 1991. "Lokar May Leave U.S. Over Flag." February 12: 15.

———. 1995. "Eroding the Constitution Does No Honor to the Flag." June 14: A34.

New York Post. 1996. "NBA Bans Abdul-Rauf for Anthem Snub." March 13: 56.

New York Public Library. 1993. *Assault on the Arts: Culture and Politics in Nazi Germany*. February 27 to May 28.

New York Times. 1916. "Social Rebels Burn All Flags." June 2: 1, 22.

———. 1916. "Swann Will Jail the Flag-Burners." June 3: 10.

———. 1917. "Jury in flag case finds White Guilty.": March 15: 1.

———. 1917. "Bouck White gets 30 days." March 16: 12.

———. 1966. April 12.

———. 1966. April 1, 2; May 10.

———. 1969. October 16.

———. 1970. March 1.

———. 1970. March 21.

———. 1972. February 3.

———. 1989. "Legislators Supporting Flag Move." July 4: 1.

———. 1989. "Votes in Congress." September 17: 54.

———. 1989. "Votes in Congress." October 8, 1989: 18.

———. 1989. "Burning the Flag Leads to Fight and Court Case." August 14: 15.

————. 1990. "Votes in Congress." June 24: 27.

————. 1990. "Senate Roll-Call Vote on Flag Burning." June 27: Section 2: 6.

————. 1990. "Supreme Court Roundup: Arguments on Flag Burning Heard." May 15: A-1.

————. 1990. July 13.

————. 1990. "The Flag and a Few Punks." April 11: A-24.

————. 1990. "Flag Burning." October 16: 24.

————. 1992. "Judge Upheld on Flag Pin." February 14: B-7.

————. 1995. "More Flag-Waving in Congress." June 12: 14.

————. 1995. "Votes in Congress [Senate]." December 17: 54.

————. 1997. "Votes in Congress [House]." June 15: 30.

————. 1999. "In Recurring Debate, House Votes to Ban Flag-Burning." June 25: A-18.

————. 1999. "Misplaced Patriotism." May 7: A-26.

————. 1999. "Declaring Star of David a Gang Symbol is Bringing a Lawsuit." August 19: A-18.

Newsweek. 1989. "A Fight for Old Glory." July 3: 18.

————. 1998. "Overheard." October 16: 23.

Nisbet, R. 1968. *Tradition and Revolt: Historical and Sociological Essays.* New York: Random House.

O'Leary, C. 1999. *To Die For: The Paradox of American Patriotism.* Princeton, NJ: Princeton University Press.

Omaha World-Herald. 1990. "A Ban on Flag-Burning Silences No One's Voice." February 25: 24A.

————. 1990. "Flag-Burning Isn't an 'Idea' Invalidation of 1989 Law: An Unfortunate Decision." June 13: 26.

————. 1999. "The Flag Was Still There." June 27: 24A.

Osborne, B. 1990. "Burning Question Reignites." *ASNE Bulletin.* July / August: 2.

Page, B., and R. Shapiro. 1992. *The Rational Public: Fifty Years of Trends in Americans' Policy Preferences.* Chicago: University of Chicago Press.

Paludan, P. 1975. *A Covenant With Death: The Constitution, Law, and Equality in the Civil War Era.* Urbana: University of Illinois Press.

Parton, J. 1864. *General Butler in New Orleans.* New York: Mason Brothers.

Patriot News (Harrisburg, PA). 1991. "Hurling Old Glory Gets Man Jail Time." November 24: A-1.

Peterson, H. C., and G. Fite. 1957. *Opponents of War, 1917–1918.* Seattle: University of Washington Press.

Phillips, D. 1989. "Constitutional Flag-Burning Ban Vexes Lawmakers." *Washington Post,* July 13: A4.

————. 1989. "House Votes to Ban Flag Desecration." *Washington Post,* September 13: A6.

Phillips, K. 1990. *Politics of the Rich and Poor: Wealth and the American Electorate in the Reagan Aftermath.* New York: Random House.

Pierce, C. S. 1931. *Collected Papers.* P. Weiss and C. Hartshone, eds. Cambridge: Harvard University Press.

Pommer, M. 1998. "Court Takes on Flag Desecration: early 1900s Law Vs. Free Speech." *Capital Times,* April 10: 4-A.

Portland Press Herald. 1995. "Superpatriots Fulminate, But Their Foolishness Falls Short." December 14: 15A.

Portland Press Herald [Maine]. 1996. "Citizens Flag Alliance Seeking to Restore National Honor: A Flag-Protecting Amendment Failed by Four Votes Last Year. If At First You Don't Succeed . . ." October 7: 7A.

Potter, G., and V. Kappeler. 1998. *Constructing Crime: Perspectives on Making News and Social Problems.* Prospect Heights, IL: Waveland Press.

Povich, E. 1989a. "House OKs Bill to Ban Flag Burning." *Chicago Tribune,* September 13: 1.

———. 1989b. "Flag Burning Ban Clears House." *Chicago Tribune,* October 13: 1.

———. 1989c. "Senate Votes No on Flag Amendment." *Chicago Tribune,* October 20: 4.

Preble, G. H. 1917. *Origin and History of the American Flag.* Philadelphia: Nicholas L. Brown.

Prosser, D. 1969. "Desecration of the American flag." *Indiana Legal Forum,* 3, 159–237.

Providence Journal Bulletin. 1995. "Happy Flag Day." June 14: B-8.

Public Papers of the Presidents of the United States. 1887–1998. Washington, DC: U.S. Government Printing.

Pullen, J. 1971. *Patriotism in America.* New York: American Heritage.

Quaife, M. 1942. *The Flag of the United States.* New York: Grosset & Dunlap.

Rabban, D. 1997. *Free Speech in Its Forgotten Years.* Cambridge: Cambridge University Press.

Raskey, S. 1990. "For Flag Vote, History Won Over Political Risk." *New York Times,* June 22: 6.

Raskin, J. 1996. *For the Hell of It: The Life and Times of Abbie Hoffman.* Berkeley: University of California Press.

Recktenwald, W., and J. Strong. 1989, "Flag Art Turning into a Federal Case." *Chicago Tribune,* March 9: Sec. 2: 9.

Refuse & Resist. n.d. *Refuse the Politics of Cruelty! Unleash a Spirit of Resistance! Join Refuse & Resist.* Flier No. 1.

Rehnquist, W. H. 1998. *All The Laws But One: Civil Liberties in Wartime.* New York: Alfred A. Knopf.

Reiman, J. 1995. *The Rich Get Richer and the Poor Get Prison: Ideology, Class and Criminal Justice.* 4th edition. Boston: Allyn and Bacon.

Reinarman, C., and H. Levine. 1997. *Crack in America: Demon Drugs and Social Justice.* Berkeley: University of California Press.

Revolutionary Worker. 1990. "Roseanne vs. The 'Sick and Dying Empire.'" August 12: 11.

———. 1991. "High Stakes in Cleveland Flagburning Case." November 10: 12–13.

———. 1991. "Battle Continues for War Parade 18."December 22: 6.

———. 1992. "War Parade 18 Trial Date Set." January 26: 15.

Rice, A. S. 1972. *The Ku Klux Klan in American Politics.* New York: Haskell House.

Richmond Times Dispatch. 1998. "Flag-Burning Protestors Are Not Criminals." A-18.

Rimer, S. 1990. "In Rap Obscenity Trial, Cultures Failed to Clash." *New York Times,* October 22: A-12.

Robb, C. S. 1995. "Robb Cites U.S. Constitution in Opposing Flag Burning Amendment." Press Release, December 12. Washington, DC.

Robins, N. 1992. *Alien Ink: The FBI's War on Freedom of Expression*. New York: William Morrow and Company.

Rose, A. 1982. *Outbreaks: The Sociology of Collective Behavior*. New York: Free Press.

Rosen, J. 1991. "Was the Flag Burning Amendment Unconstitutional?" *Yale Law Review*, 100, 4: 1073–92.

Rosenblatt, A. 1972. "Flag-Desecration Statutes: History and Analysis." *Washington University Law Quarterly*, Spring: 193–237.

Rosenstiel, T. R. 1989. "Public Found Most Interested in China, Court." *Los Angeles Times*, July 13: 6.

Ross, J. I. 1998. *Cutting the Edge: Current Perspectives in Radical/Critical Criminology and Criminal Justice*. Westport, CT: Praeger.

Ross, M. 1989. "Protestors Burn U.S. Flags at Capitol; 4 Are Arrested." *Los Angeles Times*, October 31.

Rothman, D. J. 1971. *The Discovery of the Asylum: Social Order and Disorder in the New Republic*. Boston: Little, Brown.

Rotnem, V. and F. Folsom. 1942. "Recent Restrictions Upon Religious Liberty." *American Political Science Review*, 36, 1053–58.

Rousseau, J. 1948. *The Social Contract*. M. Cranston, trans. New York: Penguin.

Royko, M. 1989. "Ah, the Flag: Such a Useful Symbol." *Chicago Tribune*, March 15, Sec. 1:3

Runes, D. 1968. *Dictionary of Philosophy*. Totowa, NJ: Littlefield, Adams, and Company.

Rushdie, S. 1989. *The Satanic Rituals*. New York: Viking.

Rutgers Focus. 1996. "Shopping Malls as Village Greens." October 25:

Sachar, E. 1991. "Cops Unflagging in War Gesture." *New York Newsday*, January 26: 6.

Sacramento Bee. 1993a. "Elk Groves Civics Lesson." May 21: B-12.

———. 1993b. "District Seeks OK to Ban Flag Mural." June 17: B-3.

———. 1993c. "Judge Refuses to Delay Mural." June 30: B-4.

Safire, W. 1989. "Fourth of July Oration." *New York Times*, July 3: 19.

Sahin, H. 1980. "The Concept of Ideology and Mass Communication." *Journal of Communication Inquiry*, 61: 3–12.

St. Louis Post Dispatch. 1991. March 25: 6.

Sanders, J. 1993a. "Flag-Burning Mural Under Fire." *Sacramento Bee*, February 12: A-1.

———. 1993b. "Plan For Flag-Burning Art Flunks Out." *Sacramento Bee*, February 17: B-1.

———. 1993c. "Flag-Burning Mural: Perilous Precedent or Free Speech." *Sacramento Bee*, July 4: B-1.

———. 1993d. "Defiant Censorship." *Sacramento Bee*, September 25: B-1.

Saussure, F. de. 1966. *Course in General Linguistics*. C. Bally and A. Secheehaye, eds.; W. Basking, trans. New York: McGraw-Hill.

Savage, D. 1990a. "Judge Rules Flag Protection Act Unconstitutional." *Los Angeles Times*, February 22: 29.

———. 1990b. "Court Is Urged to Uphold Ban on Flag Burning." *Los Angeles Times*, May 15: 1, 17.

Savio, M. 1965. "An End to History." In M. Miller and S. Gilmore, eds., *Revolution at Berkeley*, 239–43. New York: Dell.

Schneider, J., and J. Kitsuse. 1984. *Studies in the Sociology of Social Problems*. Norwood, NJ: Ablex.

Schoenfeld, A., R. Meier, and R. Griffin. 1979. "Constructing a Social Problem: The Press and the Environment." *Social Problems*, 27: 38–61.

Schur, E. 1980. *The Politics of Deviance: Stigma Contests and the Uses of Power*. Englewood Cliffs, NJ: Prentice-Hall/Spectrum.

Schwartz, B. 1971. *The Bill of Rights: A Documentary History*. New York: Random House.

Schwartz, J. 1990. "Art and First Amendment Protection in Light of *Texas v. Johnson*." *Nova Law Review*, 14: 487–502.

Schwartz, M., and D. Friedrichs. 1994. "Postmodern Thought and Criminological Discontent: New Metaphors for Understanding Violence." *Criminology*, 32, 2: 221–46.

Scott, J. 1985. *Weapons of the Weak: Everyday Forms of Peasant Resistance*. New Haven: Yale University Press.

———. 1990. *Domination and the Arts of Resistance: Hidden Transcripts*. New Haven: Yale University Press.

Seattle Times. 1999. "Protecting 'Old Glory.'" May 20: B4.

Shen, F. 1990. "Flag Desecration Bill Gains in Maryland." *Washington Post*, February 17: B8.

Shogan, R. 1992. *The Riddle of Power: Presidential Leadership from Truman to Bush*. New York: Blume Book.

Sica, M. 1990. "The School Flag Movement: Origin and Influence." *Social Education*, 54: 380–84.

Sifakis, C. 1992. *The Encyclopedia of American Crime*. New York: Smithmark.

Sleelye, K. 1995, "Conservatives Revive Bill on Protecting Flag." *New York Times*, March 22: 16.

Sloman, L. 1998. *Steal this Dream: Abbie Hoffman and the Countercultural Revolution in America*. New York: Doubleday.

Smith, C. A., and K. Smith. 1994. *The White House Speaks*. Westport, CT: Praeger.

Smith, N. 1903. *Our Nation's Flag in History and Incident*. Milwaukee: Young Churchman.

Smith, W. 1975. *The Flag Book of the United States*. New York: William Morrow & Co.

Sobel, L. 1969. *Facts on File Yearbook 1968*. New York: Facts on File, Inc.

South Bend Tribune. 1999. "Flag Amendment Would Diminish Freedom." March 28: B8.

Spector, M., and J. Kitsuse. 1977. *Constructing Social Problems*. Menlo Park, CA: Cummings.

Sperber, D. 1974. *Rethinking Symbolism*. Alice L. Morton, trans. New York: Cambridge University Press.

Spitzer, S. 1975. "Toward a Marxian Theory of Deviance." *Social Problems*, 22: 638–51.

Standard Examiner [Ogden, Utah]. 1998. "Flag Burning." May 29: 24.

Steinfels, P. 1990. "No Church, No Ministry, No Pulpit, He is Called Right's Star." *New York Times*, June 5: A22.

Stepp, L. S. 1990. "They Built on Family and Faith." *Washington Post*, August 8: C1–3.

Surette, R. 1998. *Media, Crime & Criminal Justice: Images and Realities*. 2nd edition. Pacific Grove, CA: Brooks/Cole Publishing Company.

Swank, E. 1993. "Shall We Overcome? The Sense of Movement Power Among Gulf War Protestors." *Critical Sociology*, 20, 1: 31–51.

Taylor, I. 1982. "Moral Enterprise, Moral Panic, and Law-and-Order Campaigns." In M. Rosenberg, R. Stebbins, and A. Turowitz, eds., *The Sociology of Deviance*, 123–49. New York: St. Martin's Press.

Taylor, R. N. 1990. "The Protection of Flag Burning as Symbolic Speech and the Congressional Attempt to Overturn the Decision." *Cincinnati Law Review*, 38: 1056.

Thomas, W. I. 1923. *The Unadjusted Girl*. Boston: Little, Brown.

———, and F. Znaniecki. 1927. *The Polish Peasant in Europe and America*. Chicago: University of Chicago Press.

Tiefer, C. 1992. "The Flag Burning Controversy of 1989–1990." *Harvard Journal on Legislation*, 29: 366.

Time. 1991. "It's a Grand Old (Politically Correct) Flag." February 15: 55.

Tiner, S. 1998. Testimony to the U.S. Senate Subcommittee. March 25. Washington, DC: American Society of Newspaper Editors.

Toner, R. 1989. "Bush and Many in Congress Denounce Flag Ruling." *New York Times*, June 23,: 8.

———. 1989. "President to Seek Amendment to Bar Burning the Flag." *New York Times*, June 28.

———. 1989. "Flag Fight: From Rhetoric to Reality." *New York Times*, July 24: A-13.

———. 1989. "Spirit of '89: The Uproar Over What America Owes Its First Allegiance To." *New York Times*, July 2, Section 4: 1.

———. 1989. "Senate Debates Bill Outlawing Flag Burning." *New York Times*, October 5: Section 2: 12.

———. 1989. "Momentum Shifts on Flag Amendment." *New York Times*, October 18: 1.

———. 1990. "Politicians Forced to Confront Issue of Defacing Flag." *New York Times*, June 17: 1.

Trillin, C. 1989. "Uncivil Liberties." *New York Newsday*, July 11: 6, part II.

Trippett, F. 1989. "A Few Symbol-Minded Questions." *Time*, August 28: 72.

Tulsa World. 1997. "Fun With the Flag." March 1: A12.

Tunnell, K. 1992. "Film at Eleven: Recent Developments in the Commodification of Crime." *Sociological Spectrum*, 12: 293–313.

Turner, R. 1974. "The Theme of Contemporary Social Movements." In R. S. Denisoff, ed., *The Sociology of Dissent*, 21–30. New York: Harcourt Brace Jovanovich.

Tushnet, M. 1990. "The Flag-Burning Episode: An Essay on the Constitution." *University of Colorado Law Review*, 61: 39–53.

Twain, M. 1895. "Fenimore Cooper's Literary Offenses." *North American Review*, July, 10–22.

Union Leader [New Hampshire]. 1999. "Flag Burning and Free Speech: And a NH Woman's Pledge of Allegiance." June 27: 18.

United States Code, 40 *Statutes* 555 (Sedition Act of 1918).

USA Today. 1989. "Voices: Do We Need Stronger Laws to Protect the Flag?" March 22: 10A.

Useem, B., and M. Zald. 1982. "From Pressure Group to Social Movement." *Social Problems*, 30: 144–56.

Van Alstyne, W. 1991. "Freedom of Speech and the Flag Anti-Desecration Amendment: Antinomies of Constitutional Choice." *Free Speech Yearbook*, 29: 96–105.

Vecsey, G. 1991. "Lokar's Last Point Was His Best." *New York Times*, February 15: A-26.

Von Stein, L. 1964. *The History of the Social Movement in France, 1789–1850*. Kaethe Mengelberg, ed., trans. Totowa, NJ: Bedminster Press.

Waldman, M. S. 1989. "House Passes Flag-Burning Bill: Move Aimed at Heading off Constitutional Amendment." *New York Newsday*, September 13: 15.

Walker, S. 1990. *In Defense of American Liberties: A History of the ACLU*. New York: Oxford University Press.

Wallach, A. 1991. "Hitler Didn't Like It." *New York Newsday*, March 31: Part II, 1, 18.

Wanta, W., and J. Foote. 1994. "The President–News Media Relationship: A Time Series Analysis of Agenda Setting." *Journal of Broadcasting and Electronic Media*, 38, 4: 437–46.

Warner, James. 1989. "When They Burned the Flag Back Home." *Washington Post*, July 11: A21.

Warr, M. 1995. "Poll Trends: Public Opinion on Crime and Punishment." *Public Opinion Quarterly*, 59: 296–310.

Warren (Ohio) Tribune-Chronicle, July 11, 1991: 12.

Washington Post. 1969. June 5.

———. 1970. March 18.

———. 1989. "Flag Games." June 14: A22.

———. 1989. "Flag-Burner Seeks Release From Prison." July 2: A3.

———. 1989. "Lawyer Committee Urges Congress Not to Outlaw Flag." August 4: A7.

———. 1990. "GOP Advice on Flag Upsets Candidate." June 20: A28.

Watkins, T. H. 1993. *The Great Depression*. Boston: Little, Brown.

Weekly Compilation of Presidential Documents, 25, no. 26, July 3, 1989: 1006–8

Welch, M. 1992. "The Flag-Burning Controversy: Protection of a Venerated Object as Social Control." *American Journal of Criminal Justice*, XVII, 1: 1–17.

———. 1996a. *Corrections: A Critical Approach*. New York: McGraw-Hill.

———. 1996b. "Critical Criminology, Social Justice, and an Alternative View of Incarceration." *Critical Criminology: An International Journal*, 7, 2: 43–58.

———. 1998. "Critical Criminology, Social Control, and an Alternative View of Corrections." In J. Ross, ed., *Cutting the Edge: Current Perspectives in Radical/Critical Criminology and Criminal Justice*, 107–21. Westport, CT: Praeger.

———. 1999a. "Deconstructing the Flag-Burning Controversy: Contributions of Robert J. Goldstein in Review." *Saving Old Glory, Burning the Flag*, and *Desecrating the Flag*." *Social Pathology*. In press.

———. 1999b. *Punishment in America: Social Control & the Ironies of Imprisonment*. Thousand Oaks, CA: Sage.

———. 2000. "Social Movements and Political Protest: Exploring Flag Desecration in the 1960s, 1970s, and 1980s." *Social Pathology*. In press.

————, and J. Bryan. 1997. "Flag Desecration in American Culture: Offenses against Civil Religion and a Consecrated Symbol of Nationalism." *Crime, Law, and Social Change*, 26: 77–93.

————, and J. Bryan. 1998. "Reactions to Flag Desecration in American Society: Exploring the Contours of Formal and Informal Social Control." *American Journal of Criminal Justice*, 22, 2: 151–68.

————, and J. Bryan. 2000. "Moral Campaigns, Authoritarian Aesthetics, and Escalation: An Examination of Flag Desecration in the Post-*Eichman* Era." *Journal of Crime and Justice*. In press.

————, N. Bryan, and R. Wolff. 1999. "Just War Theory and Drug Control Policy: Militarization, Morality, and the War on Drugs." *Contemporary Justice Review*, 2, 1: 49–76.

————, M. Fenwick, and M. Roberts. 1998. "State Managers, Intellectuals, and the Media: A Content Analysis of Ideology in Experts' Quotes in Featured Newspaper Articles on Crime." *Justice Quarterly*, 15, 2: 219–241.

————, M. Fenwick, and M. Roberts. 1997. "Primary Definitions of Crime and Moral Panic: A Content Analysis of Experts' Quotes in Feature Newspaper Articles of Crime." *Journal of Research in Crime and Delinquency*, 34, 4: 474–94.

————, R. Wolff, and N. Bryan. 1998. "Decontextualizing the War on Drugs: A Content Analysis of NIJ Publications and their Neglect of Race and Class." *Justice Quarterly*, 15, 4: 719–42.

Wicker, T. 1989. "Bravely Do Nothing." *New York Times*, July 21: A-29.

Wilkerson, I. 1989. "Art That Offends, Laws That Retaliate." *New York Times*, June 11, Section 4: 4.

Wilkins, L. 1965. *Social Deviance*. Englewood Cliffs, NJ: Prentice-Hall.

Williams, R. H., and N. J. Demerath, III. 1991. "Religion and Political Process in an American City." *American Sociological Review*, 56, 4: 417–31.

Wills, G. 1990. *Under God: Religion and American Politics*. New York: Simon and Schuster.

Wilson, W. 1899. "Spurious Versus Real Patriotism in Education." *School Review*, 603–4.

Wimberley, R. C. 1980. "Civil Religion and the Choice of President: Nixon in '72." *Social Forces*, 59, 1: 44–61.

Young, J. 1982. "The Role of the Police as Amplifiers of Deviancy, Negotiators of Reality and Translators of Fantasy." In S. Cohen, ed., *Images of Deviance*, 44–61. New York: Penguin Books.

Zabell, M. 1990a. "Flag-burning Retaliation May Come Cheap." *Chicago Tribune*, June 22: 13.

————. 1990b. "Romeoville Backs Off on Flag-burning." *Chicago Tribune*, June 27: 7.

Zeitlin, I. 1968. *Ideology and the Development of Sociological Theory*. Englewood Cliffs, NJ: Prentice-Hall.

Zelinsky, W. 1988. *Nation into State: The Shifting Symbolic Foundations of American Nationalism*. Chapel Hill: University of North Carolina Press.

Zielbauer, P. 1999. "In a Tidy Town, Tiny Flags Make Waves: Neatness Counts in Stratford, Where Deli Fights Order to Furl Old Glories." *New York Times*, August 17: B1, B6.

Cases Cited

Alford v. Sacramento Judicial District, 102 Cal. Reptr. (1972), 51

Carpenter v. State, 597, So. 2d (Ala. 1992), 85

Cary v. U.S., 90-5183 (1990), 63

Cohen v. California, 403 U.S. (1971), 59

Commonwealth v. Bricker, 666 A. 2d (Pa. 1995), 94, 95

Commonwealth of PA. v. Cox, 312, Mag. Dist. No. 37-3-02 (Pa. 1991), 95

Commonwealth v. Lorenc, 281 A. 2d (1971), 57

Crosson v. Silver, 319 F. Supp. 1084 (1970), 52

Debs v. United States, 249 U.S. 211 (1919), 26

Deeds v. State, 474 S.W. 2d (1971), 52, 54

Delorme v. State, 488 S.W. 2d (1973), 55

Dimmett v. City of Clearwater, 782 F. Supp. (1991), 89

Dunn v. Carroll, 40 F. 3d (1994), 90

Dwares v. City of New York, 985 F. 2d (1993), 95, 96

Ex Parte Starr, 263 F. (1920), 6, 26, 38

FCC v. Pacifica, 438 U.S. (1978), 5

Fordyce v. City of Seattle, 840 F. Supp. (1993), 87

Franz v. Commonwealth, 86 S.E. 2d (1972), 54

Goguen v. Smith, 471 F. 2d (1972), 55, 56

Halter v. Nebraska, 205 U.S. (1907), 6, 23, 54, 58

Herrick v. Commwealth, 188 S.E. 6d (1972), 56

Hoffman v. U.S., 445 F. 2d (1971), 53, 54

In re Old Glory Condom Corp., Serial No. 74/0004 (1993), 89

Johnson v. State, 706 S.W. 2d (1986), 7, 12, 15, 24, 69, 70, 77, 79, 81, 89, 116, 130, 157, 160

Korn v. Elkins, 317 F. Supp. (1970), 57

Koser v. County of Price, 834 F. Supp. (1993), 8

Long Island Vietnam Moratorium Committee v. Cahn, 437 F. (1970), 56

Markgraf v. Elk Grove Unified School District, Order Granting Plaintiffs' Motion for Preliminary Injunction, 533340 (1993), 9, 92

Miami v. Wolfenberger, 265 So. 2d (1972), 56

Minersville School District v. Gobitis, 310 U.S. (1940), 29, 39

Monroe v. State, 295 S.E. 2d (1982), 68

Monroe v. State Court of Fulton County, 739 F2 (1984), 68

New York Times v. Sullivan, 376 U.S. (1964), 5

Parker v. Morgan, 415 U.S. (1971), 55

People v. Cowgill, 396 U.S. (1970), 54

People v. Keough, 290 N.E. 2d (1972), 57

People v. Lindsay, 282 N.E. 2d 431 (1972), 58

People v. Payne, 565 N.Y.S. 2d (1990), 85

People v. Vaughan, 514 P. 2d (1973), 55

Renn v. State, 495 S.W. 2d (1973), 56

Ruhstrat v. People, 57, N.E. 41 (1900), 23

Russo v. Central School District No. 1, 469 F.2d 623 (1972), 40

Schenck v. United States, 249 U.S. 47 (1919), 26, 138

Sims v. City of Bradview Heights, 93-3410 (1994), 89

Smith v. Goguen, 415 U.S. 566 (1974), 7

Spence v. Washington, 418 U.S. (1974), 7, 56, 67, 89

State v. Claxton, 501 P. 2d (1972), 55

State v. Farrell, 233 N.W. 2d (1974), 52, 54

State v. Hershey, 289 N.E. 2d (1972), 57

State v. Hodsdon, 289 A. 2d (1972), 57

State v. Jimenez, 828 S.W. 2d (1992), 94

State v. Kasnett, 283 N.E. 2d (1971), 55

State v. Kent, No. 36, Hawaii Circuit Court, Dec. 9 (1966), 56

State v. Kool, 212 N.W. 2d (1973), 56

State v. Lessin, 620 N.E. 2d (1993), 87

State v. Liska, 291 N.E. 2d (1971), 56

State v. Mitchell, 288 N.E. 2d (1972), 55

State v. Nicola, 182 N.W. 2d (1971), 56

State v. Saionz, 261 N.E. 2d (1969), 54

State v. Saulino, 277 N.E. 2d (1971), 56

State v. Van Camp, 282 A. 2d (1971), 55

State v. Waterman, 190 N.W. 2d (1971), 54

State v. Zimmelman, 301 A. 2d (1973), 56

Street v. New York, 394 U.S. (1969), 7, 51, 52, 56, 67

Stromberg v. California, 283 United States Reports, 259 (1931), 29, 67

Sutherland v. DeWulf, 323 F. Supp. (1971), 52, 54

Terminiello v. Chicago, 337 U.S. (1949), 5

Texas v. Johnson, 109 S.Ct. (1989), 7, 62, 70, 71, 107, 113, 179, 180, 183, 185, 186

Tinker v. Des Moines Indep. Comm. School Dis., 393 U.S. (1969), 59

Troster v. Pennsylvania State Dept. of Corrections, 65 F. 3d (1995), 41, 90

U.S. v. Eichman, 110 S.Ct. (1990); 496 U.S. (1991), 7, 8, 15, 59, 66, 73, 74, 75, 77, 79, 81, 106, 110, 157, 180, 185, 186

U.S. v. Haggerty, 89-1434 (1989), 74, 75, 106, 180, 185, 186

U.S. v. Kime, 459 U.S (1982), 67, 68

U.S. v. O'Brien, 391 U.S. (1968), 59, 67, 89

U.S. v. Radich, 385 F. Supp. (1970), 58

U.S. v. Wilson, 33 M.J. (1991), 88

West Virginia Board of Education v. Barnette, 319 U.S. (1943), 6, 29, 30, 39, 67, 71

NAME INDEX

Abdul-Rauf, M., 40, 41
Ackerman, G., 12, 173
Adams, L., 19, 58
Alpert, H., 33
Alvarez, L., 8, 136, 178
American Civil Liberties
    Union, 9, 13, 39, 44,
    50, 65–69, 74, 76, 77,
    92, 98, 104, 178, 182–
    184, 188
Ames, E., 28
Andersen, W., 40
Andrews, E., 34
Anthony, D., 33
Aronowitz, S., 62
Augusta Chronicle, 171
Avakian, B., 65, 77
Avni, B., 95
Ayres, B.D., 93

Bailey, F., 108
Baker, J., 20
Balch, G., 42
Baldwin, C., 58
Ballinger, J., 93
Baltimore Sun, 84, 168
Bangor Daily News, 168
Barak, G., 108, 156, 175
Baranek, P.M., 156
Barber, H.W., 39
Barry, J.W., 37
Barthes, R., 10, 11
Baudrillard, J., 10, 11
Becker, H.S., 116, 131,
    179
Beckett, K., 131, 164, 174
Bellah, R., 10, 24, 31, 32,
    33

Bentley, B., 188
Ben-Yehuda, N., 5, 65,
    102, 108, 109, 110,
    113, 114, 115, 117,
    120, 121, 122
Berkman, A., 26, 27
Best, J., 115, 117, 125, 131,
    151
Blackmun, H., 71
Blalock, D., 180
Bloom, L., 70
Blumenthal, S., 11
Blumer, H., 48, 49, 65, 66
Bonner, R., 63
Bonwell, D., 67
Boston Globe, 89, 170
Bourquin, G.M., 38
Brace, P., 132
Bradley, B., 140
Brennan, W., 7, 67, 71,
    75, 160, 184
Brinkley, A., 17
Broad, D., 81
Brownstein, H., 124
Bryan, J., 22, 32, 34, 36,
    38, 43, 104, 106, 115
Bryan, N., 80, 24
Buchanan, P., 79, 104
Burkhardt, H., 93
Bush, G., 22, 44, 62, 63,
    64, 73, 80, 124, 128–
    131, 150, 164
Business Wire, 93
Butler, B., 22

Calavita, K., 62
Camposeco, M., 93, 106
Capital, 172

Carlos, J., 3, 4
Cary, W.C., 63
Cavender, G., 108, 175
Chafee, Z., 25, 29
Chalmers, D., 21
Chan, J.B.L., 156
Chapman, S., 158
Chen, E., 134
Chermak, S., 125, 156,
    164, 165, 174
Chiasson, L., 166
Chicago Tribune, 153,
    157–160, 162,
    163, 167
Chiricos, T., 124, 125
Chomsky, N., 43
Citizens Flag Alliance, 8,
    79, 96, 112, 113, 119,
    123, 151, 171
Cleary, P., 97
Clark, R., 187
Clines, F., 37, 44, 162
Cohen, J.E., 131, 132
Cohen, S., 5, 59, 101, 102,
    104, 106, 108, 109,
    110, 113, 114, 124,
    125, 155, 179
Colgrove, C., 34
Collins, R., 75
Colwell, B., 64
Commercial Appeal, 168
Congressional Record, 11,
    12, 34, 47, 72, 73, 101,
    105, 106, 109, 115,
    127, 128, 133, 137–
    152
Cottman, M., 90
Cox, M., 95

Craig, B.J., 80
Crow, T., 58
Curti, M., 17
Curtis, M.K., 17, 19, 26, 32, 71
Cutrone, R., 93

Daily Oklahoman, 172
Daley, S., 133, 134, 163
Dallas Morning News, 169
Dalton, P., 82
Danzig, R., 40
Daughters of the American Revolution, 23, 34, 36
Debs, E., 26
Dedman, B., 160
Deeds, G., 52, 113
Degenerate Art, 75
Deidtman, T., 27
Delgado, K., 95
Demerath III, N.J., 33, 43
Derrida, J., 10, 11
Dershowitz, A., 181
Detroit News, 166
Dewar, H., 163
Dickey, C., 63
DiFazio, W., 62
Dillon, S., 63
Dix, J., 21
Dole, B., 144, 158
Donner, F., 27
Drew, C., 70, 136, 158, 163
Dubin, S., 7, 8, 30, 31, 58, 75, 135, 173, 178, 182
Dukakis, M., 22, 63, 64, 133
Dunn, J., 90, 91
Durkheim, E., 10, 33, 115
Dwares, S., 103
Dye, T., 178

Eaton, W.J., 135, 163
Eco, U., 10
Edelman, M., 131

Editor & Publisher, 166
Edwards, H., 14
Edwards, W., 15
Efron, S., 84
Eggenberger, D., 22
Ehrlich, T., 152
Eichman, S., 66, 74, 75, 76, 82, 180, 188
Emergency Committee to Stop the Flag Amendment and Laws, 182, 183, 188
English, R., 75
Ericson, R.V., 156, 164, 165
Erikson, K., 155
Erwin, D., 93
Ewick, P., 50, 96

Fennell, W., 40
Fenwick, M., 102, 108, 109, 125, 131, 156, 164, 165, 174
Ferrell, J., 9, 96, 126, 155
Finkelman, P., 18, 177
Finley, L., 76
First Amendment Center, 127
Fishman, M., 108, 126, 156, 174, 175
Fite, G., 25, 38, 39
Folsom, F., 32, 40
Foote, J., 131, 132
Ford, J.H., 103
Fort Wayne Journal Gazette, 165
Foucault, M., 10, 96
Franz, E., 54
Fredua-Agyman, J., 152, 175
Fried, C., 184, 187
Friedrichs, D., 62
Frisbie, R., 57
Fritz, S., 155, 156, 159
Fuld, S., 58
Fulton, J., 77
Fulwood, S., 173

Gallup Poll, 31
Gamson, W., 173
Gans, H., 166
Garbus, M., 182
Gaubatz , M., 131
Gelderman, G.W., 131
Gerstenzang, J., 163
Getlin, J., 159
Ghiglione, L., 166
Gibbs, N., 32
Gibson, M., 19
Gilkey, R.C., 39
Gilmore, S., 47
Gingerich, N., 11
Glasser, I., 44
Goeas, E., 135
Goldman, E., 26, 27
Goldstein, R.J., 6, 7, 12, 17, 18, 22, 23, 25, 26, 27, 29, 32, 35, 36, 50, 51, 58, 71, 93, 106, 107, 113, 122, 137, 154, 165, 172, 174, 177, 183, 184, 185
Gomberts, J., 183
Gonzenbach, W., 131
Goode, E., 5, 65, 102, 108, 109, 110, 113, 114, 115, 117, 119–122
Goodwyn, L., 23
Gottdiener, M., 10, 11
Gramsci, A., 125
Grand Army of the Republic, 23
Greek, C., 175
Green, M., 13, 30
Greenawalt, K., 71
Greenberg, J., 43
Greenhouse, L., 32, 102, 160, 188
Greensboro News & Record, 169
Grinnell, F., 40
Griffin, R., 54
Grinnell, F., 40
Guenter, S., 17, 20, 21, 22, 23, 27, 32, 34, 35, 36,

Guenter, S. (*continued*)
  37, 38, 41, 42, 59, 111,
  122, 123
Gusfield, J., 116, 155
Guthrie, W., 37

Hale, E., 95, 108
Hall, S., 109, 113, 121,
  124, 125, 156, 165,
  174
Hammond, P.E., 33
Harrington, M., 62
Harvin, A., 41
Hayes, C., 43
Haywood, B., 30
Helms, J., 128
Henderson, R., 12
Hendricks, J., 58
Henkel, A., 28
Henry, S., 175
Hentoff, N., 5, 32, 186
Herman, E.H., 43
Hernandez, H., 166
Hertzberg, H., 12
Hess, E., 32, 76
Hickman, M., 125
Hinckley, B., 132
Hitchens, C., 11
Hochfield, S., 76
Hoffman, A., 53, 54
Hoge, P., 9, 92
Hollywood, B., 125
Holmes, S.A., 133, 134
Homcy, B., 152
Hoover, J.E., 40, 41
Hopkins, W., 50
Howlett, D., 98
Hubner, , E., 57
Hughey, M., 33
Humphries, D., 125, 156
Hyde, H., 132, 133, 142,
  173

In Re Old Glory Con-
  dom Corp., 89
Ingram, C., 133, 151
Irons, P., 5

Jackson, R., 40
Jaffe, J., 25, 29, 39
Jansenn, M., 9, 96, 97
Jefferson, T., 19
Jenkins, P., 125, 155
Johns, C., 80
Johnson, G.L., 14, 68
Johnson, J.E., 21
Johnson, R., 7, 71, 76
Johnson, S., 17, 64
Johnson, W., 17, 18
Jones, R., 97
Jones, S., 22
Judson, H.F., 12

Kahn, R., 63
Kansas City Star, 170
Kappeler, V.E., 108, 165
Kasinsky, R.G., 164, 165
Katz, J., 32, 97, 104
Kazin, M., 43
Kennedy, A., 71
Kent, N., 188
Kenworthy, T., 108, 173
Kerrey, J., 145, 147, 149
Ketter, W.B., 166
Kevelson, R., 10
Kilborn, P.T., 63
Kime, T., 67
Kimmelman, M.
Kitsuse, J., 117
Kittrie, N., 47
Klehr, H., 64, 65, 66
Klugman, C., 166
Knoxville-New Sentinel,
  171
Koser, A., 8, 94
Kramer, H.,,, 58
Kraska, P., 124
Krasnow, A., 93
Kropp, A., 188
Kunstler, W., 83, 177,
  184–187

Larrain, J., 125
Las Vegas Review-Journal,
  169

Leahy, P., 135
Lefcourt, J., 59
Lerner, M., 43
Leutzek E., 17
Levin, M., 118
Levine, H., 116, 124
Levi-Strauss, C., 10
Lewis, A., 25, 39, 65
Lewis, N.A., 154, 163
Lippard, L., 58
Lipsyte, R., 3, 4
Locin, M., 156
Loewy, A., 71
Lofland, J., 64
Lokar, M., 41
Los Angeles Times, 153,
  157–159, 161, 162,
  178

Macon Telegraph, 169
Madigan, C., 173
Makalani, M., 82
Manchester Union Leader,
  175
Manis, J., 116
Mann, M., 10, 15
Manwaring, D., 39, 42
Marcus, R., 161
Margolick, D., 40, 185
Marion, N., 131
Marshall, T., 71
Marx, Gary T., 4, 159, 179
Marx, K., 10, 125
Massey, C., 71
Mastai, B., 17, 18, 23, 32
Mathisen, J.A., 33
Mayer, D., 18, 177
McDonough, A., 175
McKay, S., 175
McKinley, W., 22
McLuhan, M., 172
McPherson, J., 17, 18, 21
McQueen, M.P., 84
Meier, B., 69
Mennel, J., 152
Merton, R., 127
Miami Herald, 104

Michelman, F., 71
Miller, C.E., 141
Miller, C.K., 35, 36
Miller, M.V., 47
Millet, K., 93
Million, E., 29
Mills, C.W., 123
Milovanovic, D., 10
Monroe, D., 67
Moore, T., 22
Morey, G.K., 37
Morrel, M., 57
Mortellito, K., 175
Mullins, M., 71
Mumford, W.B., 5, 22
Murphy, P., 25, 39, 50
Murray, R., 29

Nahmod, S., 32, 33, 41, 43
Nation, 11
National Association For the Advancement of Colored People, 184
National Observer, 59
Neidermayer, L., 175
Neitzche, F., 41
Neuborne, B., 50
New Orleans Times-Picayune, 104
New Republic, 7
Newsweek, 72, 102, 134

O'Leary, C., 17, 21, 22, 24, 32–36, 41, 42, 111, 122, 123
Omaha World-Herald, 170, 171
Osborne, B., 166

Page, B., 131
Palmer, A.M., 26
Paludan, P., 21
Parton, J., 22
Patino, A., 152
Patriot News, 95
People for the American

Way, 182, 184, 188
Peterson, H.C., 25, 38, 39
Phillips, D., 62, 162, 185
Pierce, C.S., 10
Pommer, M., 9, 96, 97
Pontell, H., 62
Portland Press Herald, 170, 172
Potter, G.W., 108
Povich, E., 133, 158, 159
Preble, G.H., 17, 18, 21, 22, 32
Price, E., 175
Prosser, D., 32
Providence Journal Bulletin, 170
Public Papers of the Presidents of the United States, 109, 127–131
Pullen, J., 59

Quaife, M., 17, 32

Rabban, D., 26, 27, 77
Radich, S., 57
Raimondo, E., 152, 175
Raskey, S., 154
Raskin, J., 53, 54
Reade, P., 35
Reagan, R., 3, 14, 62, 63, 68, 80, 128, 131, 181
Recktenwald, W., 77
Rehnquist, W.H., 27, 43, 71, 72, 106
Reinarman, C., 116, 124
Revolutionary Communist Party, 14, 61, 64, 113, 122, 140, 181
Revolutionary Worker, 61, 66, 81, 87, 182, 183
Rice, A.S., 21
Richmond Times Dispatch, 168
Riera, P., 13
Rimer, S., 178

Robb, C.S., 111
Robbins, T., 27, 33
Roberts, M., 102, 108, 110, 125, 131, 156, 164, 165, 174
Robins, N., 27
Rocha, E., 93, 106
Rocker, L., 98
Rorke, A., 28
Rose, A., 118
Rosenstiel, T.R., 165
Ross, B., 17, 37, 42, 144
Ross, M., 177
Rothberg, E., 93
Rotnem, V., 32, 40
Royko, M., 76
Runes, D., 11
Rushdie, S., 44
Rutgers Focus, 81

Sachar, E., 91
Sacramento Bee, 93
Safire, W., 31
Sahin, G., 125
Sanders, J., 9, 92
Sassi, J., 175
Saussure, F., 10
Savage, D., 160
Savio, M., 47
Scallia, A., 71
Schneider, J., 117
Schur, E., 115
Schwartz, B., 18, 177
Scott, D., 73, 76, 77, 78, 93, 96, 142, 180
Seaman, B., 77
Seattle Times, 168
Senate Joint Resolution, 121
Shapiro, R., 131
Shen, F., 188
Shiffler, G., 20
Shogan, R., 132
Shoshu, N., 36
Sica, M., 43
Sifakis, C., 27
Silbey, S., 50, 96

Simmons, W.J., 20
Sleelye, K., 173
Sloan, L., 54
Smith, C.A., 132
Smith, J.M.C., 25
Smith, N., 22
Smith, T., 3, 4
Smith, W., 17, 32, 42
Sobel, L., 4
Spatola, M., 152
Spence, H., 56
Sperber, D., 10, 33
Standard Examiner, 169
Starr, E.V., 5, 27, 38
Starr, K., 106, 110, 154, 161
Steiner, L., 175
Steinfels, P., 178
Stepp, L.S., 178
Stevens, J., 160
Stone, R., 8
Street, S., 51, 52
Stromberg, Y., 29
Strong, J., 77
Surette, R., 108, 156
Swank, E., 81

Tambellini, E., 51
Taylor, I., 131
Taylor, K., 178
Taylor, R.N., 184
Thomas, W.I., 121
Tiefer, C., 184

Tillman, R., 62
Time, 80, 81, 91
Tiner, S., 166
Toner, R., 135, 163, 165, 167, 187
Tribe, L., 183
Trillin, C., 101
Trippett, F., 12
Tulsa World, 170
Tunnell, K., 174
Tunney, K., 175
Turner, R., 51
Tushnet, M., 71
Twain, M., 3

Union Leader, 171
United States Code, 26
USA Today, 103, 109
Useem, B., 118
Urgo, J., 82, 83, 180

Vecsey, G., 41

Waldman, M.S., 44, 78
Walker, S., 25, 26, 27, 39, 65, 177
Wallach, A., 75
Wanta, W., 131, 132
Warner, J., 151
Warr, M., 131
Warren Tribune Chronicle, 95
Washington Post, 63, 134, 144, 156–160, 162, 166
Washington, G., 42
Watkins, T.H., 38, 39
Wearing, E., 40
Wedlock, E., 47
Welch, M., 6, 7, 32, 34, 38, 43, 49, 62, 64, 66, 102, 104, 108, 115, 124, 125, 131, 156, 164, 165, 174, 179
White, B., 27, 28
Wicker, T., 185
Wilkerson, I., 78
Wilkins, L., 155, 179
Willard, A.M., 17
Williams, R.H., 33, 43
Wills, G., 32
Wilson, W, 34, 88
Wimberley, R.C., 33
Wolff, R.P., 80, 124

Yoder, J., 134
Young, J., 101, 179
Yatron, G., 144

Zabell, M., 104
Zald, M., 118
Zelinsky, W., 17, 32, 33, 36
Ziegler, H., 178
Zielbauer, P., 89
Znaniecki, F., 121

SUBJECT INDEX

Advertising, 88–90
Age of protest, 48–49
Agenda-setting, 130–132, 163–165
Antebellum America and the flag, 19–21
Antigovernment messages, 82–88
Antiwar messages, 82–88
Artistic expression, 91–94
Authoritarian aesthetic, 49–55
  and moral panic, 147–149

Civil religion, 31–44, 32–36
  as informal control, 38–41
  in the debate over flag desecration, 141–143
Collective behavior, 117–118
Commerce, 88–90
Constructionism, 116–117
Criminal justice, and the role in flag protection, 146–147
Criminalization of protest, 127–151
  resisting, 177–188
Cultural expression, 91–94

Defense of dissent, 181–187
Desert Storm and the New World Odor, 80–81
Diversionary politics, 135

Flag as a venerated object, 31–44
Flag burning, 50–52, 61–78
  and the media, 155–165
  criminalization of, 132
Flag commercialism, prohibiting, 23–24
Flag controversies, during the world wars, 24–30
Flag debate in Congress, 137–150

Flag desecration in American history, 17–30
  roots of, 17–18
  charges of, 57–58
  Theory of Moral Panic, 121–125
Flag panic
  its contradictions, 153–174
  the media, 153–174
Flag patch controversies, 90–91
Flag Protection Act of 1989, 72–73
Flag protection
  American history of, 143–144
  Congressional voting on, 136–137
  flawed legislation, 144–145
  newspapers' editorials, 165–172
Formal flag codification, 36–38
Formal social control, 94–96
Free speech, origin of, 18–19

Historical considerations, 34–36

Military, in the debate over flag protection, 140–142
Moral entrepreneurs, 114–116, 127–151
Moral panic, 101–125
  concern, 102–103
  consensus, 105
  disproportionality, 105–107
  Elite-Engineered Model, 120–121
  grassroots model, 120
  hostility, 103–105
  Interest-Group Theory, 120
  its characters, 108–109
  over flag art, 75–77
  the media, 108
  the public, 109
  theories of, 119–125
  volatility, 107–108

Nativism and the flag, 19–21
New World Odor, 80–81
News Sources, their positions on flag
    protection, 157–161

Ontological considerations, 10–13

Partisan politics, 22–23, 133–134
Patriotic socialization, 41–43
Patriotism and dissent in the Post–
    Eichman Era, 79–98
Patriotism of George Bush, 62–64
Patriotism, in the debate over flag
    protection, 140
Persecutions, 117–118
Political cover, 134–135
Political diversion, on flag protection,
    145–146
Political iconoclasm, 61–78
Popular consensus, on presenting flag
    protection, 144
Post-*Eichman*–Era flag incidents, 81–
    96
President Bush as moral entrepreneur,
    128–132

Questioning authority, 47–59

Reagan revolution, 62–64
Revolutionary Communist Party,
    emergence of, 64–68

Semiotic considerations, 10–13
Social control
    action groups, 111–113
    agents of, 109, 113
    informal, 94–96
    ironies of, 179–181
    lawmakers, 110–111
    politicians, 110–111
Social construction of flag desecration,
    101–125
Social movements, 118–119, 48–49
    resistance of, 64–68
Special interests, 118–119

Texas v. Johnson, 68–72

U.S. v. Eichman, 73–75

Wearing the flag, 52–55

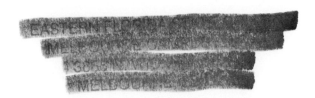